HELP YOUR KIDS WITH
Spelling and Grammar

Grammar

Punctuation

Spelling

Communication skills

PUNCTUATION

HELP YOUR KIDS WITH
Spelling and Grammar

A UNIQUE STEP-BY-STEP VISUAL GUIDE

LONDON, NEW YORK, MELBOURNE,
MUNICH, AND DELHI

Senior Project Editor Victoria Pyke

Project Editors Carron Brown, Camilla Gersh,
Matilda Gollon, Ashwin Khurana

Managing Editor Linda Esposito
Managing Art Editor Diane Peyton Jones
Publishers Laura Buller, Andrew Macintyre

Pre-production Controller Adam Stoneham
Senior Producer Gemma Sharpe

Senior Designer Jim Green

Project Designers Paul Drislane,
Hoa Luc, Mary Sandberg

Publishing Director Jonathan Metcalf
Associate Publishing Director Liz Wheeler
Art Director Phil Ormerod

Jacket Editor Manisha Majithia
Jacket Designer Laura Brim

This edition produced for the Book People Ltd,
Hall Wood Avenue, Haydock, St Helen's, WA11 9UL.

First published in Great Britain in 2013 by
Dorling Kindersley Limited
80 Strand, London WC2R 0RL

A Penguin Company

4 6 8 10 9 7 5 3
012 – 187017 – 6/13

A CIP catalogue record for this book is
available from the British Library.

ISBN: 978 1 4093 3423 1

Printed and bound by South China Printing Co. Ltd, China

See our complete catalogue at
www.dk.com

CAROL VORDERMAN M.A. (Cantab), MBE is one of Britain's best-loved TV presenters and is renowned for her skills in mathematics, and her enthusiasm and encouragement for education. She hosts numerous shows on the BBC, ITV, and Channel 4, from light entertainment with **Food Glorious Food** and **The Pride of Britain Awards** to scientific programmes such as **Tomorrow's World**. Whether hosting Channel 4's **Countdown** for 26 years or becoming the second best-selling female non-fiction author of the noughties decade in the UK, reporting to Prime Minister David Cameron in August 2010 with the far-reaching review "A World Class Mathematics Education for all our Young People", Carol has a passion for education and the value of good numeracy, literacy and communication skills. Carol was a founding trustee of NESTA, is patron for the Cambridge Science Festival, member of the Royal Institution, member of an advisory education panel for Engineering, and holder of many honorary degrees from universities around Britain. In 2010 she launched her own online maths school **www.themathsfactor.com** where she teaches parents and children how they can become the very best they can be in the language of mathematics. In 2011 she was the author of DK's **English Made Easy** series, which aims to help young children learn and practise key English language skills.

LINDA B. GAMBRELL is Distinguished Professor of Education at Clemson University. She is past president of the International Reading Association (IRA), Literacy Research Association, and the Association of Literacy Educators and Researchers. In 2004 she was inducted into the Reading Hall of Fame. She is a former classroom teacher and reading specialist. Linda has written books on reading instruction and published articles in major literacy journals, including Reading Research Quarterly, The Reading Teacher, and Journal of Educational Research.

SUSAN ROWAN is a former Head of English and Leading English and Literacy Adviser for a London borough. She has a Certificate in Education (Bishop Otter College of Education), a BA in English and History (Macquarie University, Australia) and an MBA – Education (University of Nottingham). With more than twenty-five years of teaching experience, Susan now works as an independent English and Literacy consultant supporting schools in London and south-east England.

DR. STEWART SAVARD is an eLibrarian in the Comox Valley of British Columbia. He has written a number of papers on the development of school libraries, the use of online and paper resources and how to work with students to prevent plagiarism. Stewart also has extensive experience as a classroom and Learning Assistance teacher. He has worked on almost twenty books.

Foreword

Hello,

The three decades I spent working on *Countdown* taught me to love the use of words and how language evolves. Today, we see poor English everywhere, from shop windows and advertisements to job applications. Some think it doesn't matter, but it does. The ability to speak and write well is invaluable in everyday life, at school and at work.

The rules of grammar, punctuation and spelling can seem complicated, and learning the skills needed to communicate effectively can be a daunting prospect – both for students and parents. Many parents may feel nervous about explaining the countless uses of commas, or lack confidence when deciding whether to say "you and me" or "you and I". This book presents clear examples and explanations that make even the most complex of concepts easy for everyone to understand.

Once you've got to grips with the rules, you can use them to get your message across in any situation – from writing an essay or an autobiography to booking a holiday or presenting a television programme.

I hope that you enjoy this book as much as we have loved putting it together.

CAROL VORDERMAN

abbreviations, accents, **acronyms**, adjectives, **adverbs**, alliteration, **apostrophes**, Arabic numerals, **articles**, asterisks, **auxiliary verbs**, brackets, **bullet points**, capital letters, **clauses**, collective nouns, **colloquialisms**, colons, **commands**, commas, **common nouns**, compound sentences, **compound words**, conditional sentences, **conjunctions**, consonants, **dangling participles**, dashes, **dialects**, direct speech, **ellipses**, exclamations, **exaggeration**, figures of speech, **first person**, fragments, **gender**, homographs, **homonyms**, homophones, **hyperbole**, hyphens, **idioms**, indefinite pronouns, **indicative mood**, indirect questions, **infinitives**, interjections, **irregular verbs**, italics, **jargon**, linking verbs, **main clauses**, misplaced modifiers, **moods**, morphemes, **negatives**, noun phrases, **nouns**, numbers, **objects**, ordinal numbers, **parentheses**, participles, **personal pronouns**, phonetics, **phrasal verbs**, phrases, **pitch**, plural nouns, **possessive determiners**, prefixes, **prepositional phrases**, present participles, **pronouns**, proper nouns, **puns**, punctuation, **question marks**, questions, **quotations**, relative pronouns, **reported speech**, rhetorical questions, **Roman numerals**, roots, **sentences**, silent letters, **singular**, slang, **subject**, subordinate clauses, **suffixes**, syllables, **tautology**, tenses, **third person**, tone, **verbs**, voices, **vowels**

CONTENTS

1 GRAMMAR

2 PUNCTUATION

3 SPELLING

4 COMMUNICATION SKILLS

5 REFERENCE

Why learn the rules?

THERE ARE MANY BENEFITS TO LEARNING AND MASTERING
THE RULES OF THE ENGLISH LANGUAGE.

The rules of English are indispensable and will help English speakers
of all ages in a variety of situations, from sending a simple e-mail and
giving travel directions to writing the next bestselling novel.

English is the main
language of **news** and
information in the world.

Ways with words

The rules or skills of English can be divided into four major
areas. These areas show how words should be organised
in a sentence, how they should be spelt and punctuated
and how they should be used in specific situations.

Grammar	Punctuation	Spelling	Communication skills
Grammar rules show how different types of words – such as nouns and adjectives – should be put together in a sentence to create fluent and clear writing.	Punctuation refers to the use of symbols – such as full stops, question marks, commas and apostrophes – to tell the reader how to read a piece of writing.	Spelling rules help English speakers to understand and remember the ways in which letters and groups of letters combine to form words.	Communication skills help English speakers to interact with others effectively: for instance, when writing a letter, passing on instructions or delivering a speech.

Access all areas

A solid grasp of English will help students
to succeed in all subject areas, not just in
English lessons. Whether writing a science
report, instructing a basketball team as
captain or auditioning for a play, English
language skills help students to fulfil
their potential.

English language skills can
help students to succeed
in all subject areas.

Report Card

Student: Paul Drislane

Course	Mark	Grade
English	97%	A
Maths	94%	A
Science	90%	A
History	92%	A
Geography	97%	A
Drama	93%	A
Sport	95%	A

Dream job

When applying for jobs, good English language skills can make all the difference. Knowing the rules will help a candidate to write a perfect application, and to speak clearly and confidently in an interview. All employers, regardless of the industry, look for candidates who can express themselves correctly and assertively because these skills are valuable in most jobs every day.

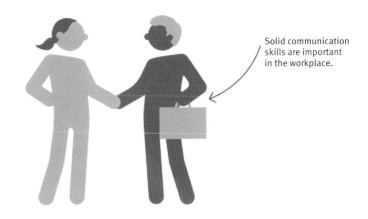

Solid communication skills are important in the workplace.

Time out

Language is used creatively in a variety of social situations, from a rowdy sports game to a sophisticated stage show. At a big game, fans sing rhyming and repetitive chants filled with playful jokes or insults to the opposite team. In the theatre, actors perform dramatic, evocative lines to express feelings of love, passion, sadness or anger. Whether watching a funny film, reading a newspaper or listening to a pop song, a person who has a good working knowledge of English will get the most out of these experiences.

Is love a tender thing? It is too rough, too rude, too boisterous, and it pricks like thorn.

William Shakespeare's character Romeo compares love to a sharp thorn, suggesting that love hurts. An audience with a good understanding of English will appreciate this subtle, visual use of language.

Travel the world

English is one of the most popular languages spoken across the globe, and it's the main language used in the business world. Fluency in the language makes it easier to travel to English-speaking places for work or holidays. What's more, a knowledge of grammatical terms makes learning other languages easier.

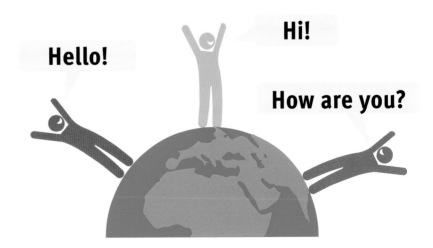

Hello!

Hi!

How are you?

Spoken and written language

BOTH WRITTEN AND SPOKEN ENGLISH HAVE UNIQUE FEATURES.

It's important to understand the differences between written and spoken language – as well as the different uses within each – to improve these two types of communication.

The **earliest known written language** was **Sumerian**, which developed in **Mesopotamia** (modern-day Iraq) in about 2600 BCE.

Written language

Pieces of writing such as novels, letters and newspaper articles are carefully constructed because writers usually have time to think about the words and sentences that they use. This means that written English is organised into complete sentences and uses formal vocabulary and correct grammar.

Dear Jane,

I am having a wonderful time in Thailand. It's a beautiful country with a fascinating culture. The sun shines every day, so we spend most of our time at the stunning beaches, sunbathing and snorkelling. I would love to come back another year.

Love from Nick x

08-01-2013

Miss Jane Palmer

2 Villa Court

London, SE4 2JK

ENGLAND

Written English should be in complete sentences.

Spoken language

In general, spoken language is more spontaneous than written language, so it contains features such as repetition, pauses and sounds like *er* or *um*. Words are often left out or shortened to speed up a conversation, and the vocabulary and pronunciation varies according to the background of the speaker.

The words *I had an* have been left out.

The words *yeah* and *awesome* are informal words used in speech.

Hey, Jane! Yeah, awesome trip, thanks. Good weather, good beaches...um... we went snorkelling, too. Can't wait to go back another time.

People often repeat words when they are speaking.

It is more common to shorten or abbreviate words in spoken language. Here, *cannot* has been shortened to *can't* and *I* has been omitted.

People pause and fill silences with sounds when they speak.

Writing spoken language

Some pieces of writing intentionally mimic the features of spoken English. For instance, the dialogue in novels or dramatic scripts is often written to sound spontaneous, and uses words and spellings that suggest the background of the characters, to make them more authentic.

Yarra Creek

Episode 14: The Big Invitation

Scene: It's a sunny day. Mario and Darren meet while collecting their mail on the driveway.

Mario: G'day Darren. D'ya wanna drop by for a barbie this arvo?

Darren: Yeah, no plans, mate. Catch ya later.

G'day is a word used in Australian speech for "hello".

The words *Do you want to* have been written as they should be pronounced by the actor.

The informal phrase *catch ya later* is used instead of *see you later*. *You* is written as *ya* to show how the word should be pronounced.

The word *barbie* means "barbeque" and *arvo* means "afternoon".

Formal or informal

In general, spoken English can be less formal than written English; however, there are important exceptions. For instance, a text message to a friend may be informal, but a work presentation should be delivered in formal language. The level of formality depends on the situation and the audience.

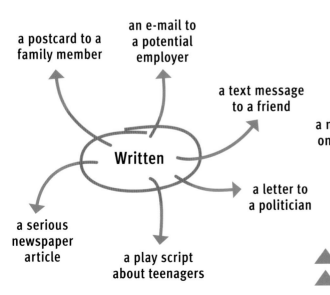

a chat to a friend on the telephone

a response in a job interview

a joke

Spoken

a work presentation

a news broadcast on the television

an interview on a talk show

a postcard to a family member

an e-mail to a potential employer

a text message to a friend

Written

a letter to a politician

a serious newspaper article

a play script about teenagers

▲ Informal

▲ Formal

△ **Formal or informal**
Some types of written English need to use formal language, while others can be informal. The same is true for spoken English. It depends on the particular situation.

English around the world

ENGLISH IS USED THROUGHOUT THE WORLD, BUT NOT ALWAYS
IN THE SAME WAY.

Many countries throughout the world use the English language,
but the way it's used – especially spoken – can differ hugely
between regions, even within the same country.

Spread the word

The English language can be traced
back to a combination of Anglo-Saxon
dialects more than 1,500 years old.
It started to spread around the world
from the 1600s onwards, when the
British began to explore and colonise,
taking their language with them. Today,
the English language continues to grow
in popularity, especially in Southeast
and eastern Asia, where English is seen
as the preferred language for business
and trade with Western countries.

1. In the Caribbean and Canada,
historical links with the UK compete
with geographical, cultural and
economic ties with the United States,
so their language reflects both British
and American forms of English.

2. Most of South America speaks
Spanish or Portuguese because Spain
and Portugal once had empires there.
However, in a few countries in Central
and South America – such as Guyana,
which achieved independence from
Great Britain in 1966 – the official
language is English.

Spot the differences

After the English language was taken to
North America, the spelling of certain
words started to change. Published in
1828, *An American Dictionary of the
English Language* established spellings
such as *center* and *color* (instead of the
British spellings *centre* and *colour*),
creating a broader acceptance of
American and British English as two
distinct entities. These variations in
spelling still exist today.

▷ **Spelling and punctuation**
British and American English use different
spellings and punctuation. For example,
verbs such as *criticise* are spelt with an *s*
in British English but a *z* in American
English. American English often uses
longer dashes and more commas in
a list than British English.

The new musical *Hello Darling* has been cancelled after
just nine performances – the shortest run in the theatre's
history. The show has been severely criticised after many
jokes caused offence. One critic described the humour
as "crude, dated and unimaginative".

British version ——————   —————— American version

The new musical *Hello Darling* has been canceled after
just nine performances—the shortest run in the theater's
history. The show has been severely criticized after many
jokes caused offense. One critic described the humor as
"crude, dated, and unimaginative."

3. North America was the first English-speaking colony, but it developed a distinct form of English with different spellings.

4. English became the dominant language in Great Britain during the Middle Ages (5th to 15th centuries).

5. A 2010 survey found that about two-thirds of Europeans can speak some English.

6. Today, English is an international language of business, and is taught in schools in many Asian countries, including Japan and China.

7. In India and parts of Africa, English was imposed as the administrative language through centuries of colonial rule, but – in most cases – it was spoken only as a second language by the local populations.

8. The expansion of the British Empire during the 1700s in Australia and New Zealand saw European populations quickly outnumber indigenous populations, and English became the dominant language.

What's that?

English speakers around the world use different words and pronunciation, according to their background, age and sense of identity. An accent is the way in which the words are pronounced, whereas a dialect refers to the use of certain vocabulary and grammatical constructions. In the UK alone, there are many distinctive dialects, such as Geordie (Newcastle), Brummie (Birmingham) and Doric (northeast Scotland). Similarly, around the world, English is spoken and written in many different ways, so that some common objects are called by different names in Britain, America, Canada and Australia.

fizzy drink
soda   pop

flip-flops
thongs

knapsack
backpack   rucksack

A path at the side of the road for pedestrians is called a *pavement* in Britain, a *sidewalk* in North America and a *footpath* in Australia.

pavement
sidewalk
footpath

jumper
sweater

The British call a knitted garment with long sleeves *a jumper*. In North America, this is called *a sweater*.

sweet pepper
bell pepper
capsicum

trousers
pants

trainers
runners   sneakers

Grammar

The purpose of grammar

THE STRUCTURE OF A LANGUAGE IS KNOWN AS ITS GRAMMAR.

Words are the building blocks of language. Grammar is a set of rules that determines how these building blocks can be put together in different combinations to create well-formed phrases, clauses and sentences, which enable and enrich conversation.

The **first** published **book** about English **grammar**, *Pamphlet for Grammar*, was written by **William Bullokar** in 1586.

Evolving languages

All languages change over time. As a language evolves, its grammar adapts to incorporate new words and ways of organising them. Different languages have different sets of rules, so sentences are formed in different ways, even if they mean the same thing. Thus, it's often difficult to translate sentences exactly from another language into English.

▷ **English word order**
This is a grammatically correct sentence in English. The verb *read* follows the subject, *I*, and the adjective *good* follows the linking verb *was*.

I read my sister's book, which was good.

▷ **Old English word order**
This sentence has been translated into Old English, and then translated directly back into modern English. The first part of the sentence still makes grammatical sense in modern English, but in the second part of the sentence, the verb is now at the end.

I read the book of my sister, which good was.

▷ **German word order**
This sentence has been translated into German, and then translated directly back into English. The word order is the same as that of the Old English sentence, because Old English is a Germanic language.

I read the book of my sister, which good was.

Learning grammar

When a child learns a language, he or she absorbs information about how that language is structured. This knowledge is refined as the child learns to read and write. Although much of this learning is subconscious, some grammatical rules simply have to be learnt.

I'm coming with you, aren't I?

Wrong! What you meant to say was, "I'm coming with you, am I not?"

Parts of speech

Words are grouped together according to the functions they perform in a sentence. There are ten parts of speech in English. Nouns (or pronouns) and verbs are essential to the structure of a sentence, but it's the other parts of speech, including adjectives, adverbs, conjunctions and prepositions, that make a sentence interesting.

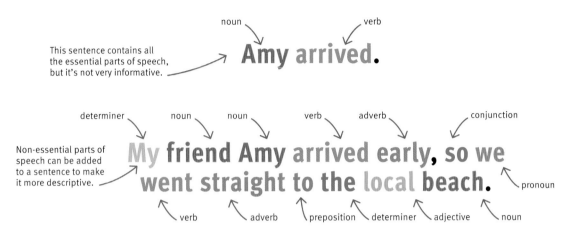

noun   verb

This sentence contains all the essential parts of speech, but it's not very informative.

Amy arrived.

determiner   noun   noun   verb   adverb   conjunction

Non-essential parts of speech can be added to a sentence to make it more descriptive.

My friend Amy arrived early, so we went straight to the local beach.

pronoun

verb   adverb   preposition   determiner   adjective   noun

Structuring sentences

Without the rules of grammar, words would be placed in a random order, and no one would be able to understand what anyone else was saying. An ability to communicate effectively comes from following these rules. A sentence must also be correctly punctuated for it to make sense. Grammar explains which order to put words in, while punctuation marks such as full stops and commas indicate how the sentence should be read.

The pronoun *I* is always capitalised, but all sentences must start with a capital letter.

Verbs always follow the noun or pronoun that is performing the action – in this case, *I*.

Adjectives usually go before the noun they are modifying.

I always put my words in the right order.

Adverbs usually go before the verb they are modifying.

Determiners, including articles, always go before the nouns they refer to – here, *words* and *order*.

Sentences always end with a full stop, a question mark or an exclamation mark.

Everyday grammar

A good grasp of grammar enables people to speak and write clearly and concisely, and to understand all kinds of reading material. These skills are invaluable when it comes to job applications, as employers will always show a preference for candidates who have submitted grammatically correct applications. Similarly, candidates who can express themselves clearly will be more successful in interviews. Good grammar improves creative writing, too, and even the best-known writers – past and present – have followed a few simple rules.

"My suffering left me sad and gloomy."

The opening line from Yann Martel's *Life of Pi* follows the rules because it starts with a noun, followed by a verb, and includes adjectives that make the sentence memorable.

Parts of speech

WORDS ARE THE BUILDING BLOCKS OF LANGUAGE, BUT
THEY MUST BE ARRANGED IN A RECOGNISABLE ORDER.

Parts of speech refer to the way in which particular words are used.
Some words can be classified as more than one word type, and they
change type according to the sentence they belong to.

SEE ALSO	
Nouns	22–23 ❯
Verbs	38–39 ❯
Voices and moods	54–55 ❯
Phrases	64–65 ❯
Clauses	66–67 ❯
Sentences	68–69 ❯

Word types

The main parts of speech are nouns, verbs, adjectives,
pronouns, adverbs, prepositions and conjunctions.
Interjections are also important, as they are used so often
in everyday speech. Nouns (or pronouns) and verbs are
the only essential components of a sentence.

▽ **Different roles**
Each type of word performs a different
function. Some depend on others for
sense; some exist solely to modify others.

Noun

A word used to name a person, animal, place or thing.

EXAMPLES
William, mouse, supermarket,
ladder, desk, station, ball, boy

ball

Adjective

A word used to describe a noun or pronoun.

EXAMPLES
shiny, dangerous, new, bouncy,
noisy, colourful, wooden

colourful ball

Verb

A word that expresses an
action or a state of being.

EXAMPLES
run, be, kick, go, think, do, play,
stumble, touch

kick the ball

Adverb

A word that describes and adds
information to a verb or a verb phrase.

EXAMPLES
quickly, soon, very, rather, too,
almost, only,
quietly   **quickly** kick the ball

Pronoun

A word that takes the place of a noun.

EXAMPLES
he, she, them, him, we, you, us,
mine, yours, theirs

kick the ball to **him**

Preposition

A word that indicates the relationship between two
people or things, usually in terms of where they are.

EXAMPLES
with, under, on, behind, into,
over, across

kick the ball **behind** you

Putting words together

For speech to make sense, words must be linked to other words in the right way to form sentences. Imagine a sports team – each player representing one word. A lone player cannot achieve very much, but, teamed with other players and following strict rules, he can achieve a lot. These rules of play are like grammar – they determine both direction and purpose.

When we are joined together, we make a great team.

Conjunction

A word used to link words and clauses.

EXAMPLES
and, but, so, yet, or, neither, nor, because

bat **and** ball

Interjection

A word that usually occurs alone and expresses emotion.

EXAMPLES
oh, hello, ah, ouch, phew, yuck, hurrah, help, er, um, oops

ouch!

Article

A word used with a noun to refer to a specific person or thing, or someone or something in general.

EXAMPLES
a, an, the

the ball

Determiner

A word used in front of a noun to denote something specific or something of a particular type. Articles are also determiners.

EXAMPLES
those, many, my, his, few, several, much

my ball

Summary sentence

article — noun — adverb — verb — determiner — adjective — noun — preposition — interjection

The boy quickly kicked his bouncy ball past a defender, but in his haste he stumbled. oops!

article — noun — conjunction — preposition — determiner — noun — pronoun — verb

Nouns

NOUNS ARE USED TO NAME PEOPLE, ANIMALS, PLACES OR THINGS.

Nouns are often known as "naming" words. Every sentence must include at least one noun or pronoun. Most nouns can be either singular or plural, and can be divided into two main groups: common and proper nouns.

Common nouns

Common nouns are used all the time to describe everyday objects, animals, places, people and ideas. They do not have a capital letter unless they appear at the start of a sentence. Every sentence must contain a noun, and this noun is usually a common noun. Nouns that describe things that can be seen and touched are known as concrete nouns.

book

goat

bread

birds

girl

piece

Abstract nouns

A type of common noun, abstract nouns are more difficult to define. Unlike concrete nouns, which refer to physical things, abstract nouns refer to ideas, feelings, occasions or time – things that can't be seen or touched.

love

happiness

bravery

trust

afternoon

health

The goat's afternoon was ruined
down and snatched the piece o

- With the exception of some abstract nouns, if the word *the* can be put **in front of a word** and the resulting combination **makes sense**, then that word is a **noun**.
- Nouns can often be recognised by their **endings**. Typical endings include **-er, -or, -ist, -tion, -ment** and **-ism**: *writer, visitor, dentist, competition, argument, criticism.*

GLOSSARY

Abstract noun The name given to something that cannot be touched, such as a concept or a sensation.

Collective noun The name given to a collection of individuals – people or things.

Concrete noun The name given to an ordinary thing, such as an animal or object.

Noun phrase Several words that, when grouped together, perform the same function as a noun.

Prepositional phrase A preposition such as *in* or *on* followed by a noun or pronoun that together act as an adjective (describing a noun) or an adverb (describing a verb) in a sentence.

Proper noun The name given to a particular person, place or thing, which always starts with a capital letter.

The word *time* is the most **commonly used noun** in the **English** language.

Identifying noun phrases

A noun phrase is made up of a noun and any words that are modifying that noun. These modifying words are usually articles such as *the* or *a*, determiners such as *my*, *this* or *most*, adjectives such as *happy* or *hungry*, or prepositional phrases such as *in the field*. Noun phrases perform exactly the same role as common nouns in a sentence.

common noun

goat

article

The goat is named Billy.

noun phrase

adjective

The **hungry goat** is named Billy.

noun phrase   prepositional phrase

The hungry **goat in the field** is named Billy.

noun phrase

Collective nouns

Another type of common noun, collective nouns refer to a group of things or people. They are usually singular words that represent a number of things. Different collective nouns refer to different concrete nouns, and the collective nouns used to describe groups of animals are especially varied.

a **swarm** of bees

a **crowd** of people

a **flight** of stairs

a **bunch** of grapes

a **flock** of birds

when a **flock of birds swooped bread from Emily's hand.**

Proper nouns

A proper noun is the name given to a particular person, place or breed of animal, or to a religious or historical concept or period. Proper nouns always start with a capital letter. This helps to distinguish them from common nouns. The most common proper nouns are the names of people or places, but titles, institutions, days of the week, and events and festivals are also proper nouns.

Type of proper noun	Examples
Names of people	John, Sally Smith, Queen Elizabeth II
Titles	Mr., Miss, Sir, Dr., Professor, Reverend
Places, buildings and institutions	Africa, Asia, Canada, New York, Red Cross, Sydney Opera House, United Nations
Religious names	Bible, Koran, Christianity, Hinduism, Islam
Historical names	World War I, Ming Dynasty, Roman Empire
Events and festivals	Olympic Games, New Year's Eve
Days of the week, months	Saturday, December

Plurals

A NOUN'S PLURAL FORM IS USED WHEN THERE IS MORE THAN ONE OF SOMETHING.

SEE ALSO	
❰ 22–23 Nouns	
Comparatives and superlatives	28–29 ❱
Verb agreement	52–53 ❱
Prefixes and suffixes	142–143 ❱

The word *plural* refers to the form a noun takes when more than one thing is being mentioned. Most nouns have distinctive singular and plural forms.

Regular plural nouns

The most common way to make a noun plural is to add *s* or *es* to the end of the singular form. Most nouns take the ending -s, except for those ending in -s, -z, -x, -sh, -ch or -ss, which take the suffix (ending) -es.

One **dragon**
Two **dragons**

One **wish**
Two **wishes**

Follow the rules

Some nouns are given different plural endings to make them easier to pronounce. In most cases, it is possible to follow a few simple rules. If a word ends in -y, for example, and it has a vowel before the final -y, the plural is formed in the usual way: an *s* is added. If the final -y is preceded by a consonant, however, the *y* must be changed to *i*, followed by the ending -es.

If a word, such as *cactus*, has been borrowed from **Latin**, the Latin **plural** form (here, *cacti*) is often used.

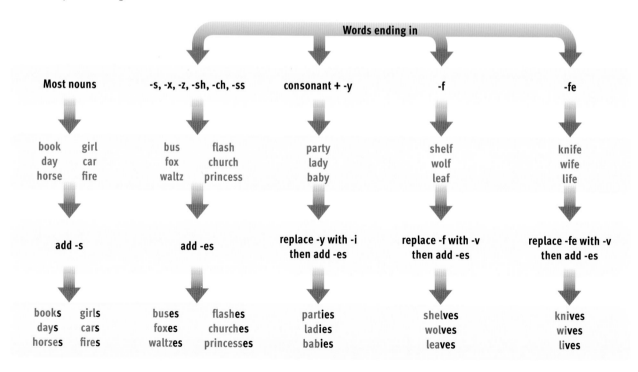

Words ending in				
Most nouns	-s, -x, -z, -sh, -ch, -ss	consonant + -y	-f	-fe
book girl day car horse fire	bus flash fox church waltz princess	party lady baby	shelf wolf leaf	knife wife life
add -s	add -es	replace -y with -i then add -es	replace -f with -v then add -es	replace -fe with -v then add -es
book**s** girl**s** day**s** car**s** horse**s** fire**s**	bus**es** flash**es** fox**es** church**es** waltz**es** princess**es**	part**ies** lad**ies** bab**ies**	shel**ves** wol**ves** lea**ves**	kni**ves** wi**ves** li**ves**

Irregular plural nouns

Some words just don't follow the rules. Although many nouns that end in -o are made plural by adding an *s*, others take the ending -es. Some nouns change their spelling completely when they become plural, while others do not change at all. Words that originate from Latin and Greek often have irregular plural endings. These exceptions have to be learnt.

- If the plural form of a **noun** is used in a sentence, the **verb** that follows it must also be **plural**.
- Do not confuse **plural** words with the **possessive**. For example, "There are **two Jasons** [plural] in my class, and this is **Jason's car** [possessive]."

Staying singular

Collective nouns such as *flock* or *crowd* have plural forms, but usually appear in the singular. Some nouns do not have a plural form at all, even though they usually represent multiple things. Furniture, for example, is a singular word, but it may encompass a table, a chair, a sofa and a wardrobe.

education

furniture

information

homework

livestock

evidence

weather

knowledge

Singular	Plural
quiz	quizzes

Words ending in -z usually take the regular -es ending.

Singular	Plural
belief	beliefs
chief	chiefs
cliff	cliffs
roof	roofs

Words ending in -f usually change their endings to -ves.

Words ending in -o usually take the -s ending.

Singular	Plural
echo	echoes
hero	heroes
potato	potatoes
tomato	tomatoes

Singular	Plural
analysis	analyses
appendix	appendices
crisis	crises

Words of Latin or Greek origin often have irregular plural forms.

Some words change their spelling completely.

Singular	Plural
child	children
woman	women
person	people
man	men
foot	feet
tooth	teeth
goose	geese
mouse	mice
ox	oxen

Singular	Plural
sheep	sheep
deer	deer
moose	moose
series	series
scissors	scissors

Some words don't change at all.

Some nouns have two plural forms.

Singular	Plural
hoof	hooves or hoofs
dwarf	dwarves or dwarfs
mango	mangoes or mangos
buffalo	buffaloes or buffalo
index	indexes or indices
focus	focuses or foci

Adjectives

ADJECTIVES ARE WORDS OR PHRASES THAT MODIFY OR DESCRIBE NOUNS OR PRONOUNS.

A noun by itself does not offer much information. If a man wanted to buy a shirt in a shop, he would need to narrow down what he was looking for by using descriptive words like *thin* or *silky*. These words are known as adjectives.

• If you are unsure whether a word is an adjective or something else, see if it answers questions such as: **What kind? Which one? How much? How many?**

• Adjectives should be used **sparingly**, for effect. Too many adjectives can make a sentence difficult to follow.

Describing words

Most adjectives describe attributes (characteristics) of nouns or pronouns and answer the question *What is it like?* They are used to compare one person or thing to other people or things. Adjectives are usually placed directly in front of the noun – a position known as the attributive position.

the weary painter

adjective in attributive position

noun

The weary painter took off his and ate a day-old Chinese

GLOSSARY

Attributive position When an adjective is placed directly in front of the noun or pronoun that it is modifying.

Clause A group of words that contains a subject and a verb.

Linking verb A verb that joins the subject of a sentence to a word or phrase – often an adjective – that describes the subject.

Predicate position When an adjective follows a linking verb at the end of a sentence.

Proper noun The name given to a particular person, place or thing, which always starts with a capital letter.

Compound adjectives

Compound adjectives are made up of more than one word. When two or more words are used together as an adjective in front of a noun, they are usually hyphenated. This shows that the two words are acting together as a single adjective.

This two-word adjective means "not fresh today".

day-old meal

"Proper" adjectives

Some nouns can be modified and used before other nouns as adjectives. These include proper nouns, such as the names of places. Adjectives formed from proper nouns should always start with a capital letter. They often end in -an, -ian and -ish.

Chinese

Australian   **English**

Roman

Identifying adjectives

Adverbs such as *very* or *extremely* can be used to exaggerate the state of a subject. These adverbs are sometimes confused with adjectives. A simple way of checking whether a word is an adjective or an adverb is to break down a sentence, pairing each descriptive word in turn with the noun to see if the resulting phrase makes sense.

A hungry, **decidedly** weary painter

A hungry painter ✓ — This is an adjective, because the phrase makes sense.

A **decidedly** painter ✗ — This is not an adjective, because the phrase doesn't make sense. It is an adverb.

A weary painter ✓ — This is also an adjective, because the phrase makes sense.

Listing adjectives

If one word is not enough to describe something, use several adjectives. Each adjective should be separated from the next by a comma. If there is a list of adjectives at the end of the clause, the last adjective must be preceded by *and*.

blue, green **and** white **overalls**

Place a comma between adjectives in a list.

The last adjective should follow the word *and*.

• Avoid using two or more adjectives together that mean the same thing: for example, "the hungry, starving, ravenous tennis player". This **unnecessary repetition** of the same idea using different words is known as **tautology**.

blue, green **and** white **overalls**
meal because he felt ravenous.

Predicate adjectives

Many adjectives can also be placed at the end of a sentence, following a verb. This is known as the predicate position. A verb used in this way is called a linking verb, because it connects a subject with a descriptive word. Common linking verbs include *seem*, *look*, *feel*, *become*, *stay* and *turn*.

he felt ravenous

linking verb

adjective in predicate position

Adjective endings

Many adjectives can be recognised by their endings. Knowing these endings can help to distinguish adjectives from adverbs and verbs.

Ending	Examples
-able/-ible	comfort**able**, remark**able**, horr**ible**, ed**ible**
-al	fiction**al**, education**al**, logic**al**, nation**al**
-ful	bash**ful**, peace**ful**, help**ful**, beauti**ful**
-ic	energet**ic**, man**ic**, dramat**ic**, fantast**ic**
-ive	attract**ive**, sensit**ive**, impuls**ive**, persuas**ive**
-less	home**less**, care**less**, end**less**, use**less**
-ous	raven**ous**, mischiev**ous**, fam**ous**, nerv**ous**

Comparatives and superlatives

ADJECTIVES CAN BE USED TO COMPARE NOUNS OR PRONOUNS.

Comparatives and superlatives are special types of adjectives that are used to compare two or more things. Most comparatives are formed using the ending -er, and most superlatives are formed using the ending -est.

• **Never use double** comparatives or double superlatives – "more prettier" and "most prettiest" are wrong.

• Not every adjective has a comparative or superlative form. *Unique*, *square*, *round*, *excellent* and *perfect* are all words that can't be graded.

Comparatives

A comparative adjective is used to compare two people or things. It is formed by adding the ending -er to all one-syllable adjectives and some two-syllable adjectives. When two nouns are being compared in a sentence, they are usually linked using the preposition *than*.

This word is used to link the two nouns being compared: the Ferris wheel and the carousel.

The Ferris wheel is bigger than the carousel.

The Ferris wheel is bigger than the the biggest ride of all. The ghost

Superlatives

Superlative adjectives can be used to compare two or more people or things. They are formed by adding the ending -est to one-syllable adjectives, and using the word *the* in front of them: "the biggest ride".

big
bigger
biggest

small
smaller
smallest

thin
thinner
thinnest

REAL WORLD

Biggest and best

Multiple superlatives are often used in advertisements to sell things, whether they're books, holidays or circus attractions. Words like *greatest*, *best* and *cheapest* enable a seller to exaggerate the quality or value of the product being sold, making it more appealing to potential customers. Superlatives should be used in moderation in formal text, however.

Identifying irregular adjective spellings

Some adjectives do not follow the rules when it comes to forming their comparatives or superlatives. If an adjective already ends in -e (*rude*), only -r needs to be added to make it comparative (*ruder*), and -st, to make it superlative (*rudest*). Words ending in -y or a vowel and a single consonant have to change their endings.

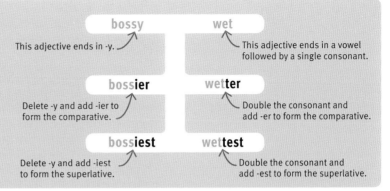

bossy

This adjective ends in -y.

wet

This adjective ends in a vowel followed by a single consonant.

bossier

Delete -y and add -ier to form the comparative.

wetter

Double the consonant and add -er to form the comparative.

bossiest

Delete -y and add -iest to form the superlative.

wettest

Double the consonant and add -est to form the superlative.

Exceptions

Some two-syllable adjectives, such as *lovely*, can take either form of the comparative or superlative (see "Awkward adjectives"). Other adjectives change completely when they are used to compare things. These comparative and superlative forms have to be learnt.

Adjective	Comparative	Superlative
good	better	best
bad	worse	worst
much	more	most
many	more	most
little	less	least
quiet	quieter or more quiet	quietest or most quiet
simple	simpler or more simple	simplest or most simple
clever	cleverer or more clever	cleverest or most clever
lovely	lovelier or more lovely	loveliest or most lovely

:arousel, but the roller coaster is :rain is the most frightening.

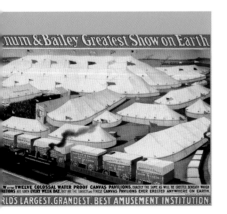

Awkward adjectives

If adding the ending -er or -est results in an odd-sounding adjective, the comparative and superlative are formed using the words *more* or *most* before the adjective. This applies to most two-syllable adjectives and all adjectives with three or more syllables.

The ghost train is the most frightening.

The superlative *frighteningest* is hard to say, so – because *frightening* has three syllables – the superlative is formed using *most*.

Articles

THERE ARE TWO TYPES OF ARTICLES: DEFINITE AND INDEFINITE.

Articles are a type of adjective and a type of determiner. They are always used with a noun. Similarly, many singular forms of nouns must be used with an article.

SEE ALSO	
❰ 22–23 Nouns	
❰ 24–25 Plurals	
❰ 26–27 Adjectives	
Determiners	32–33 ❱

The definite article

The definite article is *the*. It always precedes a noun, and refers to a specific person or thing. This person or thing may have been mentioned before, or there may be only one to talk about. Alternatively, it may be clear from the context which noun is being referred to.

the rhinoceros

There is only one rhinoceros on the bus, so the definite article is used.

In **many languages**, including French, German and Spanish, **the article** tells the reader whether a word is **feminine**, **masculine** or **neutral**. In **English**, very **few words** have a **gender**.

The rhinoceros and his best
a bus to visit the struggling

The indefinite article

The indefinite article *a* or *an* is used to refer to any one person or thing. Words that begin with consonants (*bus*) use *a*, while words that start with a vowel (*a, e, i, o* or *u*) or a silent *h*, such as *hour*, use *an* to make pronunciation easier. The indefinite article also indicates that someone or something belongs to a specific group. For example, "The animal is a giraffe" explains that this particular animal is one of many members of a group of animals known as giraffes.

The indefinite article indicates that this could be one of a number of buses, whereas the definite article *the* would refer to one particular bus.

a bus

The form *an* is used before a vowel to make it easier to say.

an elephant

Articles and adjectives

If a noun is preceded by one or more descriptive adjectives, the article goes before the adjective. The resulting phrase (article + adjective + noun) is known as a noun phrase. If the indefinite article is used in front of an adjective that begins with a vowel, the form *an* is used.

The article precedes the adjective *struggling*, which goes before the noun *ostrich*.

the struggling ostrich

The adjective *anxious* begins with a vowel, so *an* is used.

an anxious rhinoceros

Identifying when to use an article

If a singular noun can be counted, this noun will require an article – definite or indefinite. For example, "I saw elephant today" doesn't make sense. Some nouns, such as *happiness*, *information* and *bread*, do not have a plural form, and therefore cannot be counted. These nouns can be used without an article (zero article) or with the definite article. They never take the indefinite article.

elephant

This noun can be counted, so the definite or indefinite article can be used.

one elephant
two elephants

the elephant

an elephant

bread

This noun cannot be counted.

one bread
two breads

The definite article can be used for a specific piece of bread.

the bread

The zero article is used for the concept of bread in general.

bread

**riend, an elephant, took
ostrich at flying school.**

The zero article

Some words, such as *school*, *life* and *home*, take the definite article when a particular one is being referred to, and the indefinite article when one of several is being described. When these words are used to describe a general concept, such as being at school, the article is removed. This absence of an article is known as the zero article.

at flying school

This describes school as a concept – a place where a person goes to learn something – so the zero article (no article) is used.

at the flying school next to the zoo

This describes a particular school – the one next to the zoo – so *the* is required.

• Many **geographical areas** and features, including **rivers**, **deserts** and **oceans**, use the **definite article**: for example, the North Pole, the Pacific Ocean or the Rocky Mountains.

• If an **article** is at the beginning of the **title** of a work, such as *The Secret Garden*, it should start with a **capital letter**.

• **Unique things**, such as **the sun**, always take *the*.

• Watch out for words that begin with a **vowel** that **sounds like a consonant**, such as *university*. These take the indefinite article *a*, rather than *an*.

Determiners

DETERMINERS ARE ALWAYS PLACED BEFORE A NOUN,
AND HELP TO DEFINE IT.

Articles are determiners, and other determiners work in much the same way: they are used in front of nouns to indicate whether something specific or something of a particular type is being referred to.

Determiners and adjectives

Determiners are often considered to be a subclass of adjectives and, like adjectives, they belong to nouns and modify nouns. Unlike adjectives, there is rarely more than one determiner for each noun, nor can determiners be compared or graded. They precede the noun and include words like *several*, *those*, *many*, *my* and *your*, as well as articles (*the*, *a* and *an*) and numbers.

The determiner always precedes any adjectives, which, in turn, precede the noun.

several furious members
adjective — plural noun

• **Many sentences do not make sense without determiners.** Adjectives, by contrast, are optional; they colour the words rather than glue them together.

• Most **noun phrases** only use **one determiner**, but there are exceptions: for example, "all the bats" and "both my cats".

definite article

Several furious members of the broomsticks. "That witch has nine

Demonstrative determiners

Demonstrative determiners give an idea of distance between the speaker and the person or thing that he or she is referring to. *This* (singular) and *these* (plural) are used to describe things that are nearby. *That* (singular) and *those* (plural) are used for things that are further away.

This indicates a witch who is not present at the meeting. → **that witch**

The witches are discussing a noise they can hear – that of shrieking bats – so *this* is used. → **this noise**

Identifying determiners

Sometimes determiners look very similar to adjectives. One way of working out whether a word that precedes a noun is a determiner or an adjective is to try placing the word at the end of a sentence, following a linking verb such as *be*. If the sentence makes sense, that word is an adjective; if it does not make sense, it is a determiner.

Several furious members

This is an adjective, because the sentence makes sense.

The members **are furious**. ✓

linking verb

This is a determiner, because the sentence does not make sense.

The members **are** several. ✗

• Some words, such as *each* or *all*, are used both as **determiners and pronouns**. The rule to remember is that a **determiner** is always **followed by a noun**, whereas a pronoun replaces a noun.

Possessive determiners

The possessive determiners *my*, *your*, *his*, *her*, *its*, *our* and *their* are used before nouns to show ownership. They should not be confused with possessive pronouns – for example, *mine*, *yours*, *ours* and *theirs* – which replace, rather than precede, the noun.

their broomsticks

The broomsticks (plural noun) belong to the witches.

indefinite article

oven held a meeting on their hrieking bats!" they grumbled.

Numbers and quantifiers

Cardinal and ordinal numbers and other words that express quantity are considered to be determiners when they appear before a noun. These include *much*, *most*, *little*, *least*, *any*, *enough*, *half* and *whole*. Beware of determiners such as *much* (singular) and *many* (plural) that can only modify singular or plural nouns.

nine shrieking bats

This cardinal number is being used before a noun phrase (*shrieking bats*) as a determiner.

much noise

This determiner can only be used with a singular noun.

many bats

This determiner can only be used with a plural noun.

Interrogative determiners

Interrogative determiners include *which* and *what* and are used before a noun to ask a question.

Which witch?

What noise?

Pronouns

PRONOUN MEANS "FOR A NOUN", AND A PRONOUN IS A WORD THAT TAKES THE PLACE OF A NOUN.

Without pronouns, spoken and written English would be very repetitive. Once a noun has been referred to by its actual name once, another word – a pronoun – can be used to stand for this name.

Using pronouns

If the full name of a noun were used each time it had to be referred to, sentences would be long and confusing. Pronouns are useful because they make sentences shorter and therefore clearer. The noun is still required when someone or something is referred to for the first time.

noun noun
Rita loves playing the **guitar**.
She finds **it** relaxing.

This personal pronoun represents *Rita*, the subject.

This personal pronoun represents *playing the guitar*, the object.

Types of pronouns

There are seven types of pronouns, which are used for different purposes. Do not confuse these with determiners or adjectives, which modify rather than replace nouns.

• *I* is the only pronoun that is spelt with a **capital** letter.

Personal pronouns

These **represent people, places or things**. They vary according to whether the noun being replaced is the subject of a sentence (performing the action) or the object (receiving the action).

I, you, he, she, it, we, you, they (subject)
me, you, him, her, it, us, you, them (object)

This pronoun represents the singular subject.

She gave **them** a guitar lesson.

This pronoun represents the plural object.

Relative pronouns

These **link one part of a sentence to another** by introducing a relative clause that describes an earlier noun or pronoun.

who, whom, whose, which, that, what

Rita is the person **who** plays the guitar.

This pronoun is describing *Rita*, the subject.

Possessive pronouns

These **show ownership and replace possessive noun phrases**. Don't get these confused with possessive determiners such as *my* and *your*, which precede but do not replace the noun.

mine, yours, his, hers, its, ours, yours, theirs

The guitar is hers.

This pronoun replaces the possessive noun phrase *Rita's guitar*.

Reflexive pronouns

These **refer back to an earlier noun or pronoun** in a sentence, so the performing and receiving of an action apply to the same person or thing. They cannot be used without the noun or pronoun that they relate to.

myself, yourself, himself, herself, ourselves, themselves

She taught **herself**.

This pronoun refers back to the earlier pronoun *she*.

Demonstrative pronouns

These **function as subjects or objects** in a sentence, replacing nouns. Don't confuse these with demonstrative determiners, which precede but do not replace the noun.

this, that, these, those

This pronoun is acting as the subject of the sentence.

This is my instrument.

Interrogative pronouns

These are **used to ask questions** and represent an unknown subject or object.

who, whom, what, which, whose

This pronoun represents the subject, an unknown musician.

Who is playing?

Indefinite pronouns

These **do not refer to any specific person or thing**, but take the place of nouns in a sentence.

somebody, someone, something, anybody, anyone, anything, nobody, no one, nothing, all, another, both, each, many, most, other, some, few, none, such

I haven't seen anyone.

This represents an unknown person, the object of the sentence.

- As a rule, **a pronoun cannot be modified** by an **adjective** or **adverb** in the way that a noun can be: for example, "the sad I" does not make sense. Some exceptions include "**what** else" and "**somebody** nice".

- *Somebody* and *someone* **mean the same thing**, as do *anybody* and *anyone*, *everybody* and *everyone*, and *nobody* and *no one*.

Talking about myself

Many people wrongly opt for the reflexive form *myself* because they are unsure whether to use *I* or *me*. Reflexive pronouns should only be used to refer back to a specific noun or pronoun that has already been mentioned in the sentence. This noun or pronoun is usually (but not always) the subject.

I imagined myself on the stage.

This reflexive pronoun correctly refers back to the subject, *I*.

Rita performed for Ben and myself.

This wrongly used reflexive pronoun has no noun to refer back to – there is no *I* in the sentence.

Identifying when to use *I* or *me*

People often make mistakes when deciding whether to use the personal pronouns *I* or *me*. To work out which to use, split the sentence into two short sentences. It should then become clear which one is right. Remember to put others first in a sentence.

Me and Ben enjoyed the concert.

This doesn't make sense, so *me* is wrong.

Me enjoyed the concert.

This makes sense, so *I* is the correct pronoun.

Ben enjoyed the concert.

I enjoyed the concert.

Always place others first.

Ben and I enjoyed the concert.

If the pronoun follows a preposition, the object personal pronoun *me* should be used.

This is a preposition, so the subject pronoun *I* is wrong.

It was a late night **for** Ben and I.

It was a late night **for** Ben and me. ✓

The object pronoun *me* now correctly follows the preposition *for*.

Number and gender

PRONOUNS AND DETERMINERS MUST AGREE WITH THE NOUNS TO WHICH THEY RELATE.

In English, there are no personal pronouns or possessive determiners that can be used to refer to someone without identifying whether that person is male or female. This often results in mismatched combinations of singular nouns and plural pronouns or determiners.

SEE ALSO

❮ **24–25** Plurals
❮ **32–33** Determiners
❮ **34–35** Pronouns
Verbs   **38–39** ❯
Verb agreement   **52–53** ❯

👍

• If a piece of text is likely to become clumsy with the repetition of **his or her**, try using certain nouns in the **plural** form to add **variety**.

GLOSSARY

Indefinite pronoun A pronoun such as *everyone* that refers to nobody or nothing specific.

Number The term used to identify a noun or pronoun as singular or plural.

Personal pronoun A pronoun that takes the place of a noun and represents people, places or things.

Possessive determiner A word that is used before a noun to show ownership.

Matching numbers

Pronouns must agree in number (singular or plural) with the nouns they represent. Plural nouns or pronouns must be followed by plural pronouns or determiners, and singular nouns or pronouns must be followed by singular pronouns or determiners.

Pronoun	Determiner
I	my
you	your
he	his
she	her
it	its
we	our
you	your
they	their

They were preparing for thei
told **his** students that **everyon**

Indefinite pronouns

Indefinite pronouns such as *everyone* and *anything* often cause problems. Although they appear to refer to more than one person or thing, these pronouns are, in fact, singular words. One way of establishing whether a pronoun is singular or plural is to put the verb form *are* straight after it. If the resulting combination sounds wrong, then that pronoun is singular.

Singular	Plural
everyone is	both are
somebody is	all are
something is	many are
each is	most are
nothing is	others are
another is	few are

👍

• When using the word *each*, think about **"each one"**, as it makes it easier to remember that *each* is always followed by a **singular pronoun** or **determiner**.

• Some words, such as *each* and *all*, are used both as **determiners** and as **pronouns**. Remember that a determiner is always used in front of a noun, whereas a pronoun replaces a noun.

Identifying who's who

If there is more than one person or thing in a sentence, it must be clear which pronoun refers to which person or thing. If it is not clear, the sentence needs to be reworded. Alternatively, the name of the relevant person can be repeated to make it clear who is doing what.

In this case it was Anna's first climb, not Emily's, so the name *Anna* has been repeated to make this clear.

Emily wanted **Anna** to come, although it was **her** first climb. ✗

It is unclear whether it was Emily's first climb or Anna's.

Although it was **her** first climb, **Emily** wanted **Anna** to come. ✓

This sentence has been reordered so that the pronoun is next to the subject it relates to – it was Emily's first climb, not Anna's.

Emily wanted **Anna** to come, although it was **Anna's** first climb. ✓

Misusing *their*

The plural form *they* doesn't have a gender, and people often use this form when speaking or writing to avoid having to distinguish between males and females. In many cases, this results in a singular noun or pronoun being paired with a plural determiner. The only way to avoid this problem is to use *his or her* instead of *their* for the singular, or to make the noun plural and use *their*.

Everyone had to bring his **or** her **own rope.**

The indefinite pronoun *everyone* is singular, so the determiners *his* and *her* are used to refer to a group made up of males and females.

The students had to bring their **own ropes.**

The sentence has been reworded to include a plural subject (*students*), so the plural determiner *their* can be used. The object (*ropes*) has been made plural as well.

climbing expedition. The instructor had to bring his **or** her **own rope.**

Male or female?

Sometimes it's hard to know whether to use *he*, *she* or *they* when referring to both men and women. Historically, writers used the masculine pronouns and determiners *he*, *his*, *him* and *himself* to represent both sexes, but this approach is now considered outdated. Assumptions about male and female roles should also be avoided.

The instructor told his **students to bring ropes.**

This sentence refers to a specific instructor, who is known to be male, so the determiner *his* is correct.

An instructor must carry spare ropes for his **or** her **students.**

This sentence refers to an unknown instructor, who could be male or female, so the determiners *his* and *her* are required.

Instructors must carry spare ropes for their **students.**

Sometimes it is clearer to use both the noun and the determiner in the plural form.

Verbs

MOST VERBS ARE ACTION WORDS.

A verb is the most important word in a sentence; without it, the sentence would not make sense. Verbs describe what a person or thing is doing or being.

Verbs, subjects and objects

All sentences require both a verb and a subject. The subject (a noun or pronoun) is the person or thing doing the action (a verb). Many sentences also have an object. The direct object (also a noun or pronoun) is the person or thing that is receiving the action.

SUBJECT — The raccoon
The subject, a noun, is performing the action.

VERB — climbed
the action

OBJECT — the tree.
The direct object – the tree – is being climbed by the subject, the raccoon.

▷ **The indirect object**
The indirect object is the person or thing indirectly affected by the action of the verb. It always goes before the direct object, and typically right after the verb. Indirect objects never occur without a direct object.

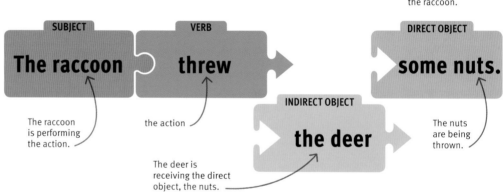

SUBJECT — The raccoon
The raccoon is performing the action.

VERB — threw
the action

INDIRECT OBJECT — the deer
The deer is receiving the direct object, the nuts.

DIRECT OBJECT — some nuts.
The nuts are being thrown.

Transitive verbs

Action verbs can be divided into two types – transitive and intransitive. A transitive verb always occurs with an object. It carries an action across from the subject to the direct object. If you can ask and answer the question *who?* or *what?* using the verb, then it is transitive.

This object answers the question "What did the fire destroy?"

A fire destroyed the forest.

SUBJECT	TRANSITIVE VERB	OBJECT

Intransitive verbs

Intransitive verbs do not need an object – they make sense on their own. Common intransitive verbs include *arrive*, *sleep* and *die*. Some verbs, such as *escape*, can be both transitive and intransitive.

Here, *escaped* is used as an intransitive verb – it makes sense without an object.

The animals escaped.

SUBJECT	INTRANSITIVE VERB

Linking verbs

A linking verb links the subject of a sentence to a word or phrase that describes the subject. Linking verbs either relate to the senses (*feel*, *taste*, *smell*, *look*, *hear*) or to a state of existence (*be*, *become*, *appear*, *remain*). The most common linking verb is *be*.

subject — This linking verb is a past form of the verb *be*. This adjective describes the state of mind of the rabbits.

The rabbits **were** **frightened.**

🔍 Identifying a linking verb

The simplest way to identify a linking verb is to substitute a form of *be* for the verb. If the resulting sentence makes sense, that verb is a linking verb. If it doesn't make sense, the verb is an action verb.

The chipmunk **looked** hungry.

Here, *looked* is a linking verb.

The chipmunk **looked** for berries.

Here, *looked* is an action verb.

substitute ***is***

✓ The chipmunk **is** hungry.

The chipmunk **is** for berries. ✗

The infinitive

The infinitive is the simplest form of a verb – the form that is used in dictionaries. It can be used on its own, but is almost always preceded by *to*. Unlike verbs, infinitives never change in form. They can be used as nouns, adjectives or adverbs in a sentence.

The chipmunk **needed** **to eat.**

subject — This infinitive is acting like a noun, such as *food*, would act because it is the object of the sentence.

He **found** a grasshopper **to eat.**

subject — This infinitive is acting like an adjective, because it is modifying the object of the sentence; it adds the information that the grasshopper is edible.

A well-known exception to the **subject–verb–object** rule comes from the Christian marriage service: "With this ring, **I thee wed**."

REAL WORLD

To boldly go or to go boldly?

Split infinitives occur when an adverb, such as *boldly*, is placed between the infinitive and the preceding *to*. It is preferable to keep the *to* next to the verb, but avoiding a split infinitive can make a sentence awkward. Split infinitives can be used sparingly for emphasis, to avoid confusion or for a more natural reading order. A famous example is from the opening lines of the 1960s *Star Trek* television series: "To boldly go where no man has gone before".

GLOSSARY

Intransitive verb A verb that does not require an object.

Linking verb A verb, such as *be*, that connects the subject of a sentence to a word or phrase – often an adjective – that describes the subject.

Object The noun or pronoun that is receiving the action of the verb.

Subject The noun or pronoun that is performing the action of the verb.

Transitive verb A verb that must be used with an object.

Adverbs

AN ADVERB MODIFIES A VERB, AN ADJECTIVE OR ANOTHER ADVERB.

The word *adverb* essentially means "to add to a verb", and this is what adverbs mostly do. They provide information about how, when, where or how often something is happening, and to what degree.

SEE ALSO	
❰ 26–27 Adjectives	
❰ 28–29 Comparatives and superlatives	
❰ 38–39 Verbs	
Conjunctions	58–59 ❱
Phrases	64–65 ❱
Clauses	66–67 ❱
Managing modifiers	76–77 ❱

When and how often?

Adverbs of time indicate when something is happening, while adverbs of frequency indicate how often it is happening. These adverbs modify verbs, and can occupy different positions in a sentence – usually at the beginning or end of a clause.

yesterday soon
today now
then later

adverbs of time

always rarely
usually again
sometimes never

adverbs of frequency

Where?

Adverbs of place work in the same way as adverbs of time and frequency. They modify verbs and tell the reader more about where something is happening.

away   nowhere   there

everywhere

abroad   upstairs

here   out

Yesterday we went out. We left
an extremely large dog saw us

Forming common adverbs

Most adverbs in English are formed by adding the ending -ly to an adjective, but there are some exceptions. Some adjectives, such as *lovely* or *holy*, also end in -ly, so it's important not to confuse these with adverbs.

Adjective ending	Rule	Adverb
-l (beautiful, wonderful)	Add -ly	beautiful**ly**, wonderful**ly**
-y (pretty, busy, hungry)	Change -y to -i, then add -ly	prett**ily**, bus**ily**, hung**rily**
-le (comfortable, reputable)	Change -e to -y	comfortabl**y**, reputabl**y**
-ic (enthusiastic, ecstatic)	Add -ally	enthusiastic**ally**, ecstatic**ally**
-ly (friendly, daily)	Use an adverbial phrase	in a friendly way, every day

How?

Adverbs that describe how actions are performed are known as adverbs of manner. They are formed from adjectives and modify verbs. These adverbs can be placed before or after the verb, or at the beginning or end of a clause. Like adjectives, most adverbs of manner and frequency can be graded by adverbs of degree, such as *very*, *quite* or *almost*. These are always placed directly before the adjective or adverb they describe.

This adverb of degree is modifying the adverb of manner *quietly* – it indicates how quietly they left.

We left very quietly

This adverb of manner is at the end of a clause, and is modifying the verb *left* – it is describing how they left.

an extremely large dog

This adverb of degree is modifying the adjective *large* – it is explaining how large the dog was.

• Some **adverbs of degree**, such as *just*, *only*, *almost* and *even*, must be placed immediately in front of the word they are modifying: for example, "I have **just** arrived."

Sentence adverbs

Sentence adverbs are unusual because they do not just modify a verb – they modify the whole sentence or clause containing that verb. They usually express the likelihood or desirability of something happening, and include words like *unfortunately*, *probably* and *certainly*. They can also be used to influence the reader.

This adverb is modifying a whole clause, meaning "it is unfortunate that an extremely large dog saw us".

unfortunately an extremely large dog saw us

ery quietly, but unfortunately We'll run more quickly next time.

Comparing adverbs

Like adjectives, adverbs of manner can be compared. To form the comparative, *more* is usually added before the adverb. In the same way, *most* is added before the adverb to form the superlative.

more quickly
most quickly

• *Then* is an **adverb of time**, and should **not** be used as a **conjunction**. When joining two clauses together, use a conjunction such as *and* before *then*.

• **Don't overuse adverbs**. In the phrase "absolutely fabulous", the adverb *absolutely* adds nothing to the adjective *fabulous*, which already implies high levels of enthusiasm for something.

The three **most common adverbs** in English are *not*, *very* and *too*.

GLOSSARY

Adverbial phrase A group of words such as "in July last year" that perform the same role as an adverb and answer questions such as: How? When? Where? How often?

Simple tenses

THE TENSE OF A VERB INDICATES WHEN AN ACTION TAKES PLACE.

Unlike most parts of speech, verbs change their form. These different forms, known as tenses, indicate the timing of an action, which is performed by the first, second or third person.

SEE ALSO

❮ **34–35** Pronouns

❮ **38–39** Verbs

❮ **40–41** Adverbs

Perfect and continuous tenses	44–45 ❯
Auxiliary verbs	48–49 ❯
Irregular verbs	50–51 ❯

Picking the right person

Each verb must express a person (first, second or third), a number (singular or plural) and a tense (past, present or future). There are three persons in English. These identify who is taking part in a conversation.

The word *tense* comes from the **Latin** word *tempus*, which means **"time"**.

▷ **The first person**
The first person represents the speaker, and uses the personal pronouns *I* or *me* if the speaker is alone, and *we* or *us* if the speaker is accompanied.

▷ **The second person**
The second person addresses the reader or listener, and uses *you* for both singular and plural.

▷ **The third person**
The third person represents everyone and everything else, and uses the singular pronouns *he* and *him*, *she* and *her*, and *it*, and the plural pronouns *they* and *them*.

The present simple tense

The present simple tense is used to express a constant or repeated action that is happening right now. It can also represent a widespread truth: for example, "I smile all the time." Regular verbs in the present tense use the infinitive, except for the third person singular, which uses the infinitive, plus the ending -s.

I smile   **We** smile
You smile   **You** smile
She smiles   **They** smile

The third person singular is formed by adding an *s*.

The first, second and third person take the same form of the verb in the past tense – for both singular and plural.

I laughed   **We** laughed
You laughed   **You** laughed
She laughed   **They** laughed

The past simple tense

The past simple tense expresses an action that began and ended in the past. Regular past tense verbs are formed using the infinitive, followed by the ending -ed.

The future simple tense

The future simple tense is used to express actions that will occur in the future. Regular verbs in the future tense are formed using the auxiliary verb *will*, followed by the infinitive, except for the first person, which uses the auxiliary verb *shall*. The first person can also be formed using *will*.

The auxiliary verb *shall* is used to create the future simple tense for the first person.

I shall cry   **We** shall cry
You will cry   **You** will cry
She will cry   **They** will cry

The auxiliary verb *will* is used to create the future simple tense for the second and third persons.

• Another way of forming the **future simple tense** is to place *am*, *is* or *are* before *going to*, followed by the infinitive. This form is useful when the action being described is definitely going to happen. For example, "**It is going to explode**."

• The three basic tenses are the present, the past and the future. Each of these tenses has a **simple** form, a **continuous** form, a **perfect** form and a **perfect continuous** form.

GLOSSARY

Auxiliary verb A "helping" verb such as *be* or *have* that joins the main verb in a sentence to the subject.

Infinitive The simplest form of a verb: the form that is used in dictionaries.

Perfect and continuous tenses

THESE TENSES GIVE MORE INFORMATION ABOUT WHEN
AN ACTION IS HAPPENING, AND HOW LONG IT GOES ON FOR.

The perfect tenses refer to actions that are completed over a period
of time. The continuous tenses are used to emphasise that an action
is ongoing at a particular point in time.

SEE ALSO	
❰ **38–39** Verbs	
❰ **42–43** Simple tenses	
Participles	**46–47** ❱
Auxiliary verbs	**48–49** ❱
Irregular verbs	**50–51** ❱

GLOSSARY

Auxiliary verb A "helping" verb such
as *be* or *have* that links the main verb
in a sentence to the subject.

Past participle The form of a verb that
usually ends in -ed or -en.

Present participle The form of a verb
that ends in -ing.

The present perfect tense

The perfect tenses describe actions
that span a period of time but have a
known end. The present perfect tense
refers either to an action that happened
at an unspecified time in the past, or to
an action that began in the past and
continues in the present. It is formed
using the past participle, preceded by
the auxiliary verb form *have* or – for
the third person singular – *has*.

This refers to an action
that happened at some
point in the past.

I have disappeared   **We** have disappeared
You have disappeared   **You** have disappeared
She has disappeared   **They** have disappeared

This refers to an
action that began in
the past and continues
in the present.

She has lived here for ten years.

The third person singular is formed
using *has* instead of *have*.

The past perfect tense

The past perfect tense describes an
action that happened in the past before
something else happened. It is formed
in the same way as the present perfect
tense, but using the auxiliary verb form
had before the past participle.

I had escaped   **We** had escaped
You had escaped   **You** had escaped
It had escaped   **They** had escaped

By the time **the guard** noticed, **I** had escaped.

This action finished before
the second action (the
guard noticing) started.

The future perfect tense

The future perfect tense describes an
action that will occur at some point in
the future before another action. For
example, "He will have offended again
before we catch him."

I will have offended   **We** will have offended
You will have offended   **You** will have offended
He will have offended   **They** will have offended

This tense is formed using the past
participle, preceded by *will have*.

The present continuous tense

Continuous or progressive tenses are used to describe actions or situations that are ongoing. The present continuous tense expresses an action that is continuing at the same time as something else is happening. This tense is formed using the present participle, preceded by *am*, *are* or *is*.

I am hiding
You are hiding
She is hiding

We are hiding
You are hiding
They are hiding

I am hiding in a tree until it gets dark.

The action *hiding* is continuing at the same time as it starts to get dark.

The past continuous tense

The past continuous tense describes a past action that was happening at the same time as another action occurred. For example, "They were falling asleep when they heard a loud crash."

I was falling
You were falling
He was falling

We were falling
You were falling
They were falling

This tense is formed in the same way as the present continuous tense, but using *was* or *were* instead of *am*, *is* or *are*.

The future continuous tense

The future continuous tense describes an ongoing action that is going to happen in the future. Like the other continuous forms, the present participle is used, but it is preceded by *will be*.

I will be watching
You will be watching
She will be watching

We will be watching
You will be watching
They will be watching

Perfect continuous tenses

Like simple continuous tenses, perfect continuous tenses describe ongoing actions. Like perfect tenses, these actions end at some point in the present, past or future. Perfect continuous tenses are also formed using the present participle.

Tense	Form	Example
Present perfect continuous	have/has been + present participle	I have been hiding since dawn.
Past perfect continuous	had been + present participle	The guard had been searching all day.
Future perfect continuous	will have been + present participle	They will have been following my trail.

REAL WORLD

Verbal dynamism

Some verbs sound strange when they are used in the continuous tenses. For something to be ongoing, it needs to be something active, such as running or eating. Verbs that do not imply an action, but instead refer to a state of affairs – for example, *know*, *own*, *love* or *feel* – cannot be used in the continuous tenses. Although it has become a familiar expression, the slogan "I'm lovin' it" is grammatically wrong. Maybe that's why everyone remembers it.

Participles

PARTICIPLES ARE FORMED FROM VERBS.

There are two participles: the past and the present. They are used with auxiliary verbs such as *have* and *be* to form tenses, and on their own as adjectives. The present participle can also be used as a noun.

SEE ALSO

❰ **26–27** Adjectives
❰ **38–39** Verbs
❰ **42–43** Simple tenses
❰ **44–45** Perfect and continuous tenses
Auxiliary verbs **48–49** ❱
Voices and moods **54–55** ❱
Managing modifiers **76–77** ❱
Silent letters **160–161** ❱

Past participles as verbs

Combined with the auxiliary verb *have*, past participles are used to form the perfect tense of a verb. Regular past participles are formed in the same way as the simple past tense, using the infinitive, plus the ending -ed. Common irregular past participle endings include -en, -t or -n. The past participle of a few verbs is the same as the infinitive, and some, such as *tell*, change their spelling completely.

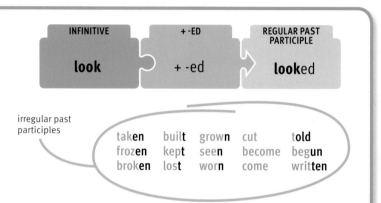

irregular past participles

tak**en**	**built**	grow**n**	cut	**told**
froz**en**	kep**t**	see**n**	become	beg**un**
brok**en**	los**t**	wor**n**	come	writt**en**

Josh had looked everywhere fo
been hoping to do some ice-

• Don't use the **wrong participle** as an **adjective**. An "interested cat" is not the same as an "interesting cat".

GLOSSARY

Auxiliary verb A "helping" verb such as *be* or *have* that joins the main verb in a sentence to the subject.

Gerund The name given to the present participle when it is used as a noun.

Linking verb A verb that joins the subject of a sentence to a word or phrase that describes the subject.

Present participles as verbs

Present participles are used with the auxiliary verb *be* to form verbs in the continuous tense. They are formed using the infinitive and the ending -ing. Unlike past participles, all present participles have the same ending. If the infinitive ends in a silent -e (for example, *hope*), the -e is dropped before the -ing ending is added.

INFINITIVE	+ -ING	PRESENT PARTICIPLE
want	+ -ing	**want**ing
hope	+ -ing	**hop**ing

Past participles as adjectives

Past participles can be used on their own as adjectives to modify nouns. They are placed either before the noun or pronoun they describe, or after it, following a linking verb.

This past participle is being used as an adjective before the noun it describes (*skates*).

his broken skates

His skates were broken.

Here, the past participle is being used as an adjective after the noun it describes (*skates*), following the linking verb *were*.

Identifying a gerund phrase

Participle phrases act as adjectives, whereas gerund phrases act as nouns, which can be described by adjectives. As gerund phrases are always singular, it is possible to check whether a phrase is a gerund phrase by substituting the pronoun *it*.

Emptying his cupboard, Josh found them.

The pronoun *it* has been substituted for the phrase, and the resulting sentence doesn't make sense, so the phrase is a participle phrase.

It, Josh found them. ✗

Emptying his cupboard, Josh found them. ✓

This participle phrase is acting as an adjective, describing Josh.

Repairing the skates was a priority.

The pronoun *it* has been substituted for the phrase, and the resulting sentence makes sense, so the phrase is a gerund phrase.

It was a priority. ✓

Repairing the skates was a priority. ✓

his broken skates. He had skating, but they were missing.

Present participles as nouns

When the present participle of a verb is used as a noun, it is called a gerund. Like nouns, a gerund (one word) or a gerund phrase (multiple words) can be used as the subject or object of a sentence.

subject

He wanted to do some ice-skating.

The gerund phrase *ice-skating* is acting as the object of this sentence.

Present participles as adjectives

Like past participles, present participles can be used as adjectives. They can be placed before or after the noun or pronoun that they modify.

This present participle is being used as an adjective after the pronoun it describes (*they*), following the linking verb *were*.

They were missing.

the missing skates

This present participle is formed from the verb *miss*, and is describing the noun *skates*.

Auxiliary verbs

SOME VERBS HELP TO FORM OTHER VERBS.

Often called "helping" verbs, auxiliary verbs can be used in front of other verbs to form tenses, negative sentences and the passive voice, or to express different moods.

SEE ALSO	
⟨ **34–35** Pronouns	
⟨ **38–39** Verbs	
⟨ **42–43** Simple tenses	
⟨ **44–45** Perfect and continuous tenses	
⟨ **46–47** Participles	
Voices and moods	**54–55** ⟩
Negatives	**80–81** ⟩
Question marks	**110–111** ⟩

Helpful properties

Auxiliary verbs are known as helping verbs because they perform several different roles. Their main job is to help form different tenses, but they are also used to create negative sentences, turn statements into questions and add emphasis to speech.

Must is the **only verb** in English to have a **present** but **no past** form.

▷ **Forming tenses**
Auxiliary verbs are used to link the main verb to the subject, helping to form different tenses. The future, perfect and continuous tenses all rely on auxiliary verbs.

The present participle is used to form the present continuous tense.

▷ **Forming negatives**
Auxiliary verbs are the only verbs that can be made negative. A negative sentence is formed by placing the word *not* between the auxiliary verb and the main verb.

▷ **Forming questions**
In a statement, the subject always comes before the verb. Auxiliary verbs can switch places with their subjects in order to form questions.

▷ **Adding emphasis**
Auxiliary verbs can also be used for emphasis, particularly when the speaker wants to contradict a previous statement.

Primary auxiliary verbs

The verbs *be*, *have* and *do* are known as the primary auxiliary verbs. Primary auxiliary verbs can be used as the main verb in a sentence, or they can be used with participles to form tenses. These verbs also have participles of their own. Auxiliary verbs are irregular verbs, and are irregular even in the present tense.

Verb form	be	have	do
Infinitive	be	have	do
First person (present)	am, are	have	do
Second person (present)	are	have	do
Third person (present)	is, are	has, have	does, do
Past participle	been	had	done
Present participle	being	having	doing

• Only the **primary auxiliaries** – **be**, **have** and **do** – can **change** their form. **Modal auxiliaries** always take the **same form**.

• *Might* is the past form of *may*, so *might* is always used when talking about something that might have happened previously.

• Sometimes modal auxiliaries are used to add **emphasis** to a decision or a command. Using *will* instead of *shall* for the **first person** future tense makes a statement sound more determined: for example, "I **will** go to the party."

Modal auxiliary verbs

Common auxiliary verbs that cannot be used on their own are known as modal auxiliary verbs. These include *can*, *will*, *should*, *may* and *must*, and they are used with action verbs to express a command, an obligation or a possibility. Modal auxiliaries are unusual because they do not have an infinitive form or participles, nor – unlike primary auxiliaries and regular verbs – do they take the ending -s for the third person singular.

He can go.

The third person singular modal auxiliary does not take an -s; "he cans" doesn't make sense.

Modal auxiliary	Use	Example
can	Used to express a person's ability to do something.	I can run fast.
could	Used to show possibility; also the past form of *can*.	I could run faster.
may	Used to ask permission to do something, or to express a possibility.	May I come?
might	Used to express a small possibility; also the past form of *may*.	I might run away.
must	Used to indicate a strong obligation.	I must come.
ought	Used to express a sense of obligation.	I ought to stay.
shall	Used to form the future simple tense, and to show determination.	I shall run faster.
should	Used to express obligation.	I should come.
will	Used to form the future simple tense, and to show determination or issue a command.	You will come!
would	Used to express a polite question or a wish, or to indicate the consequence of a conditional sentence; also the past form of *will*.	Would you like to come? I would love to come. If I were to come, I would have fun.

Irregular verbs

SOME VERBS HAVE ONE OR MORE IRREGULAR FORMS.

The past tense and past participles of all regular verbs are formed in the same way. By contrast, irregular verbs are unpredictable, and take a variety of verb endings. Some change their spelling completely. It is essential to learn these.

Forming irregular verbs

The simple past tense and past participle of regular verbs are formed using the ending -ed (or -d, if the infinitive form already ends in -e). Irregular verbs do not follow this pattern. They take different endings, and the vowel of a verb often changes to form the past tense.

regular simple past tense of
discover, with the ending -ed

Grace discovered her shoes a week after her sister had swiped them.

regular past participle
of *swipe*, with the
ending -d

irregular simple
past tense of *find*

Grace found her shoes a week after her sister had stolen them.

irregular past
participle of *steal*

SEE ALSO

❰ **38–39** Verbs
❰ **42–43** Simple tenses
❰ **44–45** Perfect and continuous tenses
❰ **46–47** Participles
❰ **48–49** Auxiliary verbs

• **Auxiliary verbs** are **irregular**, and – unlike other irregular verbs – the verbs *be*, *have* and *do* are irregular **even in the present tense**.

Some of the **most common verbs** in the **English** language are **irregular** verbs.

GLOSSARY

Auxiliary verb A "helping" verb such as *be* or *have* that joins the main verb in a sentence to the subject.

Infinitive The simplest form of a verb: the form that is used in dictionaries.

Past participle The form of a verb that usually ends in -ed or -en. It is used with the auxiliary verbs *have* and *will* to form the perfect tenses.

Identifying when to use *lie* and *lay*

The irregular verbs *lie* and *lay* are often mixed up in everyday speech. The past tense of the verb *lie* (meaning "to be in a resting position") is the same as the infinitive form of the verb *lay* (meaning "to place something" or "to enforce"). The mistake most speakers make is to use the past tense form of *lie* – "lay" – when the present tense or infinitive form is required.

I need to lay down. ✘

It is clear from the context of the sentence that the infinitive *lie* is required, rather than the infinitive *lay*.

I need to lie down. ✔

Here, the irregular past tense form of the verb *lie* has been used correctly.

I lay down. ✔

I lay down the law. ✘

I laid down the law. ✔

Here, the irregular past tense form of the verb *lay* has been used correctly.

Common irregular verbs

Many well-known verbs do not take the standard ending -ed when they are used in the past tense or as past participles. The past tense forms and past participles of some irregular verbs look very different from the infinitive form. All of these verb forms have to be learnt.

Infinitive form	Simple past tense	Past participle
be	was/were	been
become	became	become
begin	began	begun
blow	blew	blown
break	broke	broken
bring	brought	brought
build	built	built
buy	bought	bought
catch	caught	caught
choose	chose	chosen
come	came	come
cost	cost	cost
creep	crept	crept
cut	cut	cut
do	did	done
draw	drew	drawn
drink	drank	drunk
drive	drove	driven
eat	ate	eaten
fall	fell	fallen
feel	felt	felt
find	found	found
fly	flew	flown
freeze	froze	frozen
get	got	got
give	gave	given
go	went	gone
grow	grew	grown
hang	hung	hung
have	had	had
hear	heard	heard
hold	held	held
keep	kept	kept
know	knew	known
lay	laid	laid

Infinitive form	Simple past tense	Past participle
lead	led	led
leave	left	left
let	let	let
lie	lay	lain
lose	lost	lost
make	made	made
mean	meant	meant
meet	met	met
mistake	mistook	mistaken
pay	paid	paid
put	put	put
ride	rode	ridden
rise	rose	risen
run	ran	run
say	said	said
see	saw	seen
sell	sold	sold
send	sent	sent
set	set	set
shake	shook	shaken
sit	sat	sat
sleep	slept	slept
speak	spoke	spoken
spend	spent	spent
spin	spun	spun
stand	stood	stood
steal	stole	stolen
stick	stuck	stuck
swear	swore	sworn
swim	swam	swum
take	took	taken
teach	taught	taught
tear	tore	torn
tell	told	told
think	thought	thought
throw	threw	thrown
understand	understood	understood
wear	wore	worn
weep	wept	wept
win	won	won
write	wrote	written

Verb agreement

THE NUMBER OF THE SUBJECT DICTATES THE NUMBER OF THE VERB.

Like nouns and pronouns, a verb can be singular or plural in number, but it must match the subject to which it relates. Sometimes it's hard to know whether a noun is singular or plural, leading to errors in verb agreement.

Singular or plural?

The key to correct verb agreement is to follow this simple rule: if the subject is singular, the verb must be singular; if the subject is plural, the verb must also be plural.

subject

The subject is plural so the verb must be plural.

The competitors have arrived, and the Mighty Musclemen contest is about to start.

subject

The subject is singular so the verb must be singular.

• Some nouns sound plural but are actually treated as **singular**. These include *mathematics* and *politics*, as well as **proper nouns** such as the *United States* or *Philippines*.

🔍 Identifying the subject

One problem occurs when the wrong word is identified as the subject. This often happens when the subject and verb are separated by a prepositional phrase. When the prepositional phrase is removed from the sentence, it becomes clear which noun or pronoun is the true subject.

The box **of extra weights are** ready. ✗

This is a prepositional phrase, made up of the preposition *of*, the adjective *extra* and the noun *weights*.

The **box are** ready. ✗

The prepositional phrase has been removed from the sentence, so it is now clear that the subject (*box*) is singular.

The **box is** ready. ✓

The subject is singular, so the singular verb form *is* is used.

The **box of extra weights is** ready. ✓

The prepositional phrase has been put back into the sentence, and the verb now agrees with the subject.

Collective nouns

Most collective nouns (for example, *class* or *crowd*) are singular words, because they can be made plural (*classes*, *crowds*). However, some collective nouns, including *team*, *staff* and *couple*, can be singular or plural. A good general rule to follow is to consider whether the noun is acting as a unit or whether the noun is made up of individuals acting in different ways.

My team has won.

Here, the team represents a unit, so the singular form of the verb is used.

The team are divided in their feelings.

Here, the individual members of the team are acting in different ways, so the plural form of the verb is used.

Multiple subjects

If a sentence contains more than one noun, and these nouns are joined by *and*, they almost always take a plural verb. These are known as compound subjects. Phrases such as *along with* and *as well as* separate the subjects, however. In these cases, the verb should agree with the first subject, regardless of whether the second subject is singular or plural. By contrast, if a singular subject is joined to a plural subject and separated by *or* or *nor*, the verb agrees with the nearest subject.

Tyler and his brother **Matt are** competing.

◁ **Compound subjects**
The subjects *Tyler* and *Matt* are acting together, and are joined by *and*, so they take the plural form.

Matt's **size as well as** his **strength is** awesome.

◁ **Separate subjects**
The subjects *size* and *strength* are acting separately, so the verb is singular to match the first subject, *size*.

Neither Tyler's **neck nor** his **arms are** small.

◁ **Mixed subjects**
The plural subject *arms* is closer to the verb than the singular subject *neck*, so the verb is plural. With mixed subjects, always put the plural subject closest to the verb.

- When the phrase ***the number of*** precedes the subject of a sentence, the subject is considered to be singular: "The number of weights used **is** variable." In contrast, the phrase ***a number of*** makes a subject plural: "A number of different weights **are** used."

- Expressions of **quantity**, such as **time, money, weight** or **fractions**, are treated in the same way as **collective nouns**: for example, "**Half** of Tyler's allowance **is** spent on exercise equipment."

Indefinite pronouns

Most indefinite pronouns can be easily identified as singular or plural. *Both*, *several*, *few* and *many*, for example, are always plural. Some, however, are singular words that refer to plural things. These include *each*, *everyone* and *everything*.

▽ **Agreeing with prepositional phrases**
Five indefinite pronouns can be singular or plural, depending on the context. These are *all*, *any*, *most*, *none* and *some*. Only when these pronouns occur do prepositional phrases determine whether a verb should be singular or plural.

Most of the contest **is** over.

indefinite pronoun

This prepositional phrase is singular because the noun *contest* is singular, so the verb also has to be singular.

indefinite pronoun

Most of the competitors **have** left.

This prepositional phrase is plural, because the noun *competitors* is plural.

The verb is plural to match the prepositional phrase.

Number	Indefinite pronoun
singular	everybody, everyone, everything, somebody, someone, something, anybody, anyone, anything, nobody, no one, nothing, neither, another, each, either, one, other, much
plural	both, several, few, many, others
singular or plural	all, any, most, none, some

Voices and moods

SENTENCES IN ENGLISH CAN BE EXPRESSED
IN DIFFERENT VOICES AND DIFFERENT MOODS.

There are two voices in English. These determine whether
the subject of a sentence is performing or receiving an action.
Mood is the form of the verb that conveys the attitude in which
a thought is expressed.

The active voice

Verbs can be used in two different ways.
These are known as voices. The active
voice is simpler than the passive voice.
In an active sentence, the subject
is performing the action of the verb,
and the object is receiving it.

The snake is performing
the action of attacking.

The action is
being performed.

The boy is
receiving
the action.

Subject   Verb   Object

The **snake attacked** the **boy**.

The passive voice

In a passive sentence, the word order
is reversed so that the subject is
receiving the action and the object
is performing it. The passive voice is
formed using the auxiliary verb *be*
followed by a past participle. The
performer of the action is either
identified using the preposition
by or not included at all.

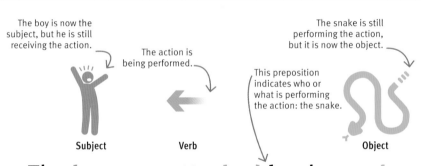

The boy is now the
subject, but he is still
receiving the action.

The action is
being performed.

This preposition
indicates who or
what is performing
the action: the snake.

The snake is still
performing the action,
but it is now the object.

Subject   Verb   Object

The **boy was attacked by** the **snake**.

Passive persuasion

The passive voice is often used on
official signs, because it is perceived
as less confrontational than the active
voice. In these situations, it is also
often unnecessary to state who is
performing the action.

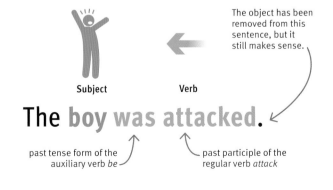

The object has been
removed from this
sentence, but it
still makes sense.

Subject   Verb

The **boy was attacked**.

past tense form of the
auxiliary verb *be*

past participle of the
regular verb *attack*

The indicative mood

There are three main moods in English. Most verbs are used in the indicative mood, which indicates an actual condition, as opposed to an intended, expected or believed condition. This mood is used to state facts.

This sentence states a fact – something that was the case at some point in the past – so it is in the indicative mood.

The boy was terrified.

The imperative mood

The imperative mood is used to give commands or make requests. Exclamations are often in the imperative mood; these always end with an exclamation mark.

This command is also an exclamation.

This is a request.

Go away! Please leave me alone.

The subjunctive mood

The subjunctive mood is rarely used in English, and it can only be identified in the third person form or with the verb *be*. It is used after verbs and phrases that express an obligation or a desire, such as *demand*, *require*, *suggest* or *it is essential that*, and it indicates that the obligation or desire may not be fulfilled.

> **GLOSSARY**
>
> **Auxiliary verb** A "helping" verb such as *be* or *have* that links the main verb in a sentence to the subject.
>
> **Exclamation** A sentence that expresses a strong emotion, such as surprise, or a raised voice, and ends with an exclamation mark.
>
> **Modal auxiliary verb** An auxiliary verb that is used with an action verb to express a command, an obligation or a possibility.
>
> **Past participle** The form of a verb that ends in -ed or -en. It is used with the auxiliary verb *be* to form the passive voice.

▷ **Third person**
To form most subjunctive verbs, the final *s* is removed from the third person form.

He demanded that the zookeeper remove the snake.

The present subjunctive follows the verb phrase *demanded that*. It is used because the zookeeper might not remove the snake.

▷ **Exception**
The main exception is the verb *be*, which takes the form *be* for the present tense and *were* for the past tense.

The zookeeper requested that the boy be quiet.

The present subjunctive follows the verb phrase *requested that*. The zookeeper wants the boy to be quiet, but the boy might not be quiet.

🔍 Identifying the subjunctive in conditional sentences

Conditional sentences are used to indicate that the action of a main clause ("going to the beach") can only happen if a certain condition, contained in a subordinate clause, is fulfilled ("if the weather is hot"). Most conditional sentences start with *if* or *unless*. If the action being described is almost certain to happen, the indicative mood is used. If the action being described is hypothetical (impossible to predict), the past tense form of the subjunctive mood is used.

Many conditional sentences start with *if*.

If the weather...

They will almost certainly go to the beach if the weather is hot, so the indicative mood is used.

If the weather is hot, we will go to the beach. ✓

If the weather were hot, we would be happier. ✓

The weather is not hot, so the belief that they would be happier is a hypothetical situation, which requires the subjunctive verb form *were*.

The modal auxiliary verb *would* usually appears in conditional sentences with the subjunctive.

Phrasal verbs

NEW VERBS ARE FORMED BY ADDING AN ADVERB OR
A PREPOSITION TO AN EXISTING VERB.

SEE ALSO	
❮ 38–39 Verbs	
❮ 40–41 Adverbs	
Prepositions	60–61 ❯
Hyphens	106–107 ❯

A phrasal verb is a compound of a verb and an adverb, a verb and
a preposition, or a verb, an adverb and a preposition. Phrasal verbs
work like regular verbs, but they are mostly used in informal speech.

Adverb phrasal verbs

Composed of an existing verb
followed by an adverb, an adverb
phrasal verb works in the same way
as a regular verb – as a single unit.
The adverb is essential to the
phrasal verb's meaning, either
intensifying the sense of the
preceding verb or changing its
meaning entirely. The adverbs
up, *down*, *out* or *off* are often
used to form phrasal verbs.

The adverb *up* changes the
meaning of the verb *get*,
resulting in a phrasal verb
that means "to rise, usually
after sleeping", rather than
"to receive or obtain".

I **got up** early.

adverb phrasal verb

Most **new verbs** in
the **English** language
are **phrasal verbs**.

• The small words used to form
phrasal verbs – **adverbs** and
prepositions – are often known
as **particles**.

• Phrasal verbs are **never
hyphenated**.

I **got up** early because Danie
We **ran into** Paulo, who wa

Prepositional phrasal verbs

Prepositional phrasal verbs consist of
a verb followed by a preposition, such
as *by*, *after*, *in*, *on* or *for*. The preposition
links the verb to the noun or pronoun that
follows – the direct object. Prepositional
phrasal verbs are always transitive, but
unlike adverb phrasal verbs, prepositional
phrasal verbs cannot usually be separated
by the direct object (see "Word order").

talk about

stand by

listen to

call on

take after

wait for

run into

Versatile verbs

Only a handful of adverbs and
prepositions are needed to
create a range of phrasal verbs
with different meanings. Using
a different phrasal verb can
completely change the
meaning of a sentence. For
example, "Paulo is looking
after the game" means that
he is in charge of the game.

Word order

Like regular verbs, phrasal verbs can be transitive or intransitive. Transitive phrasal verbs require a direct object to receive the action, while intransitive phrasal verbs, such as *get up* or *eat out*, make sense without an object. The verb and adverb in a transitive adverb phrasal verb can usually be separated by the direct object.

Daniel was taking me out for lunch.

direct object

This adverb phrasal verb is transitive, so it can be separated by the direct object.

Identifying when a phrasal verb can be separated

Some transitive phrasal verbs can be separated by a direct object; others cannot be separated. A simple way to test whether a phrasal verb is separable or inseparable is to place the pronoun *it* (representing the direct object) between the verb and the adverb or preposition. If the resulting phrase makes sense, that phrasal verb can be separated.

transitive adverb phrasal verb

transitive prepositional phrasal verb

pick up

look after

pick **it** up ✓

look **it** after ✗

This phrase makes sense, so the phrasal verb is separable.

This phrase does not make sense, so the phrasal verb is inseparable.

was taking me out for lunch.
ooking forward to the game.

look forward to
look over
look out
look through
look at
look after

Adverb-prepositional phrasal verbs

Some phrasal verbs are made up of a verb, followed by an adverb and a preposition. Like prepositional phrasal verbs, these must have a direct object, and the parts of the phrasal verb cannot be separated by this object.

verb

Paulo was looking forward to the game.

adverb   preposition   direct object

Conjunctions

A CONJUNCTION CONNECTS WORDS, PHRASES AND CLAUSES.

Also known as connectives, conjunctions are used to link two or more parts of a sentence. These parts can be of equal importance, or a main clause can be linked to a subordinate clause using a subordinator.

- Relative pronouns such as **who**, **whom**, **which** and **that** are used in the same way as subordinators.

- It is a good idea to avoid starting a sentence with conjunctions like **because** or **and** because this practice often results in **incomplete sentences**.

Co-ordinating conjunctions

Without conjunctions, writing would be made up of numerous short sentences. Conjunctions are used to create longer sentences, preventing text from becoming stilted. Co-ordinating conjunctions are used to link words, phrases or clauses of equal importance. They include the words *and*, *but*, *or*, *nor*, *yet*, *for* and *so*.

roses and sunflowers

This co-ordinating conjunction is being used to link two types of flowers.

Flora tried to water her roses and
She cut both the hedge and th

- Never use a comma to link two main clauses. **Main clauses** should only be linked using a **conjunction**, a **semi-colon** or a **colon**.

GLOSSARY

Main clause A group of words that contains a subject and a verb and makes complete sense on its own.

Subordinate clause A group of words that contains a subject and a verb but depends on a main clause for its meaning.

Pairs of conjunctions

Conjunctions can be single words or phrases, and they often appear in pairs. Pairs such as *both/and*, *either/or* and *not only/but also* are sometimes known as "correlative conjunctions" because the conjunctions work together. The two parts must be placed directly before the words they are joining.

pair of conjunctions

She cut both the hedge and the tree.

nouns being joined by the pair

Identifying when to use a semi-colon

Adverbs such as *however*, *accordingly*, *besides* and *therefore* can also be used as conjunctions to join two main clauses. Unlike co-ordinating conjunctions and subordinators, these adverbs must be preceded by a semi-colon and followed by a comma.

two main clauses

She was confident. She hadn't cut the hedge before.

co-ordinating conjunction separating two main clauses

She was confident, **but** she hadn't cut the hedge before.

This adverb is being used as a conjunction, so it must be preceded by a semi-colon and followed by a comma.

She was confident; **however**, she hadn't cut the hedge before.

Co-ordinating multiple subjects

When a co-ordinating conjunction is used to link two main clauses with different subjects, a comma should be placed before the conjunction. This helps to show where one main clause ends and another begins.

first main clause   first subject

Flora tried to water her roses and sunflowers, but the hose burst.

A comma and co-ordinating conjunction separate the two main clauses.

second subject

second main clause

unflowers, but the hose burst.
ree because they were too tall.

Subordinators

Subordinators or subordinating conjunctions are used to connect words, phrases and clauses of unequal importance. A subordinate clause adds information to a main clause, explaining why, where or when something is happening. Subordinate clauses start with subordinators such as *before*, *if*, *because*, *although* and *while*, and can be placed at the beginning or end of a sentence.

She cut both the hedge and the tree because they were too tall.

main clause

subordinator

The subordinate clause explains why Flora cut the hedge.

subordinator

A subordinate clause can also go at the start of a sentence.

Before she started, she put on some gloves.

A comma is needed to separate the two clauses when the subordinator is at the start of a sentence.

main clause

Prepositions

PREPOSITIONS CONNECT NOUNS AND PRONOUNS TO OTHER
WORDS IN A SENTENCE.

Prepositions never appear alone. They are short words that convey
the relationship of a noun or pronoun to another part of a sentence –
often the physical position of one thing in relation to another.

Simple prepositions

Prepositions are common in written and spoken English. They
usually appear as part of a prepositional phrase, and include
words like *for*, *about*, *with*, *of* and *on*. A prepositional phrase
is made up of a preposition followed by its object, which is
a noun, pronoun or noun phrase.

preposition   adjective

for a long bicycle ride

article   noun phrase and
object of the preposition

• In **formal writing**, **sentences**
should **not end** with **prepositions**,
but this practice is common in
spoken English. "What are you
talking about?" is a good example.

• **Prepositional phrases** only ever
contain the **object** of a clause.
They never contain the subject.
In the sentence "They sped **down
a hill**," *hill* is the object, and *they*
is the subject.

Daisy went for a long bicycl
a hill and through a stream

Winston Churchill,
objecting to strict
rules about
**prepositional
word order,**
famously said,
"That is nonsense
up with which
I shall not put."

Parallel prepositions

Writers can improve their sentences
by using consistent language. If
different prepositions are required
for different nouns, they must all
be included in the sentence. If
one preposition is being used to
introduce a series of nouns, it only
needs to be used before the first
noun. The same preposition can
be used before each noun, but
this is repetitive.

The noun objects *hill* and *stream*
require different prepositions, so both
must be included in the sentence.

They raced down a hill
and through a stream.

This preposition applies to both
nouns, so it only needs to appear
before the first item in this list.

They sped through
a stream and a forest.

Identifying prepositional phrasal verbs

A prepositional phrasal verb is made up of a verb followed by a preposition. This type of verb must have an object, but the preposition cannot be separated from its verb by this object. If the preposition part of a prepositional phrasal verb is removed, the sentence will not make sense.

Daisy was **annoyed** and **afraid of** Ed's poor cycling skills. ✗

If the phrase *and afraid* is removed, the sentence does not make sense.

Daisy was **annoyed of** Ed's poor cycling skills. ✗

This phrasal verb does make sense on its own.

Daisy was **afraid of** Ed's poor cycling skills. ✓

The correct preposition has been added into the sentence.

object, a noun phrase

Daisy was **annoyed by** and **afraid of** Ed's poor cycling skills. ✓

Using prepositional phrases

Prepositional phrases can be used like adjectives and adverbs to modify nouns or verbs. They can offer more detail about an object so that the reader knows what or whom is being referred to, or they can point to where something is, or when or why something happened.

This prepositional phrase is working as an adjective because it is describing a noun, *eagle.*

Daisy saw an eagle **in** a tree.

This prepositional phrase is working as an adverb, because it is describing where they raced.

They raced **down** a hill.

ide **with** Ed. They raced **down** nd stopped **next to** a bridge.

Complex prepositions

Sometimes simple prepositions are used with one or two other words to form complex prepositions, which act as a single unit. Like one-word prepositions, these come before nouns or pronouns in prepositional phrases and can act as adjectives or adverbs.

except for **next to**

out of **as for** **in front of**

in spite of **along with**

GLOSSARY

Adjective prepositional phrase A prepositional phrase that describes a noun.

Adverb prepositional phrase A prepositional phrase that describes a verb.

Noun phrase A phrase made up of a noun and any words that are modifying that noun, such as articles or adjectives.

Object The noun or pronoun that is receiving the action of the verb.

Prepositional phrasal verb A verb followed by a preposition, which together act as a single unit.

Prepositional phrase A preposition followed by a noun, pronoun or noun phrase that together act as an adjective (describing a noun) or an adverb (describing a verb) in a sentence.

Interjections

INTERJECTIONS ARE WORDS OR PHRASES THAT
OCCUR ALONE AND EXPRESS EMOTION.

SEE ALSO	
❮ **20–21** Parts of speech	
Sentences	**68–69 ❯**
Colloquialisms and slang	**86–87 ❯**
Commas	**96–99 ❯**
Exclamation marks	**112–113 ❯**

Interjections are considered a part of speech, but they play no
grammatical role in a sentence. They are single words or phrases
that are used to exclaim, protest or command, and rarely appear
in formal writing.

Emotional words

Interjections occur frequently in spoken English. They are
useful in informal writing – particularly in narratives or
scripts – as they help to convey the emotions of a character,
but they are only used in formal writing as part of a direct
quotation. New interjections to describe different emotions
are invented all the time, and they vary from region to region.

Emotion	Interjection
pain	ouch, ow, oh
disgust	yuck, ugh, ew
surprise	eek, yikes, ooh, wow, eh, well, really
elation	hurrah, yippee, ha, woo-hoo, whoopee
pleasure	mmm, yeah
relief	phew, whew, whoa
boredom	blah, ho-hum
embarrassment	ahem, er
disappointment	aw, meh, pfft
dismay	oh no, oh, oops
panic	help, ah, uh oh
irritation	hmph, huh, hey, oy
disapproval	tsk-tsk, tut-tut
realisation	aha, ah
pity	dear, alas, ahh
doubt	hmm, er, um

• **Use interjections in moderation,**
or not at all. They rarely improve a
piece of writing.

Using interjections

Interjections that express strong emotions such as
dismay or surprise usually function as exclamations,
appearing alone as single words or phrases followed
by an exclamation mark. Milder emotions tend to be
expressed using an interjection followed by a comma.

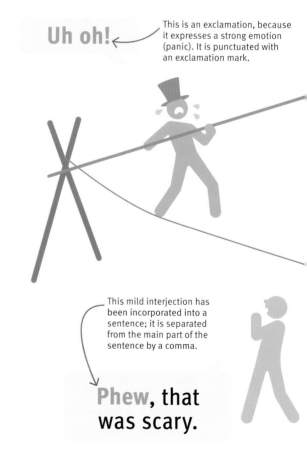

Uh oh!

This is an exclamation, because
it expresses a strong emotion
(panic). It is punctuated with
an exclamation mark.

This mild interjection has
been incorporated into a
sentence; it is separated
from the main part of the
sentence by a comma.

**Phew, that
was scary.**

Eureka!

Albert Einstein is reputed to have uttered the interjection *Eureka!* on coming up with his special theory of relativity. *Eureka* is a Greek word, meaning "I have found it". Similar moments of revelation may be marked by interjections like *hurrah!* or *aha!* – the benefit being that a single-word interjection conveys much more emotion than a simple sentence.

Greetings

Everyday greetings like *hello*, *hi*, *goodbye* and even *yoo-hoo* are interjections, functioning on their own or as part of a sentence. Like other interjections, if a greeting is removed from a sentence, the meaning of that sentence is not affected.

Hello, what are you doing?

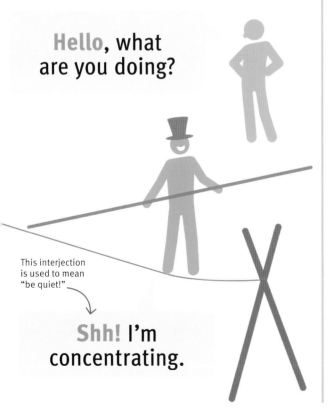

This interjection is used to mean "be quiet!"

Shh! I'm concentrating.

Interruptions and introductions

Many English speakers use the interjections *er* or *um* to fill pauses in their speech, such as when they are unsure of what to say. These are sometimes called hesitation devices. *Yes*, *no* and variations of the two are also interjections, as are other introductory expressions such as *indeed* and *well*. These can be used alone in response to a question or statement.

I, er, have no idea what has happened to, um, the snake charmer.

Commas are used on either side of a mild interjection, such as a hesitation device, if it appears in the middle of a sentence.

Yes, he's been gone for ages. Where is he?

The interjections *yes* and *no* are used at the start of a sentence, followed by a comma, or on their own.

Asides

Interjections are often used in brackets to indicate an aside or an action. This is particularly useful in a play script, because it indicates the tone of a sentence and gives directions to the actors.

The snake charmer is (cough!) temporarily unavailable.

This aside tells the speaker to pause and cough – in this case, indicating that the speaker doesn't necessarily believe what he or she is saying.

Phrases

A PHRASE IS A GROUP OF WORDS THAT MAKE UP PART OF A SENTENCE.

Phrases add information to a sentence, but they only make complete sense as part of a sentence. A phrase does not contain a verb, and it can perform the function of an adjective, an adverb or a noun.

SEE ALSO

❮ **22–23** Nouns
❮ **26–27** Adjectives
❮ **40–41** Adverbs
❮ **46–47** Participles
❮ **60–61** Prepositions
Managing modifiers **76–77** ❯

Adjectival phrases

Like adjectives, adjectival phrases describe nouns or pronouns. An adjectival phrase usually starts with an adverb or a preposition. It can be placed before or after the noun or pronoun it describes.

very red-faced

adverb

This adjectival phrase is made up of an adverb followed by an adjective, and it can be used after the noun it describes.

the very red-faced drummer

This adjectival phrase can also be placed before the noun it describes.

of the band

preposition

This is an adjectival phrase because it is giving more information about the members, a noun.

The drummer, very red-faced
The shocked members of the band

• **Phrases** can be used **instead of one-word adjectives** or **adverbs** to make a piece of writing more **interesting**.

Most **dictionary definitions** are **adjectival phrases**.

Noun phrases

A noun phrase is made up of a noun and any words that are modifying that noun, including articles, determiners, and adjectives or adjectival phrases. Noun phrases work in exactly the same way as nouns in a sentence.

This is a noun phrase because it is performing the action of the verb – hiding. This noun phrase is the subject of the sentence.

the shocked members of the band

This adjectival phrase forms part of the noun phrase.

the drummer

article

This is a simple noun phrase consisting of an article and a noun.

Adverbial phrases

Like adverbs, adverbial phrases describe verbs, adjectives and other adverbs. They answer questions such as: How? When? Why? Where? How often?

angrily across the stage

This is an adverbial phrase because it is describing how (*angrily*) and where (*across the stage*) the drummer strode.

behind their instruments

This is an adverbial phrase because it is describing where the members of the band hid.

trode angrily across the stage.
id behind their instruments.

Prepositional phrases

Prepositional phrases are the most common type of phrase, but they always act as either adjectives or adverbs in a sentence, modifying nouns or verbs. They are therefore contained within – or make up – adjectival or adverbial phrases. A prepositional phrase is made up of a preposition, along with the noun or noun phrase that follows it.

behind their instruments

preposition

This prepositional phrase is acting as an adverb, because it is modifying the verb *hid*.

across the stage

preposition

This prepositional phrase is also acting as an adverb, because it is modifying the verb *strode*.

of the band

preposition

This prepositional phrase is acting as an adjective, because it is describing the noun *members*.

Clauses

A CLAUSE IS THE KEY ELEMENT OF A SENTENCE.

A clause is a group of words that contains a subject and a verb.
It can form part of a sentence, or a complete simple sentence.
Clauses can be main or subordinate, and they can behave like
adjectives or adverbs.

Main clauses

Also known as an independent
clause, a main clause includes a
subject and a verb and expresses
a complete thought. Main clauses
are the same as simple sentences,
because they have to make sense
on their own.

Subordinate clauses

A subordinate clause (also called
a dependent clause) contains a
subject and a verb, but it does not
make sense on its own. It depends
on a main clause for its meaning.
Subordinate clauses often explain or
add more information about where or
when things happen, or how they are
done. Relative and adverbial clauses
are types of subordinate clauses.

Identifying main and subordinate clauses

Both main and subordinate
clauses have a subject and
a verb, but only main clauses
make sense on their own.
The easiest way to identify a
subordinate clause is to look
for relative pronouns, such as
which or *that*, or subordinators,
such as *because* or *although*.

This sentence is made
up of two clauses.

This is a main clause, because it
contains a subject and a verb, and
makes complete sense on its own.

This is a subordinate clause, because
it contains a subject (here, a pronoun),
a verb and a subordinator, and it does
not make sense on its own.

Relative clauses

Relative clauses are also known as adjective clauses, and they are a type of subordinate clause. Like adjectives and adjectival phrases, relative clauses describe nouns and pronouns. Unlike adjectives, they can only be placed after the noun or pronoun they are modifying. Relative clauses always start with one of the relative pronouns *who*, *whom*, *whose*, *which* or *that*, which acts as the subject or the object of the clause.

▽ **Subject**
The relative pronoun *which* is the subject of this relative clause, which can be used to describe a noun.

▷ **Object**
Here, the relative pronoun *which* is the object of the clause – it is receiving the action of the verb *did*.

Adverbial clauses

An adverbial clause is a type of subordinate clause that behaves like an adverb. It gives additional information about how, when, where and why something is happening. Adverbial clauses start with subordinators such as *because*, *although*, *after*, *while*, *as* and *until*.

▷ **Why?**
This adverbial clause explains why the cat did something, but it does not make sense without a main clause.

SUBJECT	VERB	OBJECT
as ▷ the cat	wanted	breakfast

subordinator

▷ **When?**
This adverbial clause explains when the cat did something, but it does not make sense without a main clause.

subordinator

SUBJECT	VERB	OBJECT
after ▷ the cat	had eaten	breakfast

GLOSSARY

Adverbial phrase A group of words that behave in the same way as an adverb and answer questions such as: How? When? Why? Where? How often?

Object The person or thing that is receiving the verb's action.

Relative pronoun A pronoun that links one part of a sentence to another by introducing a relative clause, which describes an earlier noun or pronoun.

Subject The person or thing that is performing the action.

Subordinator A conjunction used to connect words, phrases and clauses of unequal importance.

• A **main clause** can be turned into a **subordinate clause** by adding a **subordinator** – for example, "**because** the cat slept".

Sentences

THERE ARE MANY DIFFERENT TYPES OF SENTENCES, VARYING IN COMPLEXITY.

A sentence is a unit of written language that contains a subject and a verb and makes complete sense on its own. It must begin with a capital letter and end with a full stop, exclamation mark or question mark.

SEE ALSO	
❰ **38–39** Verbs	
❰ **54–55** Voices and moods	
❰ **64–65** Phrases	
❰ **66–67** Clauses	
Compound sentences	**70–71** ❱
Complex sentences	**72–73** ❱
Full stops and ellipses	**94–95** ❱
Question marks	**110–111** ❱
Exclamation marks	**112–113** ❱

Simple sentences

A simple sentence is the same as a main clause. It must have a subject and one main verb, and it must express a single idea. The subject is the person or thing that does the action (the verb), but one subject can be made up of more than one person or thing. Most simple sentences also include an object, which is the person or thing receiving the action.

capital letter

A full stop ends the sentence.

The chef cooked.

subject   verb

Descriptive words and phrases can be added to give more information, but if there is still only one verb, it remains a simple sentence.

The chef and his friends ate the delicious meal.

The subject can represent more than one person or thing.

object

Statements

A statement is a sentence that conveys a fact or piece of information. The subject always comes before the verb. Most simple sentences are statements, and statements end with a full stop.

The pie had exploded.

This is a statement because it states a fact and ends with a full stop.

- **Shorter sentences** tend to be **more effective** at getting a message across.
- It is important to **vary the sentence construction** in a piece of writing, so that it does not become monotonous.
- **Simple sentences** can be used to **create tension** in a story.

Questions

A question is a sentence that asks for information and ends with a question mark. Unlike a statement, the subject is placed after the verb. Only auxiliary verbs can change places with their subjects, so a question must include an auxiliary verb such as *be*, *do* or *can*. Many questions also start with question words such as *why*, *when*, *where* and *how*.

question word   subject   main verb

Why did the pie explode?

auxiliary verb

This is a question because it asks for information and ends with a question mark.

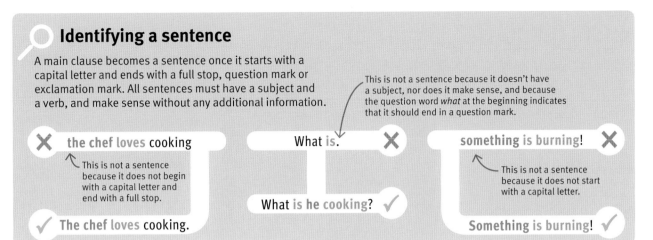

Identifying a sentence

A main clause becomes a sentence once it starts with a capital letter and ends with a full stop, question mark or exclamation mark. All sentences must have a subject and a verb, and make sense without any additional information.

✗ the chef loves cooking

This is not a sentence because it does not begin with a capital letter and end with a full stop.

✓ The chef loves cooking.

What is. ✗

This is not a sentence because it doesn't have a subject, nor does it make sense, and because the question word *what* at the beginning indicates that it should end in a question mark.

What is he cooking? ✓

something is burning! ✗

This is not a sentence because it does not start with a capital letter.

Something is burning! ✓

Commands

A command is a sentence that gives an order or an instruction. Instructions are most effective when they are written in simple sentences. The subject in a command is implied, rather than present – it is the person who is receiving the command. Orders usually end with an exclamation mark, while instructions tend to end with a full stop.

This sentence gives an order, so it ends with an exclamation mark.

Do not open the oven!

The implied subject is the person who is being told not to open the oven.

Please do not touch the pie.

The implied subject is the person who is being asked not to touch the pie.

This sentence gives a polite instruction, so it ends with a full stop.

Exclamations

An exclamation works in the same way as a statement, but it expresses a strong emotion, such as surprise or horror. Exclamations always end with an exclamation mark.

The pie had exploded!

The use of an exclamation mark instead of a full stop adds emotion to a statement, making it seem more dramatic.

The **shortest complete sentence** in the **English** language is "**I am.**"

"Careful you must be..."

When the simple rules of sentence construction are not followed, sentences become very hard to understand. The *Star Wars* character Yoda's speech is a good example. Instead of speaking in sentences that follow the subject–verb–object pattern, Yoda muddles his sentences so that the object comes first, followed by the subject, and then the verb. The result is confusing.

GLOSSARY

Auxiliary verb A "helping" verb such as *be* or *have* that joins the main verb in a sentence to the subject.

Main clause A group of words that contains a subject and a verb and makes complete sense on its own.

Object The person or thing that is receiving the action of the verb.

Subject The person or thing that is performing the action of the verb.

Compound sentences

A COMPOUND SENTENCE IS A SENTENCE THAT HAS MORE
THAN ONE MAIN CLAUSE.

Compound sentences are made up of two or more main clauses,
but no subordinate clauses. The main clauses are linked using
conjunctions, and the resulting sentence conveys different
ideas of equal importance.

Joining main clauses

Compound sentences are a useful way
of connecting two or more ideas of
equal importance. They help to improve
the flow of a piece of writing, as many
successive simple sentences can be
uncomfortable to read. To form most
compound sentences, two main
clauses – each containing a subject
and a verb – are joined together using
a co-ordinating conjunction such as
and, *but* or *so*. A comma is used before
the co-ordinating conjunction to
separate the two clauses.

This is a main clause because
it has a subject (*Ali*) and a verb,
and makes sense on its own.

This is also a
main clause.

Ali loves swimming

Aidan builds robots

and

co-ordinating
conjunction

Ali loves swimming, **and Aidan builds** robots.

A comma is used to show
where one main clause
ends and the next begins.

The conjunction *and* has been used to
connect the two main clauses. It shows
that they are of equal importance.

Using conjunctions

There are seven main co-ordinating
conjunctions, and these are used in
different ways. The conjunction *and*
is used to join two things that are
alike, or to show that one thing follows
the other. *But* is used to contrast one
idea with another, while *so* indicates
that the second thing occurs as a
result of the first. *Yet* is used to
mean "nevertheless", *or* and *nor*
are used to link alternatives, and
for is used in compound sentences
to mean "because".

The second clause is the case
despite the first clause.

Ali loves swimming,
yet she swims rarely.

The second clause happens
because of the first clause.

Ali loves swimming,
so she swims often.

Ali might go swimming,
or she might see her friends.

The two clauses offer
alternative actions that
the subject might do.

The two clauses offer
alternative actions that
the subject might do.

or   yet   so

for   but

and   nor

The second clause makes
a statement that contrasts
with the first clause.

Ali loves swimming,
but she hates
running.

Ali loves swimming,
for she grew up
near the sea.

The second clause
explains the first clause.

The two clauses offer
alternative actions that
the subject did not do.

Ali did not go swimming,
nor did she see her friends.

The two clauses give
similar information that
is of equal importance.

Ali loves swimming,
and she loves hot weather.

Joining multiple main clauses

Sometimes three (or more) main clauses are joined together. If the resulting sentence is a list of main clauses containing similar ideas, a comma is used to separate the first two main clauses, and a conjunction is used before the third clause.

A comma is used to separate the first two main clauses in a list of three clauses.

Ali loves swimming, **Aidan builds** robots, **and Sophie enjoys** reading.

A co-ordinating conjunction is used to join the third main clause to the second main clause.

Using semi-colons

Another way to form a compound sentence is to link two main clauses using a semi-colon. A semi-colon performs the same role as a conjunction, and can therefore be replaced by a conjunction. It shows that two clauses are closely related and equally important.

The two main clauses are giving two different, but closely related, pieces of information about Aidan, so they can be linked using a semi-colon.

Aidan builds robots; **he** also **repairs** motorcycles.

The same two clauses can also be linked using a conjunction.

Aidan builds robots, **and he** also **repairs** motorcycles.

Using colons

A colon can also be used to form a compound sentence. Rather than connecting two similar ideas, a colon is used to show that the second main clause is an explanation of the first main clause. Unlike a semi-colon, a colon cannot be replaced by a conjunction.

Aidan has an unusual hobby: **he builds** robots.

These two main clauses are linked using a colon, because the second clause is an explanation of the first clause.

GLOSSARY

Co-ordinating conjunction A word that connects words, phrases and clauses of equal importance.

Main clause A group of words that contains a subject and a verb and makes complete sense on its own.

Subject The person or thing that is performing the action of the verb.

Subordinate clause A group of words that contains a subject and a verb but depends on a main clause for its meaning.

• **Never use a comma to join two main clauses.** Main clauses can only be connected using a conjunction, a semi-colon or a colon.

• If the two **main clauses** use the **same subject** and are linked using a **conjunction**, the subject can be left out of the second clause. If the sentence is short, no comma is required before the conjunction. For example, "Ali loves swimming **but** hates running."

Complex sentences

A COMPLEX SENTENCE CONTAINS AT LEAST ONE
SUBORDINATE CLAUSE.

Unlike a compound sentence, which contains only main clauses,
a complex sentence is made up of a main clause and one or more
subordinate clauses. The subordinate clause depends on the main
clause for its meaning.

Ranking ideas

Complex sentences are useful because they can be used to
indicate that one idea is more important than another. The
secondary idea is contained in a subordinate clause, which
has a subject and a verb, but does not make sense without
the main clause to which it is attached. Subordinate clauses
add information to main clauses.

main clause

Zoe put on her coat ↙
because it was cold.

This is a subordinate clause
because it explains why Zoe
put on her coat, but does not
make sense on its own.

Linking subordinate clauses

Subordinate clauses usually start with
a relative pronoun such as *which* or *that*,
a participle such as *dancing* or *shouting*,
or a subordinator such as *because* or
although. Many subordinators, including
where, *when* and *while*, give a clear
indication of the type of information
they are offering.

MAIN CLAUSE

**Zoe had fun at
the dance class**

SUBORDINATE CLAUSES

where she met a new friend.

which finished late.

while the music played.

although she was tired.

until it was time to go home.

dancing with her friends.

Identifying dangling participles

Subordinate clauses often start with
a participle, which describes the action
being performed by the subject of the
main clause. If a subordinate clause
that starts with a participle is put in
the wrong place in a sentence, it is
described as "dangling", because
it has no subject to hold on to. The
clause should always be placed next
to the subject it describes.

Talking to a friend, the music deafened Zoe. ✗

This is a dangling participle because it is
modifying the wrong noun – *music*.

The music was **talking to a friend.** ✗

Check which noun the subordinate clause is modifying
by moving the noun so that it relates to the clause.

Zoe was **talking to a friend.** ✓

The correct noun is now
being modified.

Talking to a friend, Zoe was deafened by the music. ✓

Rewrite the sentence so that the correct
noun is next to the subordinate clause.

Clause order

Subordinate clauses that start with relative pronouns always follow the noun or pronoun they are describing. If a subordinate clause starts with a subordinator or a participle, however, it can occupy different positions in a sentence.

▷ **Ending a sentence**
When a subordinate clause is placed at the end of a sentence, no comma is required to separate the clauses unless the sentence is long and would otherwise be confusing.

The subordinate clause is separated from the main clause by a subordinator, so no comma is required.

Rob hid in a corner **because he hated dancing.**

This subordinate clause is at the beginning of the sentence, so a comma is required to separate the two clauses.

▷ **Starting a sentence**
If the subordinate clause is placed at the start of a sentence, however, it must be separated from the main clause that follows by a comma.

Until the class was over, Rob hid in a corner.

This subordinate clause has split the main clause into two parts, so commas are required to show which parts belong to which clauses.

▷ **Sitting in the middle**
Similarly, if a subordinate clause breaks up a main clause, a comma is required at the start and end of the clause to separate it from the main clause.

Rob, **feeling bored,** hid in a corner.

Multiple subordinate clauses

As long as a complex sentence contains at least one main clause, more than one subordinate clause can be used. The easiest way to construct a complex sentence is to start with a main clause and then add the subordinate clauses, one at a time.

Tim missed the class.

main clause

A subordinate clause has been added to make this a complex sentence.

Although he loved dancing, Tim missed the class.

main clause

subordinate clause

main clause

Although he loved dancing, Tim missed the class, **which was full.**

A second subordinate clause has been added.

GLOSSARY

Main clause A group of words that contains a subject and a verb and makes complete sense on its own.

Relative pronoun A pronoun that links one part of a sentence to another by introducing a relative clause, which describes an earlier noun or pronoun.

Subject The person or thing that is performing the action of the verb.

Subordinate clause A group of words that contains a subject and a verb but depends on a main clause for its meaning.

Subordinator A conjunction used to connect words, phrases and clauses of unequal importance.

Using clauses correctly

CLAUSES MUST BE PUT IN A CERTAIN ORDER FOR A SENTENCE
CONTAINING SEVERAL CLAUSES TO MAKE SENSE.

SEE ALSO
❮ 64–65 Phrases
❮ 66–67 Clauses
❮ 68–69 Sentences
❮ 70–71 Compound sentences
❮ 72–73 Complex sentences

A main clause must make complete sense on its own, while
a subordinate clause only makes sense when it is connected
to a main clause. When clauses are put in the wrong place
in a sentence, the meaning of that sentence changes.

Breaking sentences down

Certain rules must be followed for a complex
sentence to make sense. If a sentence is
broken down into its component parts, it has
to be clear which clause refers to which
subject. Each clause must have its own
subject and verb, and a main clause must
express a complete thought.

This is a main clause because
it makes sense on its own.

This subordinate clause explains
why Lauren (the subject of the
sentence) was upset.

Lauren was upset **because she had
lost her swimsuit,** which was new.

This subordinate clause is placed at
the end of the sentence because it
describes the swimsuit, not Lauren.

Identifying a misplaced clause

If a clause describes someone or something, it needs to be placed as
close as possible to the person or thing it describes. Sometimes a
phrase or another clause gets in the way, and the whole meaning of
a sentence changes as a result. When this happens, the sentence
should be reworded so that the potentially confusing clause is
placed next to the person or thing that it describes.

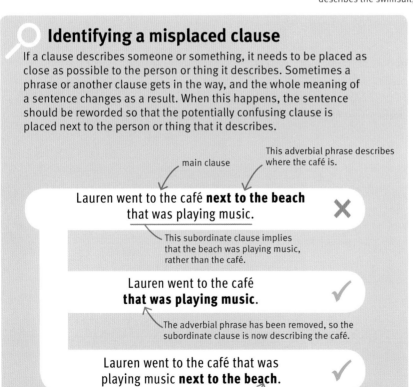

main clause

This adverbial phrase describes
where the café is.

Lauren went to the café **next to the beach**
that was playing music. ✗

This subordinate clause implies
that the beach was playing music,
rather than the café.

Lauren went to the café
that was playing music. ✓

The adverbial phrase has been removed, so the
subordinate clause is now describing the café.

Lauren went to the café that was
playing music **next to the beach.** ✓

The adverbial phrase has been put back into the
sentence, and the sentence now makes sense.

GLOSSARY

Adverbial phrase A group of words
such as "in July last year" that perform
the same role as an adverb and answer
questions such as: How? When? Why?
Where? How often?

Main clause A group of words that
contains a subject and a verb and
makes complete sense on its own.

Subject The person or thing that is
performing the action of the verb.

Subordinate clause A group of words
that contains a subject and a verb
but depends on a main clause for
its meaning.

Split subject and verb

Some subordinate clauses can be placed in the middle of a sentence, separating the different parts of a main clause. If the subject of a sentence is too far away from its verb, the meaning of that sentence will be difficult to follow, so long subordinate clauses are best placed at the beginning or end of a sentence.

▷ **Separated**
This sentence is hard to follow, because the verb, *felt*, is separated from its subject, *Lauren*, by a long subordinate clause.

Lauren, after walking to the café, buying two scoops of ice cream, and eating them hungrily, **felt ill.**

▷ **Reunited**
The sentence has been re-organised so that the subject of the main clause, *Lauren*, is now next to its verb.

After walking to the café, buying two scoops of ice cream, and eating them hungrily, **Lauren felt ill.**

Avoiding sentence fragments

Sentence fragments are parts of sentences that do not contain all the pieces needed to make a complete sentence. In the context of a conversation, sentence fragments can be meaningful. Once the context has been removed, however, sentence fragments make no sense at all, so they are rarely used in writing.

▽ **Recognising fragments**
Many sentence fragments do not contain a subject or a verb, and they only make sense in context: for example, as the answer to a question.

What would you like?

Vanilla and fudge ice cream.

sentence fragment

▽ **Making sentences**
If a sentence fragment has been removed from its context, the subject and verb need to be reinstated. A written sentence should never have to rely on the sentences around it for its sense.

subject

I would like vanilla and fudge ice cream.

verb

REAL WORLD

Fragmented advertising

Sentence fragments are often used in advertising, as the product being advertised provides the context. An advertiser's main concern is that the brand is prominent, so the name of this brand normally appears at the start or in the middle of the sentence fragment. Sometimes advertisements are more memorable simply because they sound wrong.

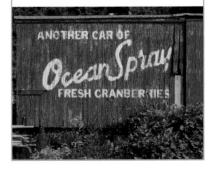

Managing modifiers

A MODIFIER IS A WORD, PHRASE OR CLAUSE THAT
DESCRIBES ANOTHER WORD, PHRASE OR CLAUSE.

SEE ALSO

❮ 26–27 Adjectives
❮ 40–41 Adverbs
❮ 46–47 Participles
❮ 64–65 Phrases
❮ 66–67 Clauses
❮ 74–75 Using clauses correctly

Used correctly, modifiers make sentences more descriptive and
therefore more interesting. If a modifier is put in the wrong place in
a sentence, however, it can alter the whole meaning of that sentence.

Misplaced adverbs

Common one-word modifiers include the adverbs
only, *almost*, *just* and *nearly*. These adverb modifiers
are usually placed right before the word they modify.
If a modifier is in the wrong place, the intended
meaning may not be clear, and the modifier may
end up modifying the wrong person or thing.

This means that I spoke to Maria very
recently, and asked her to lunch.

I just asked Maria to lunch.

I asked just Maria to lunch.

This means that I asked Maria
to lunch, and no one else.

This means that I was
tempted to eat a whole pie,
but I didn't eat any of it.

I almost ate a whole pie.

This means that I ate the
pie, and ate most of it.

I ate almost a whole pie.

The comedian Groucho Marx
humorously used a **misplaced
modifier**: "One morning I shot an
elephant **in my pyjamas**. How he got
into my pyjamas I'll never know."

Misplaced adjectives

Like adverb modifiers, adjective modifiers should be
placed as close as possible to the person or thing they
describe. Misplaced adjectives tend to occur when
a noun is described by several words.

This adjective is describing a
silver woman, not a silver bracelet.

Jim found a silver woman's bracelet.

Jim found a woman's silver bracelet.

The adjective is now describing a silver
bracelet that belongs to a woman.

GLOSSARY

Dangling participle When a modifying phrase or clause
that starts with a participle is put in the wrong place in
a sentence, it is described as "dangling", because it has
no subject to hold on to.

Main clause A group of words that contains a subject and
a verb and makes complete sense on its own.

Misplaced modifier A modifier that has been placed so
far from the person or thing it is intended to modify that
it appears to modify a different person or thing.

Participle The form of a verb that ends in -ing (present
participle) or -ed or -en (past participle).

Subject The person or thing that is performing the
action of the verb.

Subordinate clause A group of words that contains a subject
and a verb but depends on a main clause for its meaning.

Misplaced prepositional phrases

Prepositional phrases often end up in the wrong place. If a modifier is a phrase, it should still be placed next to the person or thing it is modifying. If a prepositional phrase is placed elsewhere in a sentence, it may not convey the intended message.

Laura went for a walk with the dog in her new boots.

This prepositional phrase is modifying the dog, so the dog is wearing the new boots.

Laura went for a walk in her new boots with the dog.

This prepositional phrase is now modifying the main clause, "Laura went for a walk", so it is Laura who is wearing the boots.

> • When writing, always **re-read** a finished piece of text before showing it to anyone. As the writer, it's **easy to overlook** potentially **amusing** or **misleading word order**.
>
> • A good way to check for **misplaced modifiers** in a sentence is to **single out** any **modifying words** or phrases by **underlining** or **highlighting** them. It is then easier to see which modifiers relate to which nouns, and **move** any that are in the **wrong place**.

Identifying squinting modifiers

If a modifier is placed between two phrases or clauses, it can be difficult to work out which phrase or clause it relates to. This type of modifier is often referred to as a squinting modifier, because it looks in two different directions at the same time. The only way to resolve this ambiguity is to move the modifier so that there can be no confusion.

This adverb could be modifying the verb *swim*, in which case the sentence is saying that the people who often swim are the ones who will get fitter.

People who swim **often** will get fitter. ✗

Alternatively, *often* could be modifying the phrase "will get fitter", in which case the sentence is saying that people in general will often get fitter if they swim.

People who **often** swim will get fitter. ✓

The modifying adverb has been moved so that there is no ambiguity, and the people who often swim are the ones who will get fitter.

People who swim will **often** get fitter. ✓

The modifying adverb has been moved to avoid confusion, and the sentence is saying that people in general will often get fitter if they swim.

Dangling participles

Subordinate clauses that start with a participle often cause confusion. This type of clause must be next to its subject, which should also be the subject of the sentence. If the clause is put in the wrong place, it will modify the wrong thing; similarly, if the intended subject is left out of a sentence, that sentence will not make sense. When these errors occur, they are known as dangling participles.

Driving past, the camel was asleep.

In this sentence, the sleeping camel is doing the driving. The intended subject (the person who was driving) has been left out of the sentence.

Driving past, he saw a sleeping camel.

The sentence has been reworded so that the participle *driving* now modifies a subject, *he*, which is also the subject of the sentence.

Commonly misused words

SOME GRAMMATICAL ERRORS OCCUR FREQUENTLY.

It is common to make grammatical mistakes when speaking, but when these mistakes are transferred to writing, the meaning of a sentence is often affected. Most of these problems result from confusion between two words.

That or which?

Use *that* for restrictive relative clauses, which introduce essential information, and *which* for non-restrictive relative clauses, which introduce additional, non-essential information.

The cats **that are black** are sleeping.

The cats, **which are black**, are sleeping.

May or might?

The auxiliary verb *may* implies a possibility that something will happen, while *might* indicates a real uncertainty. If something is unlikely to happen, use *might*.

I **may** go for a swim later.

You **might** encounter a shark.

Can or may?

Can refers to a person's ability to do something, whereas *may* is used to ask permission. These auxiliary verbs are not interchangeable.

Can you cook?

May I come?

I or me?

The simplest way to know which pronoun to use is to remove the other person from the sentence. It should then become obvious. Always remember to put the other person or people first.

Isabella, Rosie and **I** went to a café.

"I went to a café" makes sense, so this is correct.

Rosie bought coffee for Isabella and **me**.

"Rosie bought coffee for me" makes sense, so this is correct.

Who or whom?

Think of *who* as representing *he* or *she*, and *whom* as representing *him* or *her*. If in doubt, rephrase the sentence and substitute *he/she* or *him/her*.

Finn, **who** loved snow, went outside.

The substituted clause would be "he loved snow".

Finn found Greg, **whom** Finn had telephoned earlier.

The substituted clause would be "Finn had telephoned him".

Whether or if?

Whether does not mean the same thing as *if*. *Whether* is used in sentences where there are two or more alternatives, while *if* can only be used when there are no alternatives.

She couldn't decide **whether** to run **or** hide.

She doesn't know **if** anything will happen.

Its or it's?

Use the possessive determiner *its* when describing a thing that belongs to something, and the contraction *it's* to represent *it is*.

It's back! **its** back

Could have or could of?

In speech, the contracted form of *could have*, *could've*, is often mistakenly interpreted as *could of*. *Could of* is wrong and should never be used.

You **could have** told me!

Fewer or less?

Fewer is used for things that can be counted, while *less* is used for hypothetical quantities – things that cannot be counted.

I got **fewer** than ten birthday presents this year.

I have **less** work to do than he has.

Bring or take?

If an object is being moved towards the subject, the verb *bring* should be used. If it is being moved away, the verb *take* should be used.

Shall I **bring** a book to read?

You can **take** one of my books.

Good or well?

Good is an adjective, so it is used to describe nouns. *Well* is mostly used as an adverb to describe verbs, adjectives or other adverbs. However, it can also be used as an adjective to mean "healthy". *Good* does not mean "healthy", so it shouldn't be used in that sense.

A **good** chef eats **well**, so stays **well**.

This adjective is describing the noun *chef*.

This adverb is describing the verb *eats*.

This adjective means "healthy".

Literally

Literally means "actually" or "in a real sense". It should only be used to describe things exactly as they happened. Anything else is figurative, not literal.

I **literally** erupted with laughter!

Negatives

A NEGATIVE TURNS A POSITIVE STATEMENT INTO A NEGATIVE ONE.

In order to show that something is incorrect or untrue
in English, a positive statement has to be turned into a negative
one – usually by adding the word *not* after an auxiliary verb.
Double negatives should be avoided.

SEE ALSO

❰ **34–35** Pronouns
❰ **40–41** Adverbs
❰ **42–43** Simple tenses
❰ **44–45** Perfect and continuous tenses
❰ **48–49** Auxiliary verbs
❰ **52–53** Verb agreement
Apostrophes **104–105** ❱

REAL WORLD

Satisfied?

When British rock band The Rolling
Stones sang "I can't get no
satisfaction" in 1965, they
cancelled the negative *can't* out
with the negative *no*. But despite
the double negative, the meaning
was clear,
and listeners
worldwide
understood
the band
to be
thoroughly
dissatisfied.

Forming negative sentences

Auxiliary verbs are the only verbs that can be made negative. If a sentence
does not contain an auxiliary verb, one must be added. The negative word
not is then placed directly after the auxiliary verb. The resulting combination
is known as a negative auxiliary.

AUXILIARY VERB	NEGATIVE WORD	MAIN VERB
had **is** **will**	**not**	**been** **going** **go**

Frank had not been to a Germa
believe he wouldn't try a currie

Contractions

In negative sentences, the auxiliary
verb and the negative word *not* can
be combined and shortened to form
contractions, with an apostrophe to
represent the missing letter or letters.
Common negative contractions
include *haven't* (have not) and
can't (cannot).

Auxiliary verb	Negative word	Contraction
would	not	wouldn't
do	not	don't
should	not	shouldn't
could	not	couldn't
will	not	won't

Most negative
contractions are formed
by joining the two words
and removing the *o*
from *not*.

There are some
exceptions: here, the
i from *will* has also
been changed to *o*.

Identifying a double negative

A double negative is when two negative words appear in a single clause. Although the two negative words are usually intended to convey a single negative thought – and this usage is understood in colloquial English – in reality, one negative plus another negative equals a positive. If a clause includes two negative words, one of them should be removed.

There are two negatives in this sentence, so the resulting meaning is that Frank did want more food.

There is now only one negative in the sentence, so it conveys its intended meaning.

Frank didn't want **no** more food. ✗

didn't

no

✓ Frank didn't want more food.

Frank wanted **no** more food. ✓

The past tense auxiliary verb form *did* has been removed, so the verb *want* has to be put in the past tense.

There is now only one negative in the sentence, so it conveys its intended meaning.

• *Not* is the most common negative word, but other words can be used in the same way. These range from *never* and *no*, the most forceful, to *seldom*, *barely* and *hardly*, which reflect smaller degrees of negativity.

Negative pronouns

Some indefinite pronouns are already in a negative form, and therefore do not need to be made negative using *not*. These include *nobody*, *no one*, *nothing* and *none*.

There is no need to add the word *not* after this auxiliary verb, because *nobody* is a negative word.

Nobody could believe **he** wouldn't try **a curried sausage.**

Nobody is a singular pronoun, so the verb must be singular.

estaurant before. Nobody could ausage. He disliked spicy food.

Positive thinking

Most statements use fewer words and are more convincing if they are written in a positive way. Even negative words can be used in a positive sentence structure.

This negative word means "did not like", but it can be used in a positive sentence.

He disliked spicy food.

Negative structure	Positive structure
did not like	disliked
was not honest	was dishonest
did not pay attention	ignored
could not remember	forgot
did not start on time	started late
is not attractive	is unattractive

Relative clauses

ALSO KNOWN AS ADJECTIVE CLAUSES, RELATIVE CLAUSES MODIFY NOUNS.

Relative clauses add information to a sentence using the relative pronouns *who*, *whom*, *whose*, *that* and *which*. Restrictive relative clauses add essential details, while non-restrictive clauses add non-essential details.

• Make sure that the **relative clause** is **next** to the **noun** or **pronoun** that it is **modifying**. Otherwise, it may end up modifying the wrong person or thing.

• Sometimes a relative clause can be used to **modify** the **rest of the sentence**, rather than a single noun or pronoun. In the following sentence, the relative clause is describing the whole first part of the sentence: "Joe did not look sorry, **which was normal**."

Non-restrictive relative clauses

There are two types of relative clauses: non-restrictive and restrictive. Also known as "non-defining" or "non-essential" clauses, non-restrictive relative clauses offer additional information about a noun. They are separated from the rest of a sentence by commas, because the information they provide is supplementary, rather than essential.

Non-restrictive clauses require commas.

The principal, who hated chaos, felt calm.

This non-restrictive relative clause gives more detail about the principal, but it can be removed without affecting the meaning of the sentence.

The principal, who hated chaos, fel
Joe, whom he had summoned. Jo

Relative pronouns

Relative clauses always follow the noun or pronoun that they modify. They start with one of five relative pronouns, which act as either the subject or the object of the relative clause. *Who* always acts as the subject, while *whom* always acts as the object. The relative pronouns *who*, *whom* and *whose* are used to refer to people, while *which* and *that* are used to refer to things.

This is the object of the relative clause – the person who was summoned.

whom he had summoned

This is the subject of the relative clause.

This is the subject of the relative clause – the person who hated chaos.

who hated chaos

This is the object of the relative clause.

Identifying when a pronoun can be omitted

Sometimes a relative pronoun can be omitted from a relative clause without affecting the sense of a sentence. This only works if the pronoun is the object of the clause – the person or thing receiving the action.

restrictive relative clause

Joe had to clean up the mess **that** **the toad had made**. ✓

that the toad had made

This is the object of the relative clause, so it can be omitted without changing the meaning of the sentence.

subject

Joe had to clean up the mess **the toad had made**. ✓

The sentence makes sense without the relative pronoun and object *that*.

• Although **whom** is grammatically correct, **who** is almost always used instead in **everyday** English.

GLOSSARY

Clause A grammatical unit that contains a subject and a verb. Sentences are made up of one or more clauses.

Object The person or thing that is receiving the action of the verb.

Relative pronoun A pronoun that links one part of a sentence to another by introducing a relative clause, which describes an earlier noun or pronoun.

Subject The person or thing that is performing the action of the verb.

Which or *that*?

Historically *which* and *that* were interchangeable, and could be used for either type of relative clause. It is now usual practice to use *that* for restrictive clauses (see below) and *which* for non-restrictive clauses. This helps to differentiate one type of information from the other.

The principal felt calm, which was unusual.

This is a non-restrictive relative clause, because it gives extra – but not essential – information about the principal.

Joe held the toad that had escaped.

This is a restrictive relative clause, because it helps to identify which toad is being described.

**.alm, which was unusual. He eyed
eld the toad that had escaped.**

Restrictive relative clauses

Restrictive relative clauses are sometimes called "defining" or "essential" clauses, because they identify who or what is being referred to and are therefore vital to the meaning of a sentence. Restrictive clauses are not separated from the rest of a sentence by commas.

**Joe held the toad
that had escaped.**

This relative pronoun is acting as the subject of the relative clause – the thing that did the escaping.

This is a restrictive relative clause – it identifies which toad had escaped.

Idioms, analogies and figures of speech

CERTAIN DEVICES ARE USED TO MAKE SPEECH AND WRITING MORE INTERESTING AND PERSUASIVE.

Figures of speech are used to create different effects, usually to emphasise a point or help an audience to visualise something. Idioms would be meaningless if they were not familiar expressions, while analogies are a useful tool for explaining things.

SEE ALSO

Writing to describe	208–209 ⟩
Writing from personal experience	210–211 ⟩
Writing a narrative	212–213 ⟩

The word *metaphor* comes from the **Greek** word *metapherin*, which means **"transfer"**.

Idioms

An idiom is a word or phrase that means something completely different from the word or words it is made up of. The meanings of idioms have little or no relation to the literal meanings of their component parts, but they make sense because they are familiar expressions. Different regions have different idioms.

This idiom is used to refer to someone who watches a lot of television.

couch potato

This idiom means "to get into bed".

hit the sack

down in the dumps

This idiom is used to refer to someone who is feeling miserable.

Analogies

Analogies are used to explain what something is by likening that thing to another thing and identifying similarities. An analogy is not a figure of speech, but it works like an extended metaphor or simile: it compares an unfamiliar thing to a familiar thing, and then lists the shared characteristics. Baking a cake, for instance, can be used as an analogy for writing. Both require careful planning and specific ingredients, and are designed to suit a particular audience.

adjectives nouns verbs adverbs prepositions

Parts of speech are some of the ingredients required to create a sentence.

Figures of speech

Figures of speech are useful language tools that allow a writer or speaker to persuade, emphasise, impress or create a mental image. Words and phrases are used out of their literal contexts to create different, heightened effects. When a person claims to be "starving", for example, that person is unlikely to be dying of hunger; rather, he or she is simply very hungry.

• Try to **invent new, interesting metaphors** when writing rather than copying existing ones.

Alliteration
The same letter or sound is used at the start of multiple words for effect.

Catherine **c**arefully **c**ombined **c**old **c**offee **c**ake and **k**iwi fruit.

Simile
The words *like* or *as* are used to compare two things.

She is **as** plump **as** a peach, but she moves **like** a ballerina.

Metaphor
One thing is described as being a different thing, resulting in a comparison between the two.

Her cheeks **are** sun-blushed apples.

Euphemism
A mild word or phrase is substituted for a word or phrase that might cause offence.

She has **ample** proportions (she is overweight).

Pun
Also known as word play, the multiple meanings of a word are used to create humour.

She gave me her measurements as **a round figure**.

Hyperbole
A statement is grossly exaggerated.

She said she could **eat a rhinoceros.**

Personification
An object or animal is given human qualities.

The food **called** to her.

Oxymoron
Two terms are used together that contradict each other.

The pie looked **terribly tasty.**

Onomatopoeia
A word is used that mimics the sound of what it stands for.

She **burped** noisily.

Anaphora
A word or phrase is repeated at the start of successive clauses for emphasis.

She ate the pie; **she ate** the cake; **she ate** the kiwi fruit.

Irony
One thing is said but the opposite thing is meant, usually for humour or emphasis.

I admired her **charming** table manners (her manners were poor).

Understatement
Something is made out to be smaller or less important than it really is.

She said she had enjoyed her **light lunch.**

Colloquialisms and slang

COLLOQUIALISMS AND SLANG ARE FORMS OF INFORMAL
SPOKEN LANGUAGE.

Colloquialisms are words or phrases that are used in ordinary,
informal speech. Slang is even less formal, and is often only
recognised by the members of a particular group. Slang includes
words or phrases that may be considered taboo.

SEE ALSO

❮ 12–13 Spoken and written language
❮ 14–15 English around the world
❮ 84–85 Idioms, analogies and figures of speech

Genre, purpose and audience	190–191 ❯
Newspaper articles	198–199 ❯
The spoken word	222–223 ❯
Writing a speech	226–227 ❯

Colloquialisms

English speakers use a variety of
informal words and phrases that
differ from region to region but are
recognised by most native speakers.
These words and phrases are called
colloquialisms, which stems from
the Latin word for "conversation".

Colloquialisms are an important part
of relaxed conversation (known as
colloquial speech), but they should
not be used in formal speech or
writing. Most colloquialisms are
labelled in dictionaries as "informal"
or with the abbreviation "colloq.".

Some slang terms are
used so often that they
become **universal** –
the slang word *cool*,
meaning **"fashionable"**
or **"great"**, is one
example.

fella
dude   fellow
chap   guy
geezer
          gent
bloke

man

dosh
loot   dough
readies
bread
moola
          lolly

money

REAL WORLD

Rhyming slang

Rhyming slang, also known as
Cockney rhyming slang, originated
in the East End of London in the
nineteenth century. It is formed
by replacing a common word with
a phrase that rhymes with it. Often,
the rhyming part of this phrase is
then removed, so the resulting
slang term bears little or no
resemblance to the original
common word. The word *phone*,
for example, is translated into
rhyming slang as the phrase
"dog and bone", which is then
shortened to "dog".

Shortened forms

Some words have both a formal
meaning and a colloquial meaning.
The word *kid*, for example, can refer
to a baby goat or, informally, to a child.
Colloquialisms are often shorter and
easier to say than the word or words
they represent. Common colloquialisms
therefore include shortened forms
of longer words and words that have
been combined. They also include
abbreviations, such as *ROFL* ("rolling
on the floor laughing"), which are used
in text messages and e-mail chats in
place of longer expressions.

Shortened form	Formal term
'cos	because
ain't	is not
gonna	going to
wanna	want to
BRB	be right back
BTW	by the way
DND	do not disturb
LOL	laugh out loud
TTYL	talk to you later

Slang

Slang is only used in informal speech or, sometimes, in works of fiction. It is used in place of conventional words for things that are familiar, but possibly uncomfortable, to the speaker, and includes words that are considered taboo in most contexts. Slang words are labelled as "slang" in dictionaries. Different slang words are adopted by different groups of speakers – especially teenagers. They vary across small geographical areas and change frequently over time.

Sick! That was hardcore.

?

Slang term	Meaning
awesome	incredible, very good
bummed	depressed
chick	girl, woman
chillin'	being calm and relaxed
epic fail	a failure of huge proportions
feral	unpleasant
gross	repulsive
hardcore	intense
hater	an angry or jealous person
hissy fit	tantrum
hot	attractive
lame	unfashionable, of poor quality
my bad	it was my mistake
noob	someone unfashionable, a newcomer
sick	very good
sweet	excellent, very good
tool	someone stupid

Changing meanings

New slang words are invented all the time, and existing slang words often change their meanings from one generation to the next. For example, the slang term *busted* used to refer to something that was broken. The term then evolved to describe what happened when someone was caught doing something wrong. In modern slang, *busted* is sometimes used to refer to an unattractive person. Existing slang words are also often combined to form new ones.

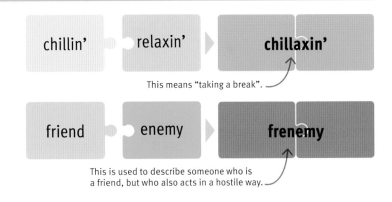

chillin' ● relaxin' ▶ **chillaxin'**

This means "taking a break".

friend ● enemy ▶ **frenemy**

This is used to describe someone who is a friend, but who also acts in a hostile way.

Jargon

Jargon is a type of slang. It is the name for the technical vocabulary that is used by a particular profession. Jargon is usually unintelligible to those outside the profession, but enables those within it to refer to things concisely and without explanation.

assistance from other officers

suspect vehicle

Call for backup! We have an S/V and the perp is on the run.

perpetrator (the person who has committed a crime)

trying to avoid being captured

Direct and indirect speech

THERE ARE TWO WAYS OF REPRESENTING SPEECH IN WRITING.

When a person's exact words are reproduced in writing within inverted commas, this is known as direct speech. When a person's speech is reported, using neither the exact words nor inverted commas, it is called indirect or reported speech.

Direct speech

Direct speech is always contained within inverted commas, indicating words that are spoken aloud by someone. Direct speech is usually written in the present tense (as it is spoken), and is accompanied by a simple clause in the past tense that tells the reader who is speaking.

What are your symptoms?

"**What are your symptoms?**" the doctor asked.

This direct speech gives the exact words of the doctor, so it is contained within inverted commas.

A comma is usually used to separate direct speech from its accompanying clause, but a question mark or exclamation mark can be used instead.

This simple clause explains who is speaking.

Indirect speech

Indirect speech is also known as reported speech, because it is an account – or report – of what someone has said. Indirect speech does not require inverted commas. It is usually written in the past tense, because it is describing what someone has said. The present tense is occasionally used when reporting something that has always been – and remains – the case.

- • **Be careful** when **converting speech** from direct to indirect. It must be clear from the **context** of the sentence or the **word order** which **pronoun** refers to which **person**.
- • When writing **dialogue**, a **new line** should be started for **each new speaker**.

▷ **Reporting back**
These are not Peter's exact words, but they recount what he said, so this is an example of indirect speech.

Peter explained that **his** thumb kept twitching.

The third person is used because Peter is not the narrator.

▷ **Stating facts**
This indirect speech is reporting an unchanging fact, so the present tense is used.

He told the doctor that **he spends** all his time playing computer games.

This means that he always has, does and will spend his time playing computer games.

Identifying characters

Alternating between different forms of speech makes a narrative more interesting to read. When converting direct speech (first person) to indirect speech (third person), it's important to take into account who is speaking, and to whom, and to change the relevant nouns and pronouns to match.

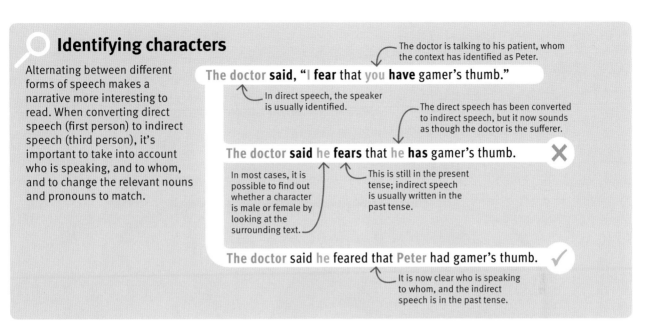

The doctor is talking to his patient, whom the context has identified as Peter.

The doctor **said, "I fear** that **you have** gamer's thumb."

In direct speech, the speaker is usually identified.

The direct speech has been converted to indirect speech, but it now sounds as though the doctor is the sufferer.

The doctor **said** he **fears** that he **has** gamer's thumb. ✗

In most cases, it is possible to find out whether a character is male or female by looking at the surrounding text.

This is still in the present tense; indirect speech is usually written in the past tense.

The doctor said he feared that Peter had gamer's thumb. ✓

It is now clear who is speaking to whom, and the indirect speech is in the past tense.

Time and space

If direct speech is being recounted (turned into indirect speech) in a different place and at a different time from where and when it happened, the adverbs and adverb phrases used must match the new situation. For example, the direct speech "Go to the hospital today!" would be recounted a week later in the following way: He was told to go to the hospital that day.

Direct speech	Indirect speech
now	then
here	there
this (morning)	that (morning)
next (week)	the following (week)
today	that day
tomorrow	the next day/the following day
yesterday	the previous day/the day before

Varying verbs

The most common verbs used to report speech are *said*, *told* and *asked*. Indirect speech can be made more interesting if the writer uses a variety of reporting verbs. The verbs used in the simple clauses that indicate who said what in direct speech can be varied in the same way.

• **Indirect speech** often uses the words *said*, *asked* or *told*, but don't **confuse** it with **direct speech**, which is always in **inverted commas**.

▷ **Descriptive direct speech**
The verb *sobbed* encourages the reader to sympathise with Peter. *Said* would not have this effect.

"I feel like a freak!" sobbed Peter.

▷ **Interesting indirect speech**
Use unusual verbs such as *promised* and *begged* to add emotion to indirect speech.

The doctor promised that Peter's symptoms were curable. Peter begged him to help.

Punctuation

What is punctuation?

PUNCTUATION REFERS TO THE MARKS USED IN WRITING THAT HELP READERS UNDERSTAND WHAT THEY ARE READING.

Sometimes words alone are not enough to convey a writer's message clearly. They need a little help from punctuation marks to illustrate relationships between words, pauses or even emotions.

Several of the main **punctuation marks** also have **uses** in **mathematical** notation.

Punctuation marks

There are twelve commonly used punctuation marks. Using punctuation marks correctly and carefully makes it possible for a writer to convey his or her message clearly. Punctuation can also enable the writer to control whether text is read quickly or slowly.

Full stop

This marks the end of a sentence.

EXAMPLE
The dog slept.

Ellipsis

This represents an unfinished sentence or omitted text.

EXAMPLE
Everything seemed calm, but then...

Comma

This joins or separates elements in a sentence.

EXAMPLE
Hearing a cat, he jumped up.

Semi-colon

This joins two main clauses or separates items in a list.

EXAMPLE
He ran after the cat; it ran up a tree.

Colon

This introduces text in a sentence.

EXAMPLE
He was interested in one thing: chasing the cat.

Apostrophe

This marks the possessive or omitted text.

EXAMPLE
The dog's owner couldn't see the cat.

Why we need punctuation

Some people might argue that writing would be simpler without punctuation. However, writers have something to say and want readers to understand exactly what they mean. Punctuation makes this possible.

	What punctuation does to writing
yes	This word has no punctuation marks. It is just a sequence of letters that together form a word. The reader can read this word in any way.
Yes.	This is a statement. It has a full stop (.), which marks the end of the sentence. This tells the reader to read the word calmly, as it states a fact.
Yes?	This is a question. It has a question mark (?) at the end of the sentence. It tells the reader to read the word as a question, with a slightly raised voice.
Yes!	This is an exclamation. It has an exclamation mark (!) at the end of the sentence, which tells the reader to read it with emotion.
y-e-s	The letters of the word *yes* are separated here by hyphens (-). These tell the reader to read the individual letters slowly and carefully.

Hyphen

This joins or separates words or parts of words.

EXAMPLE

The single-minded dog barked at the cat.

Inverted commas

These enclose direct speech or quotations.

EXAMPLE

"Come on, Fido," his owner called.

Question mark

This marks the end of a direct question.

EXAMPLE

What are you doing?

Exclamation mark

This marks the end of an exclamation.

EXAMPLE

Come here, now!

Brackets

These surround additional information in a sentence.

EXAMPLE

The dog (tail between his legs) followed his owner.

Dash

This signals extra information in a sentence.

EXAMPLE

The cat – pleased with itself – leapt out of the tree.

Full stops and ellipses

A FULL STOP ENDS A SENTENCE, WHEREAS AN ELLIPSIS INDICATES THAT A SENTENCE IS UNFINISHED.

A full stop, also known as a period, marks the end of a complete statement. It can also be used to show that a word has been abbreviated. An ellipsis represents text omitted from a sentence.

SEE ALSO

❮ **54–55** Voices and moods

❮ **68–69** Sentences

Exclamation marks **112–113** ❯

Capital letters **158–159** ❯

Abbreviations **172–173** ❯

Ending a statement

A full stop is used at the end of a statement. There is no space before a full stop, but a space is left after one. It is followed by a capital letter at the start of the next sentence.

The undersea experiment ended.

This full stop marks the end of the sentence.

• If an **abbreviation** with a full stop comes at the end of a sentence, no additional full stop is needed. For example, "The undersea experiment commenced at 4.00 p.m."

The undersea experiment ended said, "Swim to the surface

REAL WORLD

Web and e-mail addresses

The full stop is used today in website and e-mail addresses. In these situations, it is known as a "dot" and functions as a separator between the parts of the address. Unlike in normal writing, the dot is stated when the address is read aloud, so the example here would read "w-w-w-dot-d-k-dot-com".

www.dk.com

Commands

Some commands, including orders and polite requests, end with a full stop. For commands that express greater emotion, such as anger or surprise, an exclamation mark should be used.

Swim to the surface.

This full stop marks the end of this request.

Get out of the water!

This exclamation mark expresses urgency.

• When using **abbreviations**, be consistent and either always use full stops, or never use them.

• Most **acronyms**, such as **NASA** or **NATO**, should be written without full stops.

In **telegrams**, the word *STOP* was used to mark the **end of a sentence** instead of a full stop, because it **cost less** than punctuation.

Abbreviations

A full stop can be used at the ends of certain abbreviations, representing letters that have been omitted. For example, *Dr.* stands for "Doctor". Some abbreviations, such as those for metric measurements and US states, are never spelt with a full stop. It is equally acceptable to end abbreviations with no punctuation.

Washington, D.C.
D.C. stands for "District of Columbia".

Oct.
Oct. stands for "October".

Jr.
Jr. stands for "Junior".

Dept.
Dept. stands for "Department".

Dr.
Dr. stands for "Doctor".

lb. stands for "pounds".
lb.

eading scientist Dr. Fisher
Vait, I forgot to tell you..."

Ellipses

Three full stops in a row are called an ellipsis. An ellipsis indicates that a sentence has been left unfinished, as when a speaker drifts into silence or is cut off abruptly. Ellipses can also represent omitted text within quotations.

I thought...
This ellipsis means that the speaker suddenly stopped speaking. No full stop is needed.

Could I...?
A question mark or exclamation mark is kept after an ellipsis.

This ellipsis stands for the missing words from the start of the sentence in the quotation. The missing words could be "Today we heard that".

The report said that "...Dr. Fisher...is correct....The island is near...".

This ellipsis indicates missing text. Some style guides suggest placing spaces before and after the ellipsis.

A full stop is added after the inverted commas to mark the end of the sentence.

If text is omitted after a complete sentence, the ellipsis is placed after the final punctuation mark.

Commas

COMMAS ARE USED TO SEPARATE ELEMENTS
IN A SENTENCE.

Commas clarify information by separating words, phrases
or clauses. They are used to organise information into
groups, sorting it so a sentence is understood correctly.

Introductions

Sometimes, a sentence begins with
a clause, phrase or word that sets
the scene and leads the way to
where the main action begins in
the second half of the sentence.
A comma is placed after the
introduction to make the reader
pause and anticipate the main
information. An introduction to
a sentence could be a word such
as *However*, a phrase such as
Three years ago or a clause
such as *If this happens*.

This is an introductory phrase.

A comma is placed after the
introductory phrase, before the
main information is revealed.

Once upon a time,
there was a garden.

The main information
follows the comma.

This is an introductory clause.

When Lisa visited the
garden, she saw a flower.

The main
information comes
after the comma.

A comma is placed after
the introductory clause.

Working in pairs

If a sentence is interrupted by an additional phrase that is
not essential to the understanding of the sentence, a comma
is placed on either side of the phrase, like a pair of brackets.
Without the commas, the information is treated as essential.

Sometimes, the interruption is placed at the beginning
or at the end of a sentence. In these cases, only one
comma is used, since a comma is never placed at the
start or at the end of a sentence.

A flower, like a sock, can be stripy.

The interruption is placed within a pair of
commas to separate non-essential information.

A flower can be stripy, like a sock.

A comma is placed
before an interruption
at the end of a sentence.

A flower like a sock can be stripy.

Without the commas, the information becomes
part of the main sentence and changes its meaning.

A comma is placed after
an interruption at the
start of a sentence.

Like a sock, a flower can be stripy.

• Often, **quotations** are used without introductions, so no comma is needed. For example: **The guide says that this is "the best garden in France"**.

• Don't use a comma if the first part of the quotation ends with an **exclamation mark** or a **question mark**. For example: "Stop!" Tom cried. "The bridge is dangerous."

GLOSSARY

Adverb A word that describes the way something happens.

Clause A grammatical unit that contains a subject and a verb.

Conjunction A word used to connect phrases and sentences.

Direct speech Text that represents spoken words.

Interjection A word or phrase that occurs alone and expresses emotion.

Phrase A group of words that does not contain a verb.

Direct speech

In direct speech, a comma should be used between the introduction to the speech and the direct speech itself. The introduction can be at the start, end or middle of the sentence. When in the middle, use a comma on either side of the introduction, between the first and second parts of the sentence.

A comma is placed before the inverted commas, after the introduction.

Grandma asked, "Can we find more of these flowers?"

A comma is placed before the inverted commas, before an introduction.

A comma is placed before the inverted commas after the introduction.

"The flowers," Lisa said, "are always in bloom in May."

Direct address

Commas are always used when someone is spoken to directly, by name. The placement of the comma depends on where the name appears in a sentence. The commas work in the same way as around an interruption: commas to either side of the name when it appears in the middle of a sentence; a comma after the name when it starts a sentence; and a comma before the name when it comes at the end of a sentence.

• If an **interruption** is taken out of a sentence, the sentence should still make sense.

• Commas with **interjections** such as *stop* or *help* work in the same way as those for direct address.

Let's eat Grandma.

In this example, the comma is missing, so Grandma is about to be eaten.

Let's eat, Grandma.

A comma is placed before the name when it appears at the end of a sentence.

Other uses of commas

COMMAS CAN BE USED TO JOIN MULTIPLE MAIN CLAUSES, REPRESENT OMITTED WORDS AND SEPARATE ITEMS IN LISTS.

Sentences can be joined using a comma with a conjunction to create the right pace and variety in writing. A comma is also used to avoid repetition and to separate words or phrases in lists.

Joining comma

Commas are used with conjunctions to join two or more main clauses to make a sentence. The comma before the last main clause is followed by one of these conjunctions: *and*, *or*, *but*, *nor*, *for*, *yet* or *so*. If two clauses are short and closely linked, the comma can be omitted.

start of first main clause

A comma separates the first two main clauses in a set of three.

start of second main clause

Walkers turn left, joggers turn right, but cyclists go straight on.

start of third main clause

A comma is placed before the conjunction *but*.

start of first main clause

start of second main clause

Sit here and enjoy the view.

No comma is needed before the conjunction because it joins two short, closely related main clauses.

Comma butterfly

A comma is also a type of butterfly with a small, white marking on the underside of each of its wings that resembles the punctuation mark.

• Use a **semi-colon** to join two related sentences together without a conjunction.

• A **joining comma** can be used only with the **conjunctions** *and*, *or*, *but*, *for*, *nor*, *yet* or *so*.

• **Avoid** using **too many commas**. When a sentence contains a lot of pauses, it is difficult to read.

Gapping comma

When avoiding repetition that would make a sentence long and, most likely, boring, a gapping comma can be used to represent the omitted words.

A comma is placed after the introductory phrase.

In the first month of the year, the flower was orange; in the second, red; and in the third, yellow.

Each of these gapping commas represents the omitted word *month*.

Listing comma

Commas are used to separate words or phrases in a list. A good way to test if the comma is in the correct position is to replace it with one of the conjunctions *and* or *or*. If the sentence doesn't make sense with *and* or *or*, don't add a comma.

The **comma** is one of the **most misused** punctuation marks.

Each interest is separated by a comma from another interest in the list.

The last word in the list is joined by *and* instead of a comma.

My interests are walking, flowers, birds and gardening.

My interests are walking flowers, birds and gardening.

As there is no comma separating *walking* and *flowers*, the interest is *walking flowers*.

The conjunction does not require a comma because it is separating two items in a list rather than separating two main clauses.

Commas with adjectives

A list of adjectives in front of a noun can be treated in two different ways. If each adjective modifies the noun, add a comma to separate them. However, if an adjective describes a combination of words that follow it, no comma is needed. There are two ways to check if a comma should be used.

First, if *and* can be added between the adjectives, a comma should be placed between them. Second, swap the adjectives. If the meaning hasn't changed, it is correct to use a comma to separate the adjectives.

I saw a yellow, flying saucer.

By placing the comma here, each adjective describes the noun separately: the saucer is flying and yellow.

I saw a blue flying saucer.

With no comma, the adjective *blue* describes the *flying saucer*.

GLOSSARY

Adjective A word that describes a noun.

Conjunction A word used to connect phrases and clauses.

Main clause A group of words that contains a subject and a verb and makes complete sense on its own.

Noun A word that refers to a person, place or thing.

Verb A word that describes an action.

• The **Oxford** or **serial comma**, set after the second-last item of the list, is used for clarity when there are two instances of ***and*** in a sentence. For example, "The blue, pink, and black-and-white flowers have grown."

Semi-colons

SEMI-COLONS CONNECT SECTIONS OF TEXT THAT ARE
CLOSELY RELATED.

Semi-colons can be used to indicate a close relationship
between main clauses or to separate complex items in
a list. They also precede certain adverbs when they are
used as conjunctions.

• **Never use** a semi-colon to **connect a main clause to a subordinate clause**. A comma and a conjunction should be used. For example, "Sam had two red T-shirts, **which** were new."

• **Use** a semi-colon to **connect two main clauses** that are not joined by a conjunction.

Connecting

A semi-colon is used to join two main clauses and show that they are of equal importance and closely related. These clauses can stand alone as separate sentences, or they can be connected by a comma and a conjunction.

May was warm; it was pleasant.

This clause is closely related to the previous main clause because it provides information as to why May was pleasant.

May was warm; it was pleasant
cities were rainy: London; Paris

Identifying when to use a semi-colon

A lot of people have trouble deciding when to use a colon or a semi-colon. Both are used to connect two main clauses that are closely related, but the colon indicates specifically that the second sentence is a direct explanation or a result of the first.

The weather was dreadful.

It rained every day.

The weather was dreadful: it rained every day. ✓

The second clause explains why the weather was dreadful, so a colon is used to connect the two sentences.

It was freezing.

He was grateful for his coat.

The second clause does not explain why it was freezing, nor is it a direct result of it being freezing, so a semi-colon is used to connect the two sentences.

It was freezing; he was grateful for his coat. ✓

Many **writers**, such as James **Joyce**, George **Orwell** and Kurt **Vonnegut** have **refused** to use semi-colons, deeming them pointless.

GLOSSARY

Clause A grammatical unit that contains a subject and a verb. Sentences are made up of one or more clauses.

Main clause A clause that makes complete sense on its own.

Subordinate clause A clause that provides additional information but depends on the main clause for it to make sense.

REAL WORLD

Ben Jonson's *English Grammar*

English dramatist Ben Jonson (1572–1637) is widely credited as the first person to set down rules on how to use semi-colons in English. His book *English Grammar*, first published in 1640, systematically examined the full stop, comma, semi-colon and colon. Before this, there were no accepted standards on how to use these marks.

Before adverbs

A semi-colon precedes certain adverbs, such as *however*, *therefore*, *consequently* and *nevertheless*, when they are used as conjunctions to connect clauses.

However is used as a conjunction here, so it is preceded by a semi-colon.

June was hot; however, some cities were rainy.

une was hot; however, some exas; and Boston, England.

Lists

When a sentence includes a list in which some or all of the items already contain commas, semi-colons are used to separate the list items. This makes the sentence easier to follow.

Without the semi-colons, the reader might mistake *Texas* and *England* for cities.

Some cities were rainy: London; Paris, Texas; and Boston, England.

Commas separate cities from regions.

A region is needed to clarify which *Paris* the text is referring to.

A region is needed to clarify which *Boston* the text is referring to.

Colons

THE COLON SEPARATES PARTS OF A SENTENCE, WHILE ALSO
INDICATING A CLOSE RELATIONSHIP BETWEEN THEM.

A colon connects a main clause with another clause, a
phrase or a word. It can be used to provide an explanation
or for emphasis, or to introduce a list or quoted material.

SEE ALSO

❰ **70–71** Compound sentences

❰ **96–99** Commas

❰ **100–101** Semi-colons

Inverted commas   **108–109** ❱

Bullet points   **116–117** ❱

Explanations

A colon shows that what follows a main clause
is an explanation of it. The section following the
colon can be a main clause, or just a word.

This main clause provides
an explanation as to what
her secret is.

They know her secret: she is obsessed with socks.

Emphasis

A colon can be used to emphasise a point in a text, by
causing the reader to pause before reading that point.

The single word emphasises that
she's interested in only one thing.

She thinks about one thing: socks.

Lists

A colon is also used to introduce a list. The section preceding
the colon should be a complete statement, but the section
following the colon can be just a simple list of things.

Her socks have the following patterns: stripy, spotty and swirly.

This is the introduction
to the list.

The items in the list
follow the colon.

The colon is also used in mathematics
for **ratio** or **scale**. For example, **3:1** means
a ratio of **three to one**.

GLOSSARY

Clause A grammatical unit that
contains a subject and a verb.
Sentences are made up of one
or more clauses.

Main clause A clause that makes
complete sense on its own.

Subordinate clause A clause that
provides additional information but
depends on the main clause for it to
make sense.

REAL WORLD

Emoticons

In the digital world, punctuation marks, especially the colon, are used to create informal graphic representations of emotions known as "emoticons". The most frequently used marks are the colon, semi-colon and bracket, but almost any punctuation mark can be used.

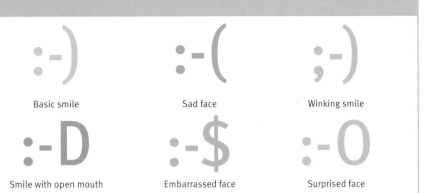

Basic smile

Sad face

Winking smile

Smile with open mouth

Embarrassed face

Surprised face

Quotes

A colon is often used to introduce quoted text, especially literary quotations, where the author's exact words are repeated.

Quoted text follows the colon.

She was quoted in the newspaper: "I love socks!"

Titles

A colon is sometimes found in the titles of works of literature, film, art and music. If the title is followed by a subtitle, a colon separates the two.

main title

The subtitle follows the colon.

Socks: The Sure-footed Life of a Collector

Bible references

When giving a Bible reference, the chapter and verse are separated by a colon.

book of the Bible

A colon separates the chapter and verse.

1 Corinthians 13:12 ← verse

chapter

- A colon never follows a **verb**.
- A **dash** can be used instead of a colon, but a **colon creates a greater pause** and a sense of anticipation for what follows it. Use a dash for emphasis and drama.
- A colon should be followed by **one space**.
- The **first word** following a colon should be **lower-case**, unless it already has a capital letter.

Apostrophes

APOSTROPHES SHOW POSSESSION OR OMISSION.

The apostrophe is used to create the possessive form of nouns and represents letters that have been omitted in contractions. It can also be used to create a few unusual plural nouns.

SEE ALSO
❮ 32–33 Determiners
❮ 48–49 Auxiliary verbs
❮ 80–81 Negatives
Other confusing words 170–171 ❯

Missing letters

An apostrophe represents missing letters in a contraction, which is when a word or words are shortened by omitting letters. There are about 100 common contractions. Only auxiliary verbs such as *be* and *have* can be used in this way.

Original form	Contracted form	Original form	Contracted form
it is	it's	he had; he would	he'd
she is	she's	I shall; I will	I'll
who is	who's	you will	you'll
I am	I'm	who will	who'll
you are	you're	is not	isn't
we are	we're	has not	hasn't
they are	they're	cannot	can't
I have	I've	could not	couldn't
we have	we've	will not	won't
would have	would've	did not	didn't

Rafael **wasn't** happy that the his name with two *f*'s o

Apostrophe catastrophe

The use of apostrophes in plurals in commercial signs is widespread. This type of mistake is sometimes called a "greengrocer's apostrophe".

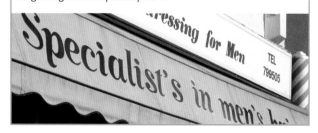

Plural forms

Occasionally, apostrophes are used to create plural forms where adding an *s* on its own would cause confusion, as when an abbreviation or a single letter is made plural. There are very few words that are pluralised in this way. Most plurals of regular nouns are formed by adding only an *s*.

with two *f*'s

Without the apostrophe, it would be unclear that the phrase is talking about the letter *f*.

• Place an apostrophe where letters have been **omitted**. This is not always where the words have joined.

• Another way to form the **possessive of a noun** is to swap the position of the owner and the item it owns and connect them with the word *of*. For example, instead of writing "the Netherlands**'s** tulips", write "the tulips **of** the Netherlands".

Apostrophes frequently appear in non-English **surnames**, such as **O'Neill**, **N'Dor** and **D'Agostino**.

Forming the possessive

An apostrophe marks a noun's possession (ownership) of something. There are two forms of possessive apostrophes. The first, an apostrophe followed by an *s* ('-s), shows possession of a singular noun. The second, an apostrophe after the *s* (-s'), shows possession of a plural noun ending in *s*.

When forming the possessive of a plural that ends in *s*, only an apostrophe is added.

grape**s'** seeds

The seeds belong to *grapes*, which is plural.

The new director belongs to the play, which is singular.

play**'s** new director

To form the possessive of a singular noun, add an apostrophe, followed by the letter *s*.

women**'s** story
people**'s** faces

If a plural word ends in any letter other than *s*, such as *e*, *i* or *n*, an apostrophe is added, followed by the letter *s*.

lay**'s** new director had spelt ocrate**s'** revised script.

Words ending in *s*

The possessive of a proper noun ending in *s* is written according to how it is pronounced. If the possessive form of a proper noun is not pronounced with an additional *s* at the end, only an apostrophe is added. If the possessive form is pronounced with an additional *s* on the end, it needs an apostrophe followed by an *s*.

Only an apostrophe is needed since an additional *s* is not pronounced after *Socrates*.

Socrate**s'** revised script

An apostrophe followed by an *s* is needed here since another *s* is pronounced.

Jes**s's** disbelief

Hyphens

HYPHENS ARE USED TO EITHER JOIN OR TO
SEPARATE WORDS OR PARTS OF WORDS.

Sometimes two terms need to be shown to be connected, so that they
are treated as one. Alternatively, a separation between terms may need
to be emphasised. A hyphen can be used for both of these purposes.

Clarity

A hyphen is essential when the
meaning of a phrase might be
confused. When a hyphen is used
between two or more words, it is
a compound modifier indicating
that the words work together to
modify another word.

big-hair society

This hyphen indicates that the
society is interested in big hair.

big hair society

Without the hyphen,
the hair society is big.

The celebrated big-hair society
for a get-together about their

• **Compound modifiers** that
contain adverbs **ending in -ly,**
such as "extraordinarily hairy
experience", are **never hyphenated.**

• Names of **centuries** used as
modifiers should be **hyphenated**
before the noun, such as
"twentieth-century issues".

• A hyphen is used to **break a long
word** in two **between two syllables**
at the **end of a line.**

Verbs into nouns

When a phrasal verb is made into a noun, it is hyphenated. Phrasal
verbs themselves are never hyphenated. For example, the phrasal verb
get together in "Let's get together and talk about it" isn't hyphenated,
but a hyphen is used when it becomes a noun: "for a get-together".

a break-in   **a get-together**

                 a hang-up   **an eye-opener**

a write-up   **a put-down**

Prefixes

Hyphens are sometimes needed in words with prefixes. Many need to be hyphenated to avoid confusion with words spelt in a similar way. A hyphen is also often added when a prefix ending in a vowel is joined to a root word beginning with a vowel, in order to avoid having two vowels side-by-side. The prefix self- is always followed by a hyphen. Finally, a hyphen is needed when adding a prefix to a capitalised word or to a date.

re-formed ← The hyphen indicates that the society formed again. Without a hyphen, the word *reformed* means "changed for the better".

co-owner ← This hyphen is needed to divide the two *o*'s because *coowner* is hard to read.

self-service ← The prefix self- always has a hyphen following it.

pre-Roman ← A hyphen follows a prefix before a capital letter.

post-1500 ← A hyphen follows a prefix before a date.

> **GLOSSARY**
>
> **Compound modifier** A term used to describe a noun that combines two or more words.
>
> **Phrasal verb** A verb composed of a verb followed by an adverb or a preposition that act together as a single unit.
>
> **Prefix** A group of letters attached to the start of a word that can change the original word's meaning.
>
> **Root word** A word to which prefixes and suffixes can be added.
>
> **Suffix** A group of letters attached to the end of a word that can change the original word's meaning.

Writing numbers

Hyphens are needed when writing out fractions, or numbers from twenty-one (21) to ninety-nine (99).

twenty-four   **three-quarters**

re-formed after twenty-four years
beard- and hair-loss issues.

Suspended hyphens

Occasionally a hyphen is found alone at the end of a word. This is called a suspended hyphen, and it occurs when two or more compound modifiers describing one noun and connected by *or*, *and* or *to* use the same word. To avoid repetition, the first instance of the word is omitted and replaced with a hyphen.

beard- and hair-loss issues

This suspended hyphen followed by *and* indicates that there were both beard-loss and hair-loss issues.

Compound modifiers

When two or more words are used together to modify another word, a hyphen is often needed to show that these modifying words are acting as a single unit. These compound modifiers are almost always hyphenated when they precede the noun, but not when they follow the noun, unless a hyphen is needed for clarity.

hair-loss issues ← noun

A compound modifier before the noun is hyphenated.

A compound modifier after the noun is not hyphenated.

issues of hair loss

Inverted commas " "

INVERTED COMMAS INDICATE DIRECT SPEECH
OR QUOTED MATERIAL.

Inverted commas, also known as quotation marks or speech
marks, are always used in pairs. Besides indicating speech
or a quotation, they can also signal unusual words.

Direct speech

Inverted commas surround direct speech (text that
represents spoken words). The material within inverted
commas can be split into two sections at either end of
the sentence, with text in the middle to explain who
is speaking. Direct speech can also be placed at the
beginning, in the middle or at the end of a sentence.

GLOSSARY

Direct speech Text that represents
spoken words.

Italics A style of type in which the
letters are printed at an angle to
resemble handwriting.

Quotation Text that reproduces
another author's exact words.

This direct speech
is at the beginning
of the sentence.

The punctuation that is part
of the direct speech is placed
within the inverted commas.

This text explains who
has just spoken.

DIRECT SPEECH

SPEAKER

"Do pandas eat meat?" **one visitor asked.**

This text explains who
is about to speak.

A comma is placed before
the direct speech.

This direct speech is at
the end of the sentence.

SPEAKER

DIRECT SPEECH

One visitor asked, **"Do pandas eat meat?"**

Do pandas
eat meat?

Unusual words

Inverted commas can be used to
separate particular words or phrases
within text. These can indicate that
another author's words are being
used, that the words are unusual or
that the author does not take the
expression seriously.

The zookeeper said that the
panda show was "thrilling",
but three pandas were asleep.

The writer has placed
inverted commas around
this word to suggest that
he or she did not find
the show as thrilling
as expected, based on
how it had been described.

Identifying where to place punctuation

In direct speech, a comma is used to separate the text that explains who is speaking from the spoken words. Only punctuation that is part of the direct speech should go within the inverted commas. If the end of the direct speech falls at the end of the sentence, only one punctuation mark is needed. When reproducing a quotation, the punctuation and capitalisation of the text should be written exactly as it appears in the original text.

The zookeeper continued "Pandas are very agile."

Inverted commas are placed around direct speech.

The zookeeper continued, "Pandas are very agile."

This introduces the speech.

A comma is placed before the direct speech.

The full stop is part of the speech. It is also at the end of the zookeeper's statement, so no additional punctuation is needed.

Can you believe the panda cub "can fit on your hand?"

Quoted material is placed within inverted commas.

Can you believe the panda cub **"can fit on your hand"?**

The question mark must go outside the inverted commas because it is not part of the quoted material.

Single inverted commas

Single inverted commas are used for quotations within quotations. Any double inverted commas within direct speech or a quotation are changed to single inverted commas to distinguish the words they surround from the rest of the speech or quotation.

- Inverted commas are used to **surround quotations** in the **same way** as they surround **direct speech**.
- **Single inverted commas** are sometimes used for **quotations** to save space. In these cases, double inverted commas are used for quotations within quotations.

The direct speech is marked by double inverted commas.

SPEAKER

DIRECT SPEECH

The zookeeper said,

"I wouldn't call pandas 'cuddly'."

The zookeeper is quoting someone else's description of pandas, so the quoted word is within single inverted commas.

REAL WORLD

Air quotes

Air quotes are inverted comma shapes created with a person's hands when speaking. They serve to highlight unusual words, as inverted commas can in writing, and carry a hint of sarcasm in the person's speech.

Titles of short works

Inverted commas are used for the titles of short works, such as essays, articles and song titles. The titles of longer works, such as books and films, are italicised.

The name of the article is in inverted commas.

The article "Panda Facts" was an eye-opener.

Question marks

A QUESTION MARK SIGNALS THE END OF A SENTENCE THAT ASKS A QUESTION.

Usually, a full stop is used to indicate the end of a sentence. However, if the sentence is a question rather than a statement, it should end with a question mark.

Direct questions

A sentence that asks a question and expects an answer in response is a direct question, and requires a question mark. In direct questions, the subject (a noun or pronoun) follows the verb. This is in contrast to the word order of a statement, in which the verb follows the subject. Many direct questions start with question words, such as *when*, *who*, *where*, *why* or *how*.

This question word signals the start of the question.

verb

subject

When did you last see your cat**?**

A question mark is placed at the end of the sentence.

Embedded questions

An embedded question is one that appears within a longer sentence, following an introductory phrase. The word order for an embedded question follows that of a statement, with the subject preceding the verb. This makes the question sound more polite. If the full sentence asks a question, it requires a question mark.

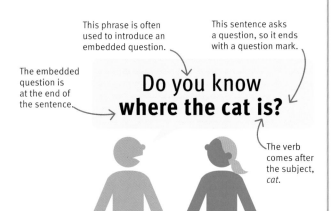

The embedded question is at the end of the sentence.

This phrase is often used to introduce an embedded question.

This sentence asks a question, so it ends with a question mark.

Do you know **where the cat is?**

The verb comes after the subject, *cat*.

Indirect questions

An indirect question always ends in a full stop. This type of question states what has been asked, rather than directly asking a question. It does not repeat the speaker's exact words, and usually does not require an answer. Indirect questions never end in a question mark.

He asked me if I knew **where the cat was.**

This is an indirect question because it does not require an answer, and it ends in a full stop.

- A question can be **just a word**, such as *Who?*, *What?*, *Where?*, *When?*, *Why?* or *How?*
- A question mark **should not** normally **be used with another punctuation mark**. One **exception** is when a **full stop** is used with an abbreviation at the end of a sentence. For example, "Shall we meet at 3.00 p.m.?"
- When a question mark appears within a title that is **italicised**, the question mark should also be italicised.

In **Spanish**, an **inverted question mark** (¿) is used to indicate the **beginning** of a question, in addition to the question mark at the end.

Tag questions

A tag question is one that can be added to the end of a statement. The speaker prompts the listener to respond in a certain way, and then adds the question to the end for confirmation. Tag questions follow a comma at the end of a statement.

Rhetorical questions

A rhetorical question is a question that is asked only to stress a point. It often contains a note of emotion or sometimes exaggeration. No response is expected, as the answer to the question is either obvious or cannot be known. Rhetorical questions are punctuated with a question mark.

This is a statement that makes sense on its own.

You don't think I'm responsible, **do you?**

This is the question, but it cannot appear on its own because it doesn't make sense without the rest of the sentence.

Do I look like a cat thief?

No response is expected, because the speaker does not think she looks like a cat thief.

Can we help you?

Occasionally, question marks are used to indicate tourist information points on signs. Signs like this exist in many places, but are particularly useful for tourists in countries where the spoken language is written in a different alphabet, such as in Japan.

GLOSSARY

Abbreviation A shortened form of a word, often with one or more full stops to represent missing letters.

Italics A style of type in which the letters are printed at an angle to resemble handwriting.

Phrase A group of words that does not contain a verb.

Question A sentence that asks for information.

Statement A sentence that conveys a fact or piece of information.

Subject The person or thing that is performing the action of the verb.

Exclamation marks

EXCLAMATION MARKS ARE USED AT THE END
OF EXCLAMATIONS.

An exclamation mark indicates the end of an exclamation,
which is a sentence that expresses a writer's strong
emotions. It can also be used for emphasis.

SEE ALSO

❮ 54–55 Voices and moods
❮ 62–63 Interjections
❮ 68–69 Sentences
❮ 110–111 Question marks
Brackets and dashes 114–115 ❯

Emotions

The exclamation mark is used at the
end of an exclamation to express a
strong emotion, such as surprise,
excitement or anger, or a raised voice.

This is so unexpected!

Surprise!

I love cheese!

Fear!

I'm allergic to cheese!

Excitement!

Stop nibbling on the cheese!

Anger!

• Use exclamation marks **sparingly**
in **formal writing**. They rarely
improve a piece of writing.

• If it is unclear whether or not
an exclamation mark is needed,
remember that it is **usually
preferable to end a statement
with a full stop.**

GLOSSARY

Exclamation A sentence expressing
a strong emotion, such as surprise,
or a raised voice.

Interjection A word or phrase that
occurs alone and expresses emotion.

Question A sentence that asks for
information.

REAL WORLD

Comics

Exclamation marks are a feature
of comic books. Some comics use
them in almost every sentence.
An exclamation mark can also
be part of an illustration, used
on its own next to a character's
head to indicate surprise, or with
interjections representing sounds,
such as *Pow!* or *Zap!*. In the 1950s,
the exclamation mark was called
a "bang". This may be because
the exclamation mark often
appeared on its own in a speech
bubble next to the barrel of a gun
to show that it had just been fired.

Exclamations

Almost any type of sentence can be made into an exclamation. The most common types of exclamations are emotional statements, commands and interjections.

Exclamation marks are **rarely** used in **names,** but the name of the Canadian town **Saint-Louis-du-Ha! Ha!** officially has two.

Statements

A statement, which normally ends in a full stop, can be made into an exclamation if it conveys an emotion. An emotional statement ends with an exclamation mark instead of a full stop.

Commands

Exclamation marks are often used in commands, especially when they are direct orders rather than polite requests.

Interjections

Interjections – words usually exclaimed in urgency or surprise – are some of the most common types of exclamations. Interjections are often single words rather than sentences.

There's a mouse in the kitchen!

Be quiet and don't move suddenly!

Help!

Emphasis

Exclamation marks are often placed next to interruptions within brackets or dashes to add emphasis to an interruption. Never use an exclamation mark alongside a question mark.

The interruption uses an exclamation mark to emphasise how grateful the speaker was.

Our hero (thankfully!) arrived just in time.

• **One exclamation mark** has a greater impact than several, so using **more than one** exclamation mark **should be avoided**.

🔍 Identifying exclamations

Sentences beginning with *what* and *how* can either ask or state something, so the only way to know which punctuation mark to use is to understand what the sentence is saying and how it is being said.

What a nightmare this is? ✘

What a nightmare this is! ✓

This sentence is stating something, not asking something. It is an exclamation, so it requires an exclamation mark rather than a question mark.

What is a nightmare! ✘

What is a nightmare? ✓

This sentence is asking something, not exclaiming something. It is a question, so requires a question mark rather than an exclamation mark.

Brackets and dashes

( ) —

BRACKETS AND DASHES INDICATE A STRONG
INTERRUPTION WITHIN A SENTENCE.

Brackets (also called parentheses) and dashes allow writers
to interrupt the normal run of a sentence and insert additional
information. Brackets are always used in pairs around the
extra text, while dashes can be used alone or in pairs.

SEE ALSO

❰ **88–89** Direct and indirect speech

❰ **96–99** Commas

❰ **106–107** Hyphens

Numbers, dates and time　　　**118–119** ❱

Abbreviations　　　**172–173** ❱

• **Brackets** can be used around
an *s* to show that there may
be **one or more** of something:
for example, "boy(s)".

Brackets for interruptions

Brackets surround extra information that
is added to a sentence. The extra text
disrupts the normal run of the sentence
but can easily be removed without
changing the meaning. Brackets can also
be used to enclose an entire sentence,
which is punctuated in the same way
as any other sentence.

(which was late)

This gives extra information, which could be removed
without affecting the overall meaning of the sentence.

The driver bought a new watch. (His old one had stopped working.)

This sentence gives more information, but
can be removed without spoiling the story.

The full stop is contained
within the brackets.

The goods train (which was lat[e] [with] lychees (exotic fruit)". Aft[er]

Square brackets

Square brackets clarify text within a quotation or
provide additional information. The information in
square brackets is not part of the original quotation.

"laden [with] lychees"

This is part of
a quotation.

Square brackets show that a
word has been changed from
or added to the original quote.

Brackets for clarification

Brackets are used around information providing
clarification, such as an alternative name or spelling,
a translation or a definition.

lychees (exotic fruit)

The information inside
these brackets defines
what lychees are.

- **Square brackets** are used within a quotation with the italicised Latin word *sic*, which is used to show that words within a **quotation** have been **reproduced exactly** as they were written. For example, "I heard that the farmer, Mr. Cwpat [*sic*], is alive."
- If using a keyboard that doesn't have a dash, a **hyphen** is an acceptable substitute. **Never use a dash** in place of a hyphen, though.

A dash is **longer than a hyphen**. On old-fashioned **typewriters**, **two hyphens** typed one after the other were used instead of a **dash**.

Dashes for interruptions

Dashes perform the same function as brackets, surrounding additional information in a sentence. Whereas brackets must always be used in pairs, only one dash is required if the interruption comes at the beginning or end of a sentence.

– by all accounts –

The sentence would still make sense without the part within the dashes, so this part could be removed.

It was a long wait – the longest I'd ever had.

There is a space on either side of the dash.

This part of the sentence gives additional information about how long the wait was.

vas – by all accounts – "laden
–6 hours, it finally arrived.

Dashes for ranges

A dash can be used to express ranges of numbers, as in the case of dates or page references. In these situations, only the first and last numbers are written. The numbers are joined with a dash, without any spaces. A dash also expresses ranges of months or days of the week, and it can be used to indicate the direction of travel.

5–6 hours

This means "5 to 6 hours". If the word *from* is written before the number, use *to*, not a dash.

Monday–Friday

This includes Tuesday, Wednesday and Thursday.

the Trys–Qysto route

This means that the route goes from Trys to Qysto.

Bullet points

BULLET POINTS DRAW THE READER'S ATTENTION TO
THE KEY POINTS IN A DOCUMENT.

Bullet points are used to create lists. Bulleted items appear
in technical documents, websites or presentations as a way of
condensing important information into brief phrases or sentences.

Key points

Bulleted items are used to emphasise
important points in a document by
separating them from the main
text and presenting them as a list.
This enables the reader to process
essential information straight away.
The bulleted text can be written as
complete sentences, phrases or
single words.

This running text
provides a lot of detail.

*We'll need to be fully prepared for the mission
briefing. We'll have to make sure the jetpack is
tuned up. We should also get the sewing kit out
to finish off the penguin costumes we started
last week. Finally, we'll need to dismantle the
kite and pack it up as kit.*

Only the most important
information from the
text is given here.

SLIDE 1

**Before the mission briefing, we'll
need to complete several tasks:**
- **tune up the jetpack**
- **finish the penguin costumes**
- **pack up the kite kit.**

Writing bulleted items

Bulleted information has a greater
impact if the items are of similar
lengths and written in the same way.
If the first item starts with a verb, for
example, the remaining items should
do the same. This creates a balanced
list that is easy to follow and gives
the items equal importance.

The bulleted items are
all of a similar length.

SLIDE 2

**On the mission, we'll have
to do the following activities:**
- **go undercover**
- **impersonate penguins**
- **follow people**
- **jump out of helicopters.**

All of the bulleted items
begin with verbs.

• **Use bullet points sparingly**: a few bulleted sections have a greater impact than many.

• **Numbered lists** are an alternative to bulleted lists. These are usually indented and punctuated in the same way as bulleted lists.

Although the most common style of **bullet point** is •, there are many other options, such as *, – or ◊.

Presentations

Speakers often use bulleted lists as visual aids when giving presentations. When addressing a large audience within a short time frame, it is important to get the message across clearly and effectively. Bulleted lists are ideal for this purpose.

Sales Interfaces
- Salesperson
- Support Engineer — Customer Facing people
- Bid Manager
- Proposal W...
- Technical Autho...
- Call centre agents
- Web designers
- Accounts
- Production
- Switchboard Operators

Punctuating bulleted text

Bulleted information should be indented from the main text. The text introducing the bullet points should be followed by a colon. Different rules apply depending on whether or not the bulleted items are full sentences.

The bulleted information is indented from the main text.

A colon is placed after the introductory sentence.

SLIDE 3

Remember to bring these items:
- a water pistol
- a unicycle
- a pogo stick
- roller skates.

These points are phrases, so they begin with lower-case letters.

The final point ends with a full stop.

Most of the points require no punctuation.

◁ **Lower-case bullets**
If the bulleted items are not full sentences, they can begin with a lower-case letter. The introductory text and the bulleted items together represent a complete sentence, so only the last item needs a full stop, as it marks the end of the sentence.

◁ **Complete sentences**
If the bulleted items are complete sentences, each one needs to begin with a capital letter and end with a full stop, question mark or exclamation mark.

SLIDE 4

The director asked these questions:
- Do I need winter clothes?
- Will there be pirates?
- Can I bring my pig?
- Will we receive any gadgets?

Each of these points is a complete sentence, beginning with a capital letter and ending with a question mark.

Numbers, dates and time

NUMBERS ARE REPRESENTED IN WRITING AS BOTH NUMERALS AND WORDS.

SEE ALSO

❮ **94–95** Full stops and ellipses
❮ **96–99** Commas
❮ **102–103** Colons
❮ **106–107** Hyphens
❮ **114–115** Brackets and dashes
Abbreviations **172–173** ❯

As well as in mathematical calculations, numerals are sometimes used in writing. They are especially useful for writing dates and time, and decimals and numbers over one hundred.

The **Arabic numbering system** is more accurate than the **Roman system** because it includes the **number zero**.

- When writing a **range of numerals**, as in page references, write the first and last page of the reference and **separate the numerals** with a dash: for example, 14–17 (which includes pages 15 and 16).

- When writing informally, **years can be abbreviated** using an apostrophe followed by the last two numerals, such as "the summer of '97".

Writing out numbers

Fractions and numbers up to one hundred should be written out as words, unless the text uses numbers frequently, as in scientific or mathematical works.

eight spaceships

The numeral 8 is written out.

GLOSSARY

Arabic numerals Everyday numerals such as 1, 2 and 3.
Roman numerals Numbers represented by certain letters of the alphabet, such as *i*, *v* and *x*.

Flying on-board eight spaceships
discovered 325 comets on 10 Apr

Arabic numerals

Everyday numerals are called Arabic numerals because Arabs introduced them to Europe from India. The ten characters are 0, 1, 2, 3, 4, 5, 6, 7, 8 and 9. These are combined to represent every possible number.

325 comets

Use Arabic numerals for numbers over one hundred.

Dates

Numerals are always used for the day and year of a date. When writing years of more than four digits, as in 10,000 BCE, a comma is used. If writing the month first, a comma is needed between the date and year, and after the year when the date appears in the middle of the sentence.

Date format	Example
day-month-year	The discovery on 10 April 2099 was exciting.
month-day-year	The discovery on April 10, 2099, was exciting.
year-month-day	The discovery on 2099 April 10 was exciting.

Identifying when to use words or numerals

If a sentence begins with a number – even a very high number – the number should be written out in words, or the sentence should be rewritten to avoid starting with a number.

325 comets were discovered. ✗

Sentences should never start with numerals.

Three hundred and twenty-five comets were discovered. ✓

This number has been written out because it is at the start of the sentence. This option is not ideal with longer numbers.

This sentence has been reworded and is the more succesful version.

The aliens discovered **325** comets. ✓

Roman numerals

Roman numerals use the letters *i* (one), *v* (five), *x* (10), *l* (50), *c* (100), *d* (500) and *m* (1,000) from the alphabet to represent numbers. Numbers over ten are a combination of these letters. Both upper- and lower-case Roman numerals are used to refer to acts and scenes in plays – for example, "Act IV, scene i". Upper-case Roman numerals are sometimes used in names of royalty, such as "King Henry VIII". Lower-case Roman numerals can be used for page references – for example, "xiv–xvii".

If a lower Roman numeral is placed before a larger one, subtract it from the larger number, so *ix* is 10 (x) minus 1 (i) = 9.

Roman	Number	Roman	Number
I, i	1	XX, xx	20
II, ii	2	L, l	50
III, iii	3	C, c	100
IV, iv	4	CD, cd	400
V, v	5	CDX, cdx	410
VI, vi	6	D, d	500
VII, vii	7	CM, cm	900
VIII, viii	8	M, m	1,000
IX, ix	9	MCMXC	1,990
X, x	10	MMXIII	2,013

he aliens from planet Squark IV
099, between 1.30 and 11 p.m.

Time

Numerals are usually used to write the time of day, with a full stop separating the hour from the minutes. A colon is sometimes used instead of a full stop to separate the hour and minutes. If expressing time in quarters or halves, or when using the phrase *o'clock*, the time should be written in words.

Between **1.30** and **11 p.m.**

time in numerals

time in words

This abbreviation stands for "post meridiem" and refers to the afternoon.

Between **half past one** and **eleven o'clock.**

• In numbers over a thousand, a **comma** is placed before every group of **three digits**, **except within addresses** – for example, **20,000** and **300,000**.

• When writing the time of day using the phrase *o'clock*, spell **out** the number – for example, "eleven o'clock".

Other punctuation

SLASHES, "AT" SIGNS, AMPERSANDS AND ASTERISKS ARE
A FEW OF THE LESS COMMONLY USED PUNCTUATION MARKS.

SEE ALSO

❮ **86–87** Colloquialisms and slang
❮ **118–119** Numbers, dates and time
Abbreviations   **172–173** ❯
Writing for the Web   **214–215** ❯

Slashes are used in web addresses, to show alternatives,
to represent a period of time and in units of measurement.
"At" signs (@), ampersands (&), asterisks (*) and hashes (#)
usually represent omitted words or letters.

The **"at" sign** was
originally used to
represent a **Spanish
unit of weight** called
an *arroba*.

Slashes in Internet addresses

Slashes are used to write Internet addresses. In this
situation, they are called "forward slashes" and link
the address of a minor page to that of a main site.

Style Skunks' main website ⎯⎯   ⎯⎯ linked "news" page

www.styleskunks.com/news

Slashes for alternatives

Slashes are used to show alternatives such as *and/or* and
he/she. These are found in technical documents, such as
forms, or where space is limited, as in newspaper articles.
It is usually better to write the alternatives out.

This means that she looked
for shoes or hats, or both.

She looked for shoes and/or hats.

"At" signs

The "at" sign is used to write e-mail addresses. It separates
the unique user name from the name of the host domain.

user name ⎯⎯

host domain ⎯⎯

questions@styleskunks.com

Ampersands

The ampersand represents the word *and*. It is found in the names
of businesses and organisations, and is used in academic references.

This could also be written
"Squirrels and Swirls".

She loved the fashion label Squirrels **&** Swirls.

Asterisks

Asterisks are used to show that there is extra information at the bottom of the page. The extra information is known as a footnote. They are also used in newspaper articles when a direct quotation includes a word that is too offensive to be written in full. An asterisk represents each letter that has been omitted from the work. This reduces the word's impact, but it remains recognisable to readers who are familiar with it.

"My Chihuahua looks amazeb***s in these clothes!"

These asterisks represent *all*, although *amazeballs* would not be considered a swear word.

- To mark the **omission of** one or more **words** from a passage, never use an asterisk; an **ellipsis (…)** should be used instead.

- If there is a need for **more than one footnote** on a page, use one **asterisk (*)** for the first footnote reference, and **two asterisks (**)** for the second, but do not use more than three in a sequence. In this case, numbering the footnotes would be a better option.

- When writing a **long Internet address** that breaks at the end of a line, break it after a slash – for example after ".com/".

Hashes

Found on every telephone keypad, the hash, also known as the number or pound sign, represents the word *number* in informal writing. It is usually preferable to write the word *number* instead.

It was the #1 fashion website in the world.

This means "number one".

Twitter

The social networking service Twitter has adopted some of the less commonly used punctuation marks and given them a new significance. The "at" sign, for example, is used before someone's user name to mention or reply to that user, while the hash is used to add "tags" to words, making them searchable by other users.

- **Slashes** are found in certain abbreviations. For example, *c/o* appears in addresses and means "care of", while *miles/hour* means "miles per hour".

- The **ampersand (&)** should never be used in place of the word *and* in formal writing, nor should the **"at"** sign be used in place of the word *at*.

Italics

ITALICS ARE LETTERS THAT ARE PRINTED AT AN ANGLE TO
RESEMBLE HANDWRITING.

Words or phrases are styled in italic letters to distinguish them
from the surrounding text. Italics may indicate a title, a foreign
word or phrase, or emphasis.

Foreign words

Foreign words or phrases that have
not been adopted into the English
language should be written in italics.
These are sometimes followed by a
translation, either within brackets or
inverted commas. Genus and species
names of living things are Latin words
and should always be italicised.
The genus starts with a capital letter,
while the species is written in
lower-case letters.

The foreign word
is italicised.

The translation is
placed in brackets.

oma (grandma)

The genus is
capitalised.

The species is written with
lower-case letters.

Bombus terrestris (bumblebee)

The scientific name
is italicised.

The common name
is placed in brackets.

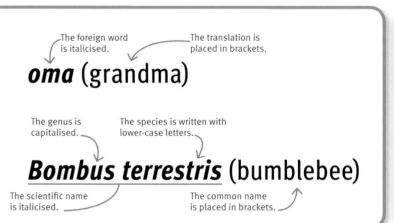

My ***oma*** (grandma) loves her

I think ***Big Beach Splash!***, a film

• If it is unclear whether a **foreign word** should be
italicised or not, look it up in a **dictionary**. If the word
is not in an English dictionary, it should be italicised.

• **Proper names** are **not italicised** even if they are
in a different language – for example, Londres
(French for London).

Punctuation

Do not italicise punctuation
following words in italics
unless it is part of the title
or phrase being italicised.

The exclamation
mark is in italics
because it is part
of the film title.

Big Beach Splash!,

The comma is not
italicised because it is
not part of the film title.

Titles

Italic type is used to write the titles of long works, such as books, journals, films or musical compositions. Shorter works, such as poems in anthologies, are written in inverted commas. The names of ships should also be italicised.

Big Beach Splash! — film title

Surfing is Simple — book title

Italicise	Do not italicise
• titles of printed matter such as books, newspapers, journals, magazines, very long poems, plays, famous speeches and collections of short stories and poems	• the name of a holy book such as the Bible or the Koran • chapters within a book, articles in a newspaper or magazine, titles of individual short stories and poems – put these in inverted commas
• titles of films, and radio and television programmes	• individual episodes of a radio or television programme – put these in inverted commas
• names of specific ships, submarines, aircraft, spacecraft and artificial satellites	• the abbreviations before a ship's name: RMS *Titanic*, USS *Arizona* • a brand of vehicle: Rolls-Royce, Boeing 747 • names of trains
• long musical compositions such as albums and operas	• titles of songs and short compositions – put these in inverted commas
• works of art such as paintings and sculptures	• buildings and monuments: the Empire State Building, the Statue of Liberty

urfing is Simple book, but bout surfing, is *much* better.

Emphasis

Italics can be used when a writer wishes to emphasise certain words or draw attention to a contrast between two terms. They may also indicate that the word or phrase should be given greater emphasis when spoken.

The film is *much* better.

This word has been italicised to emphasise how much better the speaker thinks the film about surfing is, compared to the book.

This style is called **italic** because it was first used in **Italy** in **1501**.

• When **writing by hand** or typing with a device that does not have italics, underline the word or phrase instead.

Spelling

Why learn to spell?

SPELLING IS IMPORTANT FOR BOTH READING AND WRITING.

Rules can help with spelling; however, there are many exceptions to these rules, which can sometimes make spelling difficult. Learning to spell well is worth the effort, since it helps a writer to convey meaning clearly.

Letters

There are twenty-six letters in the English alphabet, which can be written as lower-case or capital letters. These letters also make specific sounds, with some making more than one sound. In special cases, two letters – such as *c* and *h* – combine to produce one unique sound different to any individual letter sound, such as *ch* in *change*. Understanding when to use lower-case and capital letters helps to improve spelling, and better spelling increases the overall quality of writing.

The word *alphabet* comes from the **first two letters** of the **Greek** alphabet: *alpha* and *beta*.

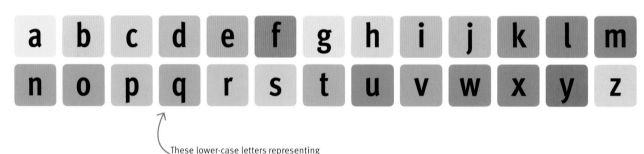

These lower-case letters representing the whole alphabet are arranged in alphabetical order.

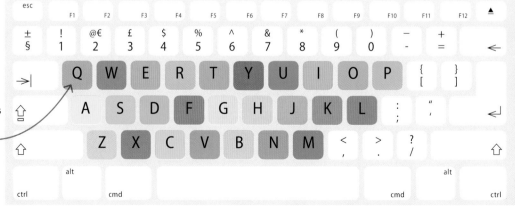

The QWERTY keyboard – named after the first six letters and arranged in capital letters – was put in this order so that the most common letters were not close together, thereby avoiding mistakes that caused jams in early typewriters.

Meanings

Many English words come from Latin or Greek, and learning to recognise these roots and understand what they mean can help with spelling. For example, *mar* is the Latin word for "sea", and it is used in the English words *marine* and *maritime*. A common Greek example is *dec*, which means "ten", and this is used in the English words *decade* and *decathlon*. Some root words, such as *build*, which comes from the Old English word *byldan*, are instantly recognisable and form the basis for other related words, including *building*, *builder* and *rebuild*.

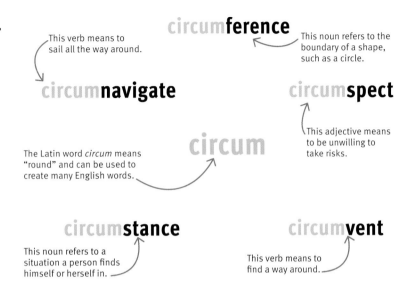

circum**ference**

This verb means to sail all the way around.

This noun refers to the boundary of a shape, such as a circle.

circum**navigate**

circum**spect**

circum

The Latin word *circum* means "round" and can be used to create many English words.

This adjective means to be unwilling to take risks.

circum**stance**

circum**vent**

This noun refers to a situation a person finds himself or herself in.

This verb means to find a way around.

Word beginnings and endings

Some words can have an extra part added to them, which results in a new word. This addition is called a prefix (word beginning) or a suffix (word ending) and can change the meaning of the word. For example, *social* acquires the opposite meaning when the prefix anti- is added, resulting in *antisocial*. However, when the suffix -ite is added to the same root word, the result is *socialite*, which refers to a person who enjoys social activities.

This prefix gives the root word the new meaning "to develop again".

root word

redevelopment

Adding a suffix to *redevelop* changes the verb into a noun that describes something that is being developed again.

Choose the right words

In some cases, spelling errors can produce a different meaning from the one expected. This is especially true when words that are spelt differently but pronounced the same (homophones) create unintentional, but sometimes amusing, results.

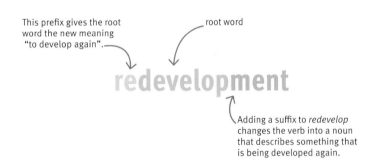

Replace with *mousse* for a type of dessert.

Replace with *yew* for a species of tree.

Replace with *current* for a body of moving water.

Mo ate a lemon **moose** under the **ewe** tree, then went for a swim. The **currant** caught him, and he let out a **whale**. Suddenly it was a scary **plaice**. If he didn't **dye**, he'd have an epic **tail**.

Replace with *wail* for a high-pitched cry.

Replace with *place* for a specific point or location.

Replace with *die* to describe the end of living.

Replace with *tale* for a type of story.

Alphabetical order

ALPHABETICAL ORDER IS A SIMPLE WAY OF ORGANISING
GROUPS OF WORDS.

From a short list of students in a classroom to a long index in a
book, alphabetical order makes information easy to store and find.

SEE ALSO

126–127	Why learn to spell?	
Capital letters		158–159 〉
Abbreviations		172–173 〉
Planning and research		186–187 〉

Sorting a list

Alphabetical order is the arranging of words based on where
their initial letters are in the alphabet. Using this system, words
are sorted by their first letters, then by their second letters, and
so on. For example, the words *buy* and *biscuit* both begin with
the letter *b*, but the second letter in each word is different: the
letter *i* in *biscuit* comes before the letter *u* in *buy*, so *biscuit*
would come before *buy* in an alphabetical list.

• If a long word has the same
letters as a short word, but then
goes further – such as *cave*
and *caveman* – the **short word
(e.g. *cave*) will always come first**
in a dictionary.

• The alphabet is **useful for locating
a seat** in a theatre or a book in a
library, as rows are usually labelled
in alphabetical order.

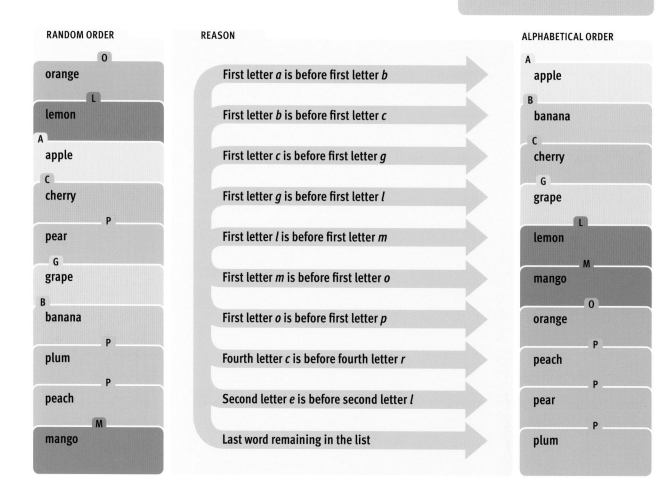

RANDOM ORDER	REASON	ALPHABETICAL ORDER
O orange	First letter *a* is before first letter *b*	A apple
L lemon	First letter *b* is before first letter *c*	B banana
A apple	First letter *c* is before first letter *g*	C cherry
C cherry	First letter *g* is before first letter *l*	G grape
P pear	First letter *l* is before first letter *m*	L lemon
G grape	First letter *m* is before first letter *o*	M mango
B banana	First letter *o* is before first letter *p*	O orange
P plum	Fourth letter *c* is before fourth letter *r*	P peach
P peach	Second letter *e* is before second letter *l*	P pear
M mango	Last word remaining in the list	P plum

Special cases

Organising words according to their initial letters does not always work. For example, abbreviations, capital letters and numerals need to be treated in special ways. In all cases, however, it is important to be consistent.

The English **alphabet** is based on the **Latin** alphabet of the **Romans**.

**king cobra
kingfisher
king penguin**

Treat capitalised words in exactly the same way as lower-case words.

**Hague, The
Hamburg
High Wycombe**

**Sacramento
St. (Saint) Helier
Salzburg**

Arrange any abbreviated terms as if they were spelt out.

Names of people are arranged by surnames, so the first name comes after the comma.

**∏ (Pi)
101 Dalmations
Toy Story**

If terms consist of more than one word, treat them as if they were written without the space. In this example, the list is arranged by looking at the fifth letter.

**blueberry
Coconut Island
date**

If a word has an article, such as *the*, ignore it and sort by the second word.

**Dahl, Roald
Meyer, Stephenie
Twain, Mark**

Collect terms with symbols or numerals at the beginning.

The dictionary

A dictionary is a collection of words and their definitions in alphabetical order. The words are arranged this way to make it easier for somebody to find a word and check its spelling or definition.

handwriting
writing done by hand, not typed or printed

The first three letters begin with the letters *han*, but the fourth letter *d* in *handwriting* comes before the letter *g* in *hang*.

hang
to support something from above

This word appears after the four-letter word *hang* because it has a fifth letter, *a*.

hangar
a very large building where aircraft are stored

Ignore the hyphen (-) and arrange the word by the fifth letter, *g*.

hang-glider
a huge kite that a person can hang from

The third letter *p* comes after the third letter *n* in *hang-glider*.

happen
to take place

The fifth letter *y* comes after the fifth letter *e* in *happen*, so this is the last word.

happy
pleased and content

Indexes

An index is a list of important topics in a reference book that is arranged in alphabetical order. Next to each key topic, a page number (or several page numbers) refers to the location of that key topic in the book. This makes it quicker and easier for the reader to find specific information.

Vowel sounds

THE ENGLISH ALPHABET CONTAINS FIVE VOWELS: *A*, *E*, *I*, *O* AND *U*.

Each vowel has a short or long phoneme, or sound. Each sound made by a vowel can be written down as a grapheme – one or more letters that represent a sound.

Short vowel sounds

A vowel can sound short, or abrupt. For example, the word *rat* has a short "a" sound and the grapheme that represents this sound is *a*. A more complex word, such as *tread*, has a short "e" sound and the grapheme is *ea*. The letter *y* sometimes takes the place of a vowel. For example, the word *gym* has a short "i" sound but the grapheme is *y*.

The **Taa language**, spoken mainly in Botswana, has **112 different sounds**.

▷ **Short "a"**
This sound is represented only by the grapheme *a*.

cat

▷ **Short "e"**
This sound is represented by the graphemes *a*, *ai*, *e*, *ea*, *eo* and *ie*.

many   said   **reptile**
head   **leopard**   friend

▷ **Short "i"**
This sound is represented by the graphemes *e*, *i*, *o*, *u* and *y*.

pretty   **insect**   **women**
busy   **rhythm**

▷ **Short "o"**
This sound is represented by the graphemes *a* and *o*.

salt   **octopus**

▷ **Short "u"**
This sound is represented by the graphemes *o*, *ou* and *u*.

dove   young   **buffalo**

Long vowel sounds

A vowel can sound long, or stretched. For example, the word *alien* has a long "a" sound at the beginning of the word and the grapheme that represents this sound is *a*. A more complex word, such as *monkey*, has a long "e" sound in its second syllable and the grapheme is *ey*.

• The letter **y is a consonant when it is the first letter of a syllable that has more than one letter,** such as *yellow*. If *y* is anywhere else in the syllable, it acts like a vowel: in the word *trendy*, it sounds like an "e".

a
▷ **Long "a"**
This sound is represented by the graphemes *a, ai, aigh, ay, a–e, ei, eigh* and *ey*.

apron snail straight ray
snake reindeer sleigh they

e
▷ **Long "e"**
This sound is represented by the graphemes *e, ea, ee, ei, ey, e–e, ie* and *y*.

he beaver cheetah ceiling
donkey these thief smelly

i
▷ **Long "i"**
This sound is represented by the graphemes *i, eigh, I, ie, igh, i–e, y, ye* and *y–e*.

bison height I pie night
pike fly eye type

o
▷ **Long "o"**
This sound is represented by the graphemes *o, oa, oe, ol, ou, ough, ow* and *o–e*.

cobra goat toe folk
soul dough crow antelope

u
▷ **Long "u"**
This sound is represented by the graphemes *u, ew, ue* and *u–e*.

unicorn chew
barbecue use

Complex vowel sounds

In addition to short and long vowel sounds, there are other complex vowel sounds in English. For example, the grapheme *oo* makes two different sounds depending on the word: a short vowel sound, as in the word *hook*, or a long vowel sound, as in the word *loot*.

Complex vowel sound	Examples
aw	awful, author
oi	toil, annoy
ow	house, cow
oo (short)	look, put
oo (long)	moot, suit

Consonant sounds

THERE ARE 21 CONSONANTS IN THE ENGLISH LANGUAGE:
THE WHOLE ALPHABET MINUS THE FIVE VOWELS.

Most consonants have one phoneme, or sound, but some
have multiple sounds. Like vowels, consonants are written
down as graphemes – letters that represent sounds.

Single consonant sounds

Single consonant sounds are sounds
that are represented by consonants.
For example, the single consonant
sound "f" is heard in the word *fan*,
and this is represented by the
grapheme *f*. However, the single
consonant sound "f" can also be
heard in the word *phase*; here, it
is represented by the grapheme *ph*.
The letters *c*, *q* and *x* do not have
single consonant sounds, but are
often paired with other letters to
form digraphs or blends.

▽ **The "b" sound**
This consonant is represented
by the graphemes *b* and *bb*.

bat   rabbit

▽ **The "d" sound**
This consonant is represented
by the graphemes *d*, *dd* and *ed*.

dog   puddle   rained

▽ **The "f" sound**
This consonant is represented
by the graphemes *f*, *ff*, *gh*
and *ph*.

flamingo   puff
laugh   dolphin

▽ **The "g" sound**
This consonant is represented by
the graphemes *g*, *gh*, *gg* and *gu*.

girl   ghost
haggle   guinea

▽ **The "h" sound**
This consonant is represented
by the graphemes *h* and *wh*.

hen   who

▽ **The "j" sound**
This consonant is represented
by the graphemes *ge*, *gg*, *gi*,
gy, *j* and *dge*.

gerbil   suggest   giraffe
gymnast jaguar   badger

▽ **The "k" sound**
This consonant is represented by
the graphemes *c*, *cc*, *ch*, *ck*, *k*
and *que*.

cat raccoon chameleon
duck kitten mosque

▽ **The "l" sound**
This consonant is represented
by the graphemes *l* and *ll*.

lion   bull

▽ **The "m" sound**
This consonant is represented
by the graphemes *m*, *mb*, *mm*
and *mn*.

mouse   lamb
hummingbird   column

▽ **The "n" sound**
This consonant is represented by
the graphemes *gn*, *kn*, *n* and *nn*.

gnome   knot   newt   sunny

▽ **The "p" sound**
This consonant is represented
by the graphemes *p* and *pp*.

pig   puppy

▽ **The "r" sound**
This consonant is represented by
the graphemes *r*, *rh*, *rr* and *wr*.

rat   rhinoceros
parrot   wren

▽ **The "s" sound**
This consonant is represented by
the graphemes *c*, *s*, *sc*, *ss* and *st*.

cell   salamander
science   hiss   whistle

▽ **The "t" sound**
This consonant is represented by the graphemes *bt*, *t*, *th*, *tt* and *ed*.

doubt tiger **thyme** cattle **jumped**

 ▷ **The "v" sound**
This consonant is represented by the graphemes *f* and *v*.

of
dove

 ▷ **The "w" sound**
This consonant is represented by the graphemes *w*, *wh* and *u*.

walrus
whale
penguin

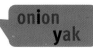 ▷ **The "y" sound**
This consonant is represented by the graphemes *i* and *y*.

onion
yak

 ▽ **The "z" sound**
This consonant is represented by the graphemes *s*, *ss*, *x*, *z* and *zz*.

please scissors **xylophone** zebra **buzz**

Digraphs

A digraph is a single sound that is made by combining two letters. For example, the word *shining* begins with the digraph "sh" and is represented by the grapheme *sh*. This digraph can appear in other words, such as *action*, but in this case it is written as *ti*.

Digraph	Grapheme	Examples
ch	ch, t, tch	**ch**icken, na**t**ure, ha**tch**
ng	n (before k), ng	monkey, hatchling
sh	ce, ch, ci, sh, ss, ti	ocean, chef, special, sheep, mission, motion
th (voiceless)	th	sloth
th (voiced)	th	feather
zh	ge, s	beige, vision

NATO phonetic alphabet

The NATO phonetic alphabet is used to avoid confusion when spelling words verbally. Each word is spoken in place of the name of the letter. Radio broadcasters in the military and aviation industries use this alphabet.

A	Alpha	N	November
B	Bravo	O	Oscar
C	Charlie	P	Papa
D	Delta	Q	Quebec
E	Echo	R	Romeo
F	Foxtrot	S	Sierra
G	Golf	T	Tango
H	Hotel	U	Uniform
I	India	V	Victor
J	Juliet	W	Whiskey
K	Kilo	X	X-ray
L	Lima	Y	Yankee
M	Mike	Z	Zulu

Blends

Consonant blends are two or more consonants that join together. They can appear at the beginning or end of a word. Like digraphs, they are never separated, but the individual sound that is represented by each letter is heard. For example, the word *bright* begins with the blend *br*, and the individual letters – *b* and *r* – are clearly heard.

Blend	Examples		Blend	Examples
bl	**bl**ock		**pl**	**pl**um
br	**br**ead		**pr**	**pr**etzel
cl	**cl**am		**pt**	ada**pt**
cr	**cr**acker		**sc**	**sc**allop
ct	perfe**ct**		**sch**	**sch**ool
dr	**dr**ink		**scr**	**scr**ape
fl	**fl**oor		**sk**	**sk**eleton
fr	**fr**uit		**sk**	whi**sk**
ft	si**ft**		**sl**	**sl**ither
gl	**gl**aze		**sm**	**sm**oke
gr	**gr**apefruit		**sn**	**sn**ack
lb	bu**lb**		**sp**	**sp**aghetti
ld	mi**ld**		**sp**	cri**sp**
lf	se**lf**		**sph**	**sph**ere
lk	mi**lk**		**spl**	**spl**atter
lm	e**lm**		**spr**	**spr**inkle
ln	ki**ln**		**squ**	**squ**id
lp	pu**lp**		**st**	**st**eak
lt	ma**lt**		**st**	toa**st**
mp	cho**mp**		**str**	**str**awberry
nd	gri**nd**		**sw**	**sw**eet
nk	dri**nk**		**tr**	**tr**out
nt	mi**nt**		**tw**	**tw**in

Syllables

BREAKING UP WORDS INTO SYLLABLES CAN HELP
WITH PRONUNCIATION AND SPELLING.

SEE ALSO

❮ **120–121** Other punctuation
❮ **130–131** Vowel sounds
❮ **132–133** Consonant sounds
Roots   **140–141** ❯
Prefixes and suffixes   **142–143** ❯

Every English word consists of one or more syllables.
Separating words into syllables helps split complex
words into simple, easy-to-remember parts.

Sounding out syllables

One way to determine the correct pronunciation of a word
is to break it up into syllables and say each part aloud.
For example, the word *melody* can be broken up into three
syllables: *me*, *lo* and *dy*. Single syllable words, such as *cook*
and *shop*, are never divided. There are certain rules about
how to break up a word.

▷ **Long vowel
sounds and consonants**
If the first part of the
word makes a long vowel
sound and a consonant
comes between two
vowels, the word is
usually divided before
the consonant.

Sa makes a
long vowel sound.
sa-ving
The consonant *v*
is between two
vowels, *a* and *i*.

▷ **Single-letter
syllables and
special sounds**
Never separate two
or more letters that
together make a single
sound. A long vowel
sounded alone forms
a syllable by itself.

Ph sounds
like an *f*.
O makes a long
vowel sound.
phys-i-o-ther-a-py
Th makes a
unique sound.

▷ **Short vowel
sounds and consonants**
If the first part of the word
makes a short vowel sound
and a consonant comes
between two vowels, the
word is usually divided
after the consonant.

Mod makes a
short vowel sound.
mod-est
The consonant *d*
is between two
vowels, *o* and *e*.

▷ **Prefixes and suffixes**
A prefix is divided from the
root word. If the word ends
in the suffix -le and this is
preceded by a consonant,
the word is divided before
the consonant.

The prefix re-
is separated
from *handle*.
re-han-dle
The suffix -le is
preceded by the
consonant *d*.

▷ **Identical
consonants and
different vowel sounds**
Two identical consonants
next to each other are
separated. The word is also
divided where two different
vowel sounds meet. Most
suffixes are separated from
the root word.

Identical consonants
(*m*) are separated.
Here, *di* and *ate*
make different
vowel sounds.
im-me-di-ate-ly
The suffix -ly
is separated
from *immediate*.

Haiku poetry

Haiku is a traditional Japanese form
of poetry that usually consists of 17
syllables. Although Japanese haiku
is printed in a vertical line (pictured),
in English it is often written over three
lines, with five syllables in the first
and third lines, and seven syllables
in the middle line.

A Haiku by Bashō
written in Kanazawa in 1689.

GLOSSARY

Consonant A letter of the alphabet
that is not a vowel.

Prefix A group of letters attached to
the start of a word that can change
the original word's meaning.

Suffix A group of letters attached to
the end of a word that can change the
original word's meaning.

Vowel One of the five letters *a*, *e*, *i*, *o*
and *u*.

Word stress

When a word has more than one syllable, one of the syllables is always louder than the others in spoken English – this is the syllable that is stressed.

Rule 1
In many English words, the stress is on the first syllable.

dam-age

Rule 2
A word with a prefix or suffix usually has the stress on the root word.

in-ter-**rup**-tion

Rule 3
In words beginning with de-, re-, in-, po-, pro- or a- the first syllable is usually not stressed.

pro-**gres**-sive

Rule 4
Two vowels together in the last syllable often indicate a stressed last syllable.

sus-**tain**

Rule 5
A word with a double consonant in the middle puts stress on the syllable before the consonant.

mid-dle

Rule 6
The stress is usually on the syllable preceding the suffixes -tion, -ity, -ic, -ical, -ian, -ial and -ious.

im-i-**ta**-tion

Rule 7
The stress is usually on the second syllable before the suffix -ate.

o-**rig**-i-nate

Rule 8
If none of 1–7 apply, in words with three or more syllables, one of the first two syllables is usually stressed.

sym-pho-ny

Iambic pentameter

Syllables are often used in literature to give sentences a lilting rhythm and to emphasise certain parts of a word. A poetic form called iambic pentameter consists of ten syllables in each line. The ten syllables are divided into five pairs of alternating unstressed and stressed syllables. The rhythm in each line resembles the "da-DUM" sound of a heartbeat.

The only English letter whose name has more than one syllable is **w**, which is pronounced **"duh-bull-you"**.

▷ **Shakespearean syllables**
Many people have used this technique, including the English playwright William Shakespeare (1564–1616). This famous line is taken from his tragedy, *Macbeth*.

Is **this** - a **dag** - ger **I** - see **be** - fore **me**

The first syllable in a pair is unstressed and represents the quieter "da" in the heartbeat rhythm.

The second syllable in the pair is stressed and represents the louder "DUM" in the heartbeat rhythm.

Morphemes

A MORPHEME IS THE SMALLEST MEANINGFUL PART OF A WORD.

All words are made up of at least one morpheme. An understanding of morphemes can help with spelling, since a morpheme in one word can apply to other similar words.

SEE ALSO	
❰ **20–21** Parts of speech	
❰ **22–23** Nouns	
❰ **24–25** Plurals	
❰ **26–27** Adjectives	
❰ **38–39** Verbs	
❰ **40–41** Adverbs	
❰ **104–105** Apostrophes	
Roots	**140–141** ❱
Prefixes and suffixes	**142–143** ❱

Free and bound morphemes

There are two types of morphemes: free and bound. Free morphemes are separate words, and can form the root of a longer word. Bound morphemes are parts of words – usually prefixes or suffixes – that attach to a free morpheme. For example, the word *cats* has two morphemes: the noun *cat* is the free morpheme and the suffix -s is the bound morpheme.

fortunate

This free morpheme is an adjective that refers to good luck or success.

fortunate**ly**

This suffix is a bound morpheme and changes the free morpheme into an adverb.

unfortunate**ly**

This prefix is another bound morpheme and gives the adverb the opposite meaning.

Adding information

A bound morpheme can add information to a free morpheme without changing the basic meaning of the word. For example, adding the bound morpheme -est to the end of the free morpheme *fast* results in the word *fastest*. The meaning has become more specific.

Rule 1
Adding the bound morpheme -s to the end of a free morpheme results in a plural word.

cup / cup**s**

The cups are very large.

Rule 2
To show possession, add the bound morpheme -s and an apostrophe to the end of a free morpheme.

swimmer / swimmer**'s**

The swimmer's goggles were too small.

Rule 3
The comparative form occurs when the bound morpheme -ier is added to the end of a free morpheme.

hungry / hung**rier**

He was hungrier than his friends.

Rule 4
The superlative form occurs when the bound morpheme -est is added to the end of a free morpheme.

long / long**est**

It was the longest day ever.

GLOSSARY

Adjective A word that describes a noun.

Adverb A word that modifies the meaning of a verb, adjective or other adverb.

Noun A word that refers to a person, place or thing.

Prefix A group of letters attached to the start of a word that can change the original word's meaning.

Suffix A group of letters attached to the end of a word that can change the original word's meaning.

Verb A word that describes an action.

Acting in a different way

Some words add more than just detail. For example, the free morpheme and adjective *kind* can combine with the bound morpheme ending -ness, which forms the noun *kindness*. The meaning of a word can also change. For example, the word *helpful* can acquire the opposite meaning when the bound morpheme un- is added, which results in the word *unhelpful*.

• Understanding morphemes can help with unfamiliar words. Take **demagnetise**: the morpheme is the noun **magnet**, but the **suffix -ise** changes it to a verb. However, the newly created word **magnetise** acquires the opposite meaning when the **prefix de-** is added, and refers to the act of making something **less magnetic**.

Rule 1

The bound morpheme ending -ness changes an adjective into a noun.

bright / bright**ness**

It is very bright in this room.

This room's bright**ness** is overwhelming.

Rule 2

The bound morpheme ending -ion changes a verb into a noun.

act / act**ion**

She wanted to act in the play.

The play contained many act**ion** scenes.

Rule 3

The bound morpheme -ful attaches to the end of a noun and changes it into an adjective.

spite / spite**ful**

The annoyed boy ignored his sister out of spite.

The spite**ful** boy became very annoyed.

Rule 4

The bound morpheme un- attaches to the start of a word to give it the opposite meaning.

helpful / **un**helpful

The helpful boy carried the bags.

The **un**helpful boy did not carry the bags.

In the field of linguistics, **morphology** is the identification, analysis and description of words that **form a language,** including root words and parts of speech.

Understanding English irregularities

THE ENGLISH LANGUAGE HAS BEEN SHAPED BY MANY LANGUAGES.

English has its foundations in Latin and Greek and continues to evolve as foreign words are adopted. With so many influences, it is understandable that English has so many spelling irregularities.

SEE ALSO

❬ **86–87** Colloquialisms and slang

Roots	**140–141** ❭
Hard and soft letter sounds	**144–145** ❭
Irregular word spellings	**164–165** ❭

Latin influences

Latin is more than 2,000 years old and originated in the Roman Empire. English has adopted Latin at different times in history. In the years of the Roman Empire (27 BCE–476 CE), contact with Rome introduced new vocabulary. During the Middle Ages (fifth–fifteenth centuries CE), Latin was the language of the Church, which exerted an enormous influence on language – in fact, the first printed books were religious texts. In subsequent centuries, people invented words for new things by combining existing Latin words.

cominitiāre — This Latin word means "to begin" and is the origin of the English word *commence*.

superbus — This Latin word means "superior" and is the origin of the English word *superb*.

verbatim — This Latin word means "word for word" and is still used today.

Greek influences

Ancient Greek literature and myths have greatly influenced the English language. Most Greek terms in English were created by combining Greek roots to describe things named in modern times, such as *dinosaur*. For this reason, Greek words are usually technical words used in medicine and science.

skeleton

This Greek word means "dried up" and is the same as the English word *skeleton*.

pharmakon

This Greek word refers to a place that dispenses medicine and is the origin of the English word *pharmacy*.

deinos and **saurus**

In Greek, the word *deinos* means "terrible" and *saurus* means "lizard". When combined, they form the origin of the English word *dinosaur*.

The Domesday Book

The Domesday Book was written in Latin and compiled in 1085–1086 CE. It is Britain's earliest public record, and was drawn up on the orders of King William I to describe the resources of late eleventh-century England. Latin was the language used for government documents and by the Church, and continued to be used for important documents up to Victorian times.

Old English influences

A more familiar-sounding form of English began when the Anglo-Saxons came from continental Europe to England in about the fifth century CE. English from this time is now referred to as Old English and it was related to German. Modern English words that derive from Old English usually have one or two syllables, and refer to everyday things, such as food, animals, parts of the body and family relationships. Old English words are usually spelt differently from the modern equivalent, but they are often pronounced in a similar way.

aepl — This is Old English for "apple".

lang — This is Old English for "long".

helm — This is Old English for "helmet".

French influences

One of the languages that has influenced English the most is French – a Latin-based language. This is because for about 300 years after the Norman Conquest in 1066, the most powerful people in England spoke a form of French called Norman. For this reason, many English words relating to government, law, money and warfare come from the French language.

parler — This French word means "to speak" and is the origin of the English word *parliament*.

recrue — This French word refers to untrained soldiers and is the origin of the English word *recruit*.

saudier — This French word refers to a person who is paid for military service and is the origin of the English word *soldier*.

Other influences

There are many other languages that have influenced English over time. For example, the English words *bangle* and *shampoo* derive from Hindi words, and *alligator* and *canoe* derive from Spanish words.

Language of origin	Examples
French	ballet, cuisine
German	hamburger, kindergarten
Italian	fresco, graffiti
Spanish	anchovy, bonanza
Dutch	cookie, tulip
Arabic	algebra, giraffe
Sanskrit	guru, karma
Hindi	bandanna, cheetah
Persian	balcony, lilac
Russian	gulag, mammoth
Czech	pistol, robot
Norwegian	fjord, ski
Dravidian (Indian subcontinent)	mango, peacock
African languages	jumbo, zombie
American Indian languages	chocolate, igloo
Chinese	ketchup, tea
Japanese	origami, tsunami

The most famous remnant of **Old English** is *Beowulf*. This epic poem survives in a **single manuscript** dating to sometime between the **eighth and eleventh centuries** CE. The author's identity remains a mystery.

Roots

THE ROOT IS THE PART OF A WORD THAT CONTAINS
MEANING, EVEN WITHOUT A PREFIX OR SUFFIX.

SEE ALSO

❮ **136–137** Morphemes
❮ **138–139** Understanding
English irregularities
Prefixes and suffixes **142–143** ❯

A root can be an existing English word or part of a word,
and it usually originates from Latin or Greek. Learning to
identify roots can help with spelling and building vocabulary.

Whole root words

English includes many whole root
words, which often stem from Greek
or Latin. These words cannot be
separated into smaller words, since
they are already in their simplest form.
However, a whole root word can be
made longer by adding a prefix or
suffix. For example, the word *build*
can become *building*, *builder* and
rebuild. Each new word has a different
meaning, but they are all related to
the whole root word.

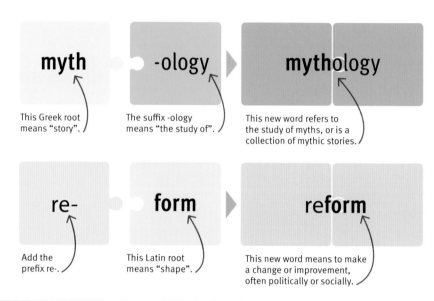

myth

This Greek root
means "story".

-ology

The suffix -ology
means "the study of".

mythology

This new word refers to
the study of myths, or is a
collection of mythic stories.

re-

Add the
prefix re-.

form

This Latin root
means "shape".

re**form**

This new word means to make
a change or improvement,
often politically or socially.

Partial root words

The root is not always a complete
English word. Adding a suffix,
or a prefix and a suffix, however,
can extend a Latin or Greek root to
create a recognisable English word.
For example, the Latin word *aud*,
meaning "hear", forms the root for
many familiar English words, including
audio, *audience*, *audition* and
auditorium. Although these words
mean different things, they are all
related to the original root word.

gen

This Greek word
means "birth"
or "production".

-etic

The suffix -etic
means "relating to".

genetic

This new word refers to
heredity encoded in genes.

lingu

This Latin word
means "tongue"
or "language".

-ist

The suffix -ist means
a person who
peforms an action.

linguist

This is a person who
studies languages.

Latin root words

There are nearly 1,000 Latin root words used in English. Many of these words were introduced through French, which stems from Latin, after the Norman conquest of England in 1066.

Latin root	Meaning	Examples
aqua, aque	water	aquarium, aquatic, aqueduct
bi	two	biannual, bicycle, binary
cent	one hundred	centipede, century, per cent
circum	round	circumference, circumnavigate, circumstance
form	shape	conform, formation, transform
jud	judgement	adjudicate, judge, judicial
liber, liver	free	liberation, liberty, deliver
liter	letter (alphabet)	literal, literate, literature
mater, matr	mother	maternity, matriarch, matronly
min	small	miniature, minimum, minority
pater, patr	father	paternal, patriotic, patron
quad	four	quadrant, quadratic, quadrilateral
terr	earth	extraterrestrial, terrain, territorial
tri	three	triangle, tricycle, trinity
uni	one	unicorn, uniform, universal

When words **share** the same root – such as *employ* in the words *employee*, *employer*, and *employment* – they are known as a **word family**.

Greek root words

There are hundreds of Greek roots used in English, especially relating to science. For example, *scope* in Greek means "to examine", and is seen in many English words, such as *microscope* and *telescope*.

Greek roots	Meanings	Examples
aero	air	aerobics, aerosol, aerospace
bibl, biblio	book	Bible, bibliography, bibliophile
bio	life	antibiotic, biography, biology
cycl, cyclo	circle	bicycle, cyclical, cyclone
dec	ten	decade, decagon, decathlon
dem, demo	people	epidemic, democracy, demography
mega	great	megalomania, megaphone, megaton
pan	all	pandemic, panorama, pantheism
path	feeling	pathology, sympathy, telepathy
phobia	fearing	agoraphobia, arachnophobia, claustrophobia
phos, photo	light	phosphorus, photograph, photosynthesis
poly	many	polygon, polymath, polytechnic
psych	spirit	psychiatry, psychic, psychology
tele	far off	telekinetic, telephone, television
therm	heat	exothermic, thermal, thermometer

• There's **no easy way** to **recognise** whether a root is **Latin** or **Greek**. The best way to find out is to look the word up in a **dictionary**. The origin of the root will be mentioned in the entry.

GLOSSARY

Prefix A group of letters attached to the start of a word that can change the original word's meaning.

Suffix A group of letters attached to the end of a word that can change the original word's meaning.

Prefixes and suffixes

PREFIXES AND SUFFIXES ARE COLLECTIVELY CALLED AFFIXES.

Prefixes are added to the start of a word and suffixes are added to the end of a word. They can change a word's meaning or its part of speech, or – combined with a partial root word – create a new word.

Prefixes

A prefix is added to the start of a root to change the meaning of that root or create a new word. For example, the root word *do* acquires the opposite meaning when the prefix un- (meaning "not") is added, resulting in the word *undo*. When the prefix demo- (meaning "common people" in Greek) is added to the partial root *crat* (meaning "rule" in Greek), it results in the whole English word *democrat*. Other prefixes can be added to the root *crat* to form the English words *aristocrat*, *autocrat* and *bureaucrat*.

SEE ALSO

❮ **106–107** Hyphens	
❮ **136–137** Morphemes	
❮ **140–141** Roots	
Words ending in -e or -y	**146–147** ❯
Words ending in -tion, -sion or -ssion	**148–149** ❯
Words ending in -able or -ible	**150–151** ❯
Words ending in -le, -el, -al or -ol	**152–153** ❯
Single and double consonant words	**154–155** ❯

• Most **prefixes** are not separated from the root by a **hyphen**. However, **ex-** (as in "former") and **self-** are **always** followed by a **hyphen**.

Prefixes	Meaning	Examples
a-, an-	not	**a**typical, **an**onymous
ab-	away from	**ab**normal
ad-	towards	**ad**vance
al-	all	**al**most
all-	all	**all**-knowing
ante-	before	**ante**room
anti-	against	**anti**social
be-	make	**be**friend
co-, col-, com-, con-	together	**co**-operate, **col**laborate, **com**munity, **con**fidence
de-	opposite	**de**tach
de-	down	**de**cline
dis-	not	**dis**embark
em-, en-	cause to	**em**battle, **en**amour
ex-	out of, from	**ex**port
ex-	former	**ex**-husband
extra-	beyond	**extra**ordinary
fore-	before	**fore**arm
im-, in-	in	**im**port, **in**come
im-, in-, ir-	not	**im**mature, **in**credible, **ir**rational
inter-	among	**inter**national
intra-	within	**intra**mural

Prefixes	Meaning	Examples
intro-	in	**intro**duction
mid-	middle	**mid**way
mis-	wrongly	**mis**conception
non-	not	**non**sense
out-	more than others	**out**standing
out-	separate	**out**house
over-	too much	**over**do
para-	beyond, beside	**para**normal
per-	through	**per**form
post-	after	**post**war
pre-	before	**pre**mature
pro-	for	**pro**active
re-	again	**re**apply
retro-	back	**retro**spective
se-	away from	**se**gregate
self-	oneself	**self**-confidence
sub-	under	**sub**marine
super-, sur-	over, above	**super**natural, **sur**vive
sus-	under	**sus**pect
trans-	across	**trans**mit
ultra-	beyond	**ultra**sound
un-	not	**un**cover
under-	beneath, below	**under**mine

Suffixes

A suffix is added to the end of a root – which is either a whole word or part of a word – and changes its meaning or its part of speech. For example, adding the suffix -ant (meaning a person who performs an action) to the end of the word *account* results in a new word with a new meaning: *accountant*. On the other hand, the verb *exist* becomes the noun *existence* when the suffix -ence ("state of") is added.

Techno-prefixes

New affixes appear in English all the time, largely due to rapidly changing technology. For example, the prefix e- (meaning "electronic") was created to form words such as *e-mail* and *e-commerce*. Similarly, the prefix cyber-, which refers to information technology, is used in the words *cyberspace* and *cybercafé*.

Suffixes	Meaning	Examples
-able, -ible	able to	sustain**able**, sens**ible**
-acy	state or quality	conspir**acy**
-age	action of	advant**age**
-age	collection	assembl**age**
-al	act of	deni**al**
-al, -ial	having characteristics of	season**al**, controvers**ial**
-ance, -ence	state of	defi**ance**, compet**ence**
-ant, -ent	person who performs an action	account**ant**, stud**ent**
-ate	become	infl**ate**
-cian	profession of	techni**cian**
-cy	state of being	accura**cy**
-dom	place or state of being	free**dom**
-ed	past tense	stopp**ed**
-en	made of	gold**en**
-en	become	bright**en**
-ent	state of being	differ**ent**
-er, -or	person who performs an action	drumm**er**, investigat**or**
-er	more	short**er**
-ery	action of	robb**ery**
-ery	place of	bak**ery**
-esque	reminiscent of	pictur**esque**
-est	the most	short**est**
-ette	small	maison**ette**
-ful	full of	cheer**ful**
-hood	state of	child**hood**
-ia, -y	state of	amnes**ia**, monarch**y**

Suffixes	Meaning	Examples
-ic, -tic, -ical	having characteristics of	histor**ic**, poet**ic**, rad**ical**
-ice	state or quality	just**ice**
-ify	make	magn**ify**
-ing	present participle	hopp**ing**
-ish	having the quality of	child**ish**
-ism	the belief in	modern**ism**
-ist	one who	art**ist**
-ite	one connected with	social**ite**
-ity, -ty	quality of	real**ity**, socie**ty**
-ive, -ative, -itive	tending to	pass**ive**, superl**ative**, sens**itive**
-less	without	use**less**
-like	resembling	child**like**
-ling	small	half**ling**
-ly	how something is	friend**ly**
-ment	condition of; act of	entertain**ment**
-ness	state of	happi**ness**
-ous, -eous, -ious	having qualities of	ridicul**ous**, naus**eous**, cur**ious**
-s, -es	more than one	otter**s**, fox**es**
-ship	state of	friend**ship**
-sion, -ssion, -tion	state of being	intru**sion**, permi**ssion**, classifica**tion**
-some	tending to	cumber**some**
-ward	in a direction	back**ward**
-y	characterised by	storm**y**

Hard and soft letter sounds

THE LETTERS *C* AND *G* CAN MAKE HARD AND SOFT SOUNDS.

SEE ALSO
❮ 130–131 Vowel sounds
❮ 132–133 Consonant sounds
Silent letters   160–161 ❯
Irregular word spellings   164–165 ❯

The letter that follows *c* or *g* determines if a word has a hard or soft sound. This sound can occur in any part of the word, not just at the beginning.

• Sometimes, **a word** has a **hard "c" sound** that is followed by the letter *e* or *i*. In these cases, the letter *h* is added to make the *c* hard. Some example words include **chemist** (the letter *e*) and **chiropractic** (the letter *i*).

The hard and soft *c*

The letter *c* makes a hard sound when it appears before any letter other than *e*, *i* or *y*. A soft *c* sounds like an *s* – as in *silly* – and can be heard in words where *c* occurs before the letters *e*, *i* or *y*.

▷ **Hard "c" sounds**
There are many words in English with a hard "c" sound. A word like *cartoon* has a hard "c" sound because *c* precedes the letter *a*.

cartoon   cow   crack
recall   uncle   porcupine

▷ **Soft "c" sounds**
These words all have a soft "c" sound. The word *cereal* has a soft "c" sound because *c* precedes the letter *e*.

cereal   circus   cyan
decent   pencil   fancy

Words with both "c" sounds

Sometimes, one word includes a hard and a soft "c" sound. These are unusual in English; however, they do follow the same rules.

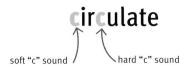
soft "c" sound   hard "c" sound

soft "c" sound   hard "c" sound

Most words with a **soft c or g** come from **Latin**.

hard "c" sound   soft "c" sound

hard "c" sound   soft "c" sound

The hard and soft *g*

The letter *g* makes a hard sound when it appears before any letter other than *e*, *i* or *y*. The soft *g* sounds like a *j* – as in *jelly* – and usually comes before the letters *e*, *i* or *y*.

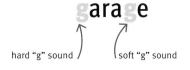

• Some words have a **hard "g" sound** that is followed by an "e" or "i" sound. In such cases, the **letter** *u* is added to make a hard "g" sound, as seen in **guess** (the letter *e*) and **guide** (the letter *i*).

▷ **Hard "g" sounds**
The hard "g" sound is common in English. The word *glue* has a hard "g" sound because *g* precedes the letter *l*.

galaxy   green   gullible

igloo   lagoon   fragrant

▷ **Soft "g" sounds**
These words have a soft "g" sound. The word *gene* has a soft "g" sound because *g* precedes the letter *e*.

gene   ginger   gymnast

angel   legible   allergy

Words with both "g" sounds

There are some words that include a hard and a soft "g" sound. There are not many words in English that have both sounds.

geography

soft "g" sound   hard "g" sound

gorgeous

hard "g" sound   soft "g" sound

garage

hard "g" sound   soft "g" sound

gigantic

soft "g" sound   hard "g" sound

Hard *g* exceptions

Some words make a hard sound even if *g* precedes the letters *e*, *i* or *y*. These exceptions to the rule just have to be learnt, so, if uncertain, check the correct spelling in a dictionary.

These are some common exceptions to the hard *g* rule.

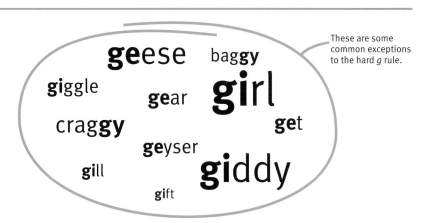

geese   baggy

giggle   gear   girl

craggy   get

geyser

gill   giddy

gift

Words ending in -e or -y

WORDS ENDING IN -E OR -Y OFTEN CHANGE
THEIR SPELLINGS WHEN A SUFFIX IS ADDED.

The final -e in words is usually silent. If a suffix
is added, the -e is sometimes dropped. A final -y
sometimes changes to an *i* when a suffix is added.

SEE ALSO

❰ **130–131** Vowel sounds	
❰ **132–133** Consonant sounds	
❰ **140–141** Roots	
❰ **142–143** Prefixes and suffixes	
Silent letters	**160–161** ❱

Words ending in -e

The silent -e serves an important function by changing the
vowel sound of the previous syllable. For example, the words
plan and *plane* are distinguished in spelling only by the
silent -e, and this difference is reflected in the way they
are pronounced. When adding a suffix, the spelling of words
ending in a silent -e follows certain rules.

Root word	Suffix	New word
argue	-ment	argument
awe	-ful	awful
due	-ly	duly
nine	-th	ninth
true	-ly	truly
whole	-ly	wholly
wise	-dom	wisdom

△ **Exceptions**
There are many exceptions to the rules,
some of which are listed in this table.

▷ **Rule 1**
If a word ends
in a silent -e, the
silent -e is dropped
when a suffix
beginning with
a vowel is added.

▷ **Rule 2**
If a word ends in a
silent -e, the silent
-e is kept when a
suffix beginning
with a consonant
is added.

▷ **Rule 3**
If a word ends
in -ce or -ge,
the silent -e must
be retained with
the suffixes -able
and -ous.

globe
fame
-al
-ous
global
famous

A silent -e produces
a long vowel sound.

Add a suffix that
begins with a vowel.

The silent -e is replaced
by a suffix that begins
with a vowel.

spite
state
-ful
-ment
spiteful
statement

A silent -e produces
a long vowel sound.

Add a suffix that begins
with a consonant.

The silent -e is
needed to retain
a long vowel sound.

courage
notice
-ous
-able
courageous
noticeable

A silent -e can follow
the letter *c* or *g*.

Add the relevant suffix.

The silent -e is needed to
retain a soft "c" or "g" sound.

• The **suffix -y acts as a vowel**, so, if adding it to words ending in a silent -e, drop the silent -e. For example, *ice* becomes *icy* and *spice* becomes *spicy*.

Words ending in -y

Words that end in -y can also change spelling when a suffix is added. The main factor that determines this spelling change is whether a word that ends in -y is preceded by a consonant or a vowel.

Root word	Suffix	New word
day	-ly	daily
dry	-ness	dryness
shy	-ly	shyly
shy	-ness	shyness
sly	-ly	slyly
sly	-ness	slyness

▷ **Exceptions**
Like words ending in -e, there are exceptions to the rules for words ending in -y.

▷ **Rule 1**
If a word ends in a consonant and -y, the -y is replaced by *i* when any suffix apart from -ing is added.

beau**ty**

app**ly**

-ful

-ance

beaut**i**ful

appl**i**ance

Here, a consonant is followed by a -y ending.

Any suffix can be added, except -ing.

The -y is replaced by the letter *i*.

▷ **Rule 2**
If a word ends in a -y preceded by a vowel, the -y is kept when a suffix is added.

ann**oy**

pl**ay**

-ed

-er

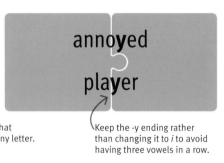

ann**oy**ed

pl**ay**er

Here, a vowel is followed by a -y ending.

Add a suffix that begins with any letter.

Keep the -y ending rather than changing it to *i* to avoid having three vowels in a row.

▷ **Rule 3**
If a word ends in a -y, the -y is kept when the suffix -ing is added.

fly

copy

-ing

-ing

fl**y**ing

cop**y**ing

This word ends in -y.

Add the suffix -ing.

The -y ending is needed to avoid a double *i*.

Words ending in -tion, -sion or -ssion

THREE DIFFERENT SUFFIXES CAN REPRESENT THE "SHUN" SOUND AT THE END OF A WORD.

The suffixes -tion, -sion and -ssion make a "shun" sound. Certain rules are helpful when choosing the correct ending to put at the end of a word.

SEE ALSO

❮ **22–23** Nouns
❮ **38–39** Verbs
❮ **130–131** Vowel sounds
❮ **132–133** Consonant sounds
❮ **136–137** Morphemes
❮ **140–141** Roots
❮ **142–143** Prefixes and suffixes

GLOSSARY

Consonant A letter of the alphabet that is not a vowel.

Noun A word that refers to a person, place or thing.

Suffix A group of letters attached to the end of a word that can change the original word's meaning.

Verb A word that describes an action.

Vowel One of the five letters *a*, *e*, *i*, *o* and *u*.

Words ending in -tion

The suffix -tion means "the act of": for instance, *digestion* means "the act of digesting". Most verbs that take the -tion ending already end in -t, so only -ion needs to be added. This suffix is the most common ending.

▷ **Rule 1**
If a verb ends in -t, then add -ion to avoid a double *t* before the suffix.

This verb ends with a -t.

This suffix borrows the *t* from the verb.

This is the newly formed noun.

▷ **Rule 2**
If a verb ends in -te, then remove the *e* and add -ion.

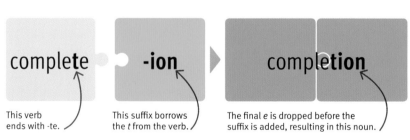

This verb ends with -te.

This suffix borrows the *t* from the verb.

The final *e* is dropped before the suffix is added, resulting in this noun.

▷ **Rule 3**
Some verbs drop the last letter and add an extra vowel before the suffix. To find out which vowel to add, always check a dictionary.

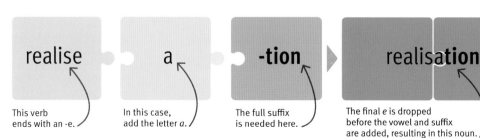

This verb ends with an -e.

In this case, add the letter *a*.

The full suffix is needed here.

The final *e* is dropped before the vowel and suffix are added, resulting in this noun.

Words ending in -sion

The suffix -sion means "the state of": for example, *conclusion* means "the state of concluding". There are about 50 words in common use that end in -sion. Most verbs change their endings in order to add the suffix.

▷ **Rule 1**
If the verb ends in -se, then remove the e and add -ion because s is already present.

This verb ends with -se.

This suffix borrows the s from the verb.

The final e is dropped before the suffix is added, resulting in this noun.

precise → **-ion** ▶ **precision**

▷ **Rule 2**
This suffix is used when the verb ends in -d, -l, -r, -s or -t. Usually, the last letter of the verb is dropped in order to add -sion and turn the verb into a noun.

extend → **-sion** ▶ **extension**

This verb ends with -d.

The full suffix is needed here.

The final d is dropped before the suffix is added, resulting in this noun.

Words ending in -ssion

This suffix -ssion means "the result of": for example, *impression* means "the result of impressing". Usually, a verb needs to change its ending before the suffix is added.

▷ **Rule 1**
If a verb ends in -ss, then just add -ion.

This verb ends with -ss.

This suffix borrows the ss from the verb.

This is the newly formed noun.

discuss → **-ion** ▶ **discussion**

▷ **Rule 2**
If the verb ends with a -t, then remove it and add -ssion.

omit → **-ssion** ▶ **omission**

This verb ends with -t.

The full suffix is needed here.

The final t is dropped before the suffix is added, resulting in this noun.

Unusual spellings

Some words that end with a "shun" sound do not follow the rules and just need to be learnt. If unsure about the correct spelling, always check a dictionary.

Ending	Examples
-sian	A**sian**, Rus**sian**
-xion	comple**xion**, crucifi**xion**
-cion	coer**cion**, suspi**cion**
-cean	crusta**cean**, o**cean**

The only words in which the **"sh" sound** at the start of the last syllable is spelt with the letters *sh* are *cushion* and *fashion*.

Words ending in -able or -ible

SPELLING WORDS WITH SIMILAR-SOUNDING SUFFIXES CAN BE CONFUSING.

SEE ALSO

❮ **26–27** Adjectives
❮ **136–137** Morphemes
❮ **140–141** Roots
❮ **142–143** Prefixes and suffixes
❮ **144–145** Hard and soft letter sounds
Single and double consonant words **154–155** ❯

The suffixes -able and -ible both mean "able to". For example, *adaptable* means "able to adapt". However, it can be difficult to decide which suffix to use, as they are not interchangeable.

GLOSSARY

Adjective A word that describes a noun.

Suffix A group of letters attached to the end of a word that can change the original word's meaning.

Syllable A unit of pronunciation that has one vowel sound.

Verb A word that describes an action.

Vowel One of the five letters *a*, *e*, *i*, *o* and *u*.

Words ending in -able

The suffix -able is usually added to complete words to turn them into adjectives. Learning a few simple rules makes it easier to decide which suffix to use. More words end in -able than -ible, so, if in doubt, choose -able. Best of all, check the correct spelling in a dictionary.

▷ **Rule 1**
Words ending in -able are usually formed from two separate words that make sense individually.

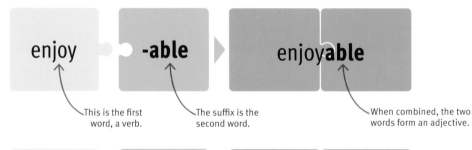

This is the first word, a verb.

The suffix is the second word.

When combined, the two words form an adjective.

▷ **Rule 2**
When -able is added to a word that ends in -e, the e is usually removed.

This verb ends in -e.

Remove the e and add the suffix.

The e is removed to form the new adjective.

▷ **Rule 3**
Often, if a word ends in -y, the y is replaced with an *i* before the suffix -able is added.

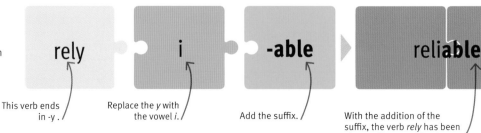

This verb ends in -y.

Replace the y with the vowel *i*.

Add the suffix.

With the addition of the suffix, the verb *rely* has been changed into an adjective.

Words ending in -ible

The suffix -ible is usually added to partial root words, many of which have Latin or Greek origins, but it can also be added to complete words. Several rules help to distinguish words that end in -ible from those that end in -able.

▷ **Rule 1**
Most words ending in -ible cannot be divided into two English words that make sense on their own. The suffix is needed in order to make a whole word.

vis — -ible ▸ vis**ible**

This Latin root means "see".

Add the suffix after the root.

This is the newly formed adjective.

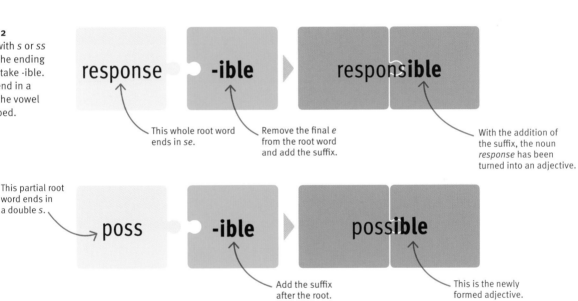

▷ **Rule 2**
Words with *s* or *ss* before the ending usually take -ible. If they end in a vowel, the vowel is dropped.

response — -ible ▸ respons**ible**

This whole root word ends in *se*.

Remove the final *e* from the root word and add the suffix.

With the addition of the suffix, the noun *response* has been turned into an adjective.

This partial root word ends in a double *s*.

poss — -ible ▸ poss**ible**

Add the suffix after the root.

This is the newly formed adjective.

Soft and hard "c" and "g" sounds

Words that end in -able usually have a hard "c" or "g" sound. In contrast, words that end in -ible usually have a soft "c" or "g" sound.

Hard "c" or "g" sounds	Soft "c" or "g" sounds
ami**cable**	for**cible**
communi**cable**	invin**cible**
despi**cable**	redu**cible**
indefati**gable**	le**gible**
navi**gable**	tan**gible**

The word ***uncopyrightable*** is the **longest** English **word** in normal use that contains no letter more than **once**.

• Many words that **begin with** *a* use the **suffix** that also begins with *a*: -able. Some common examples include ***adorable***, ***advisable*** and ***available***.

Words ending in -le, -el, -al or -ol

THESE WORD ENDINGS ARE NOT USUALLY SUFFIXES.

SEE ALSO

❮ **22–23** Nouns
❮ **26–27** Adjectives
❮ **38–39** Verbs
❮ **136–137** Morphemes
❮ **140–141** Roots
❮ **142–143** Prefixes and suffixes

Similar-sounding word endings like -le, -el, -al and -ol can cause spelling difficulties. However, there are some guidelines that can help with using them. As with all tricky spellings, a dictionary is a valuable checking tool.

Words ending in -le

The most common of these word endings is -le. This word ending is not a suffix because it does not change the meaning or part of speech of a root word. The -le word ending is usually found in nouns (such as *table*), verbs (such as *tickle*) and adjectives (such as *vile*).

edi**b**le

The letter *b* has a stick and comes before -le.

sam**p**le

The letter *p* has a tail and comes before -le.

wrin**k**le

The letter *k* has a stick and comes before -le.

dan**g**le

The letter *g* has a tail and comes before -le.

△ **The rule**
Words ending in -le are often preceded by a letter with a stick or tail – part of the letter reaching high, as in *b*, or low, as in *p*.

Some other **common words** that end with **-ol** are spelt *oo* to create a long vowel sound, such as *cool*, *pool*, *school* and *tool*.

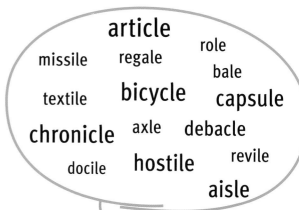

article

missile   regale   role

bale

textile   bicycle   capsule

chronicle   axle   debacle

docile   hostile   revile

aisle

Of course, a number of words that end with -le do not follow this rule. Some commonly used ones are listed here.

GLOSSARY

Adjective A word that describes a noun.

Noun A word that refers to a person, place or thing.

Root The smallest part of a word without a prefix or suffix attached.

Suffix A group of letters attached to the end of a word that can change the word's meaning.

Verb A word that describes an action.

Vowel One of the five letters *a*, *e*, *i*, *o* and *u*.

Words ending in -el and -al

As is the case with -le, the word endings -el and -al generally do not act as suffixes because they are not changing a root word's meaning or part of speech.

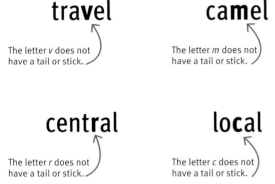

travel

The letter *v* does not have a tail or stick.

camel

The letter *m* does not have a tail or stick.

central

The letter *r* does not have a tail or stick.

local

The letter *c* does not have a tail or stick.

△ **The rule**
Words ending in -el and -al are often preceded by a letter without a stick or tail (part of the letter reaching high or low).

-el exceptions	-al exceptions
angel	acquittal
bagel	betrayal
chapel	capital
compel	coastal
decibel	frugal
gel	fundamental
gospel	homicidal
hostel	hospital
hotel	judgemental
model	mental
nickel	municipal
parallel	orbital
propel	petal
scalpel	portal
snorkel	verbal

△ **Exceptions to the rule**
As with words ending in -le, there are a number of exceptions, which end in -el or -al but do not follow this rule.

The -al ending as a suffix

The word ending -al can also be used as a suffix because it can sometimes change the meaning of a root word. Words that end with this suffix are usually nouns or adjectives.

▽ **The rule**
The -al ending can act as a suffix that attaches to a root word, which can be a whole word or part of a word.

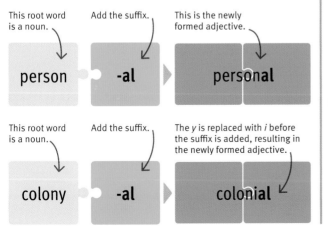

This root word is a noun.

Add the suffix.

This is the newly formed adjective.

person ▸ -al ▸ personal

This root word is a noun.

Add the suffix.

The *y* is replaced with *i* before the suffix is added, resulting in the newly formed adjective.

colony ▸ -al ▸ colonial

Words ending in -ol

On rare occasions, -ol is also used as a word ending. This ending is usually found in nouns and verbs. If in doubt, always check the spelling in a dictionary before using it.

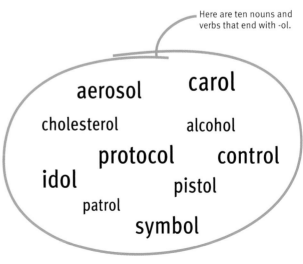

Here are ten nouns and verbs that end with -ol.

aerosol   carol
cholesterol   alcohol
protocol   control
idol   pistol
patrol
symbol

Single and double consonant words

SINGLE AND DOUBLE CONSONANTS USUALLY SOUND THE SAME.

It is not always obvious if a word contains a single or a double consonant – some spellings just have to be learnt. However, there are a few rules that can help.

Consonants and short vowel sounds

In words with more than one syllable, if the first syllable is stressed and has a short vowel sound, then the following consonant is doubled. For example, the word *letter* has a double *t* because the first syllable, *let*, is stressed and has a short vowel sound. Compare this to *retire*, which does not have a double *t*. This is because the stress is on the second syllable, *tire*, which has a long vowel sound.

• The letters *h*, *w*, *x* and *y* are **never** doubled, even when a suffix beginning with a **vowel** is added. For example, the consonant is not doubled in the words **washed**, **drawer**, **fixable** and **flying**.

depart

The letter *p* is not doubled because the stress is on the second syllable, *part*.

hammer

The letter *m* is doubled because the stress is on the first syllable, *ham*.

prepare

The letter *p* is not doubled because the stress is on the second syllable, *pare*.

valley

The letter *l* is doubled because the stress is on the first syllable, *val*.

Exceptions to the rule

Many words do not follow the rule above. In most cases, these are root words and are therefore not attached to a prefix or suffix. Some of these words, such as *melon*, have a single consonant after a short vowel sound. Double consonants can also occur after unstressed syllables, such as *correct*. These exceptions can make spelling difficult, so check a dictionary if uncertain.

Single consonant	Double consonant
comet	accept
domino	accumulate
epic	correct
galaxy	effect
lizard	necessary
melon	occur
palace	recommend
radish	sufficient
valid	terrific

Double consonants and suffixes

Consonants that come at the end of a word are often doubled when a suffix is added. This mostly applies to verbs. For example, the final consonant of the verb *sit* is doubled after adding the suffix -ing, which results in the word *sitting*.

• Consonants are **doubled** when adding a **prefix** or **another word** that ends in the same letter as the first letter of the root. For example, the prefix **mis-** and root *spell* combine to make *misspell*.

▷ **Rule 1**
When adding a suffix that begins with a vowel, such as -er, to a verb that has one syllable and ends with a short vowel sound and a consonant, the final consonant is often doubled.

The syllable *run* has a short vowel sound and ends with a consonant.

Add a suffix that begins with a vowel.

The consonant *n* is doubled.

▷ **Rule 2**
When adding a suffix that begins with a vowel, such as -ing, to a verb with more than one syllable, which ends with a short vowel sound and a consonant, the final consonant is usually doubled.

The second syllable, *gin*, ends with a short vowel sound and a consonant.

Add a suffix that begins with a vowel.

The consonant *n* is doubled.

▷ **Rule 3**
When adding a suffix that begins with *e*, *i* or *y* to a verb that ends in *c*, the final consonant is not doubled. Instead, the letter *k* is added after *c* in order to keep the hard "c" sound.

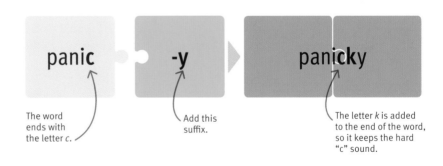

The word ends with the letter *c*.

Add this suffix.

The letter *k* is added to the end of the word, so it keeps the hard "c" sound.

GLOSSARY

Consonant A letter of the alphabet that is not a vowel.

Prefix A group of letters attached to the start of a word that can change the original word's meaning.

Suffix A group of letters attached to the end of a word that can change the original word's meaning.

Syllable A unit of pronunciation that has one vowel sound.

Vowel One of the five letters *a*, *e*, *i*, *o* and *u*.

In English, ***bookkeeper*** and ***bookkeeping*** are the only words with **three** consecutive **double letters**.

The "*i* before *e* except after *c*" rule

THE "*I* BEFORE *E* EXCEPT AFTER *C*" RULE IS USED
TO REMEMBER SPELLINGS CONTAINING *IE* OR *EI*.

This rule has been used for more than 150 years, and
it works in the majority of cases. There are, however,
many exceptions to the rule, and it's best to learn
these and to be aware of them.

SEE ALSO

❮ **130–131** Vowel sounds

❮ **138–139** Understanding English irregularities

Irregular word spellings **164–165**❯

• There are **no *cein*** words in
the English language. If a *c* is
followed by an *ie/ei* combination
then an *n*, the spelling should
always be *ie*, as in *science*.

The rhyme

A useful rhyme was created to help
people remember the "*i* before *e*"
rule. Originally, it consisted of only
two lines, but it has been expanded
over the years to include some
exceptions to the rule.

The start of the rhyme means that
i usually comes before *e* in words that
contain an "ee" sound, such as *thief*.

The *e* also goes first
when the sound in
the word is "ay",
as in *eight*.

I before e,
Except after c
When the sound is "ee"
Or when sounded as "ay",
As in neighbour and weigh,
But leisure and seize
Do as they please.

However, when the "ee"
sound comes after the
letter *c*, the *e* goes before
the *i*, as in *receive*.

The end of the rhyme
notes that there are some
words that don't follow
any particular rule.

REAL WORLD
Loan words

A word that has been borrowed
from another language is called
a loan word. Many loan words
use an *e* before *i* spelling.
These words include *geisha*
from Japanese, *sheikh* from
Arabic, and *rottweiler* from
German. Many names borrowed
from foreign languages are also
spelt with the *e* first, such as
Keith, *Heidi*, *Neil* and *Sheila*.

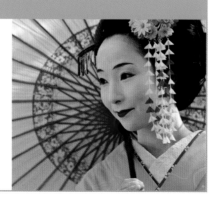

• If in **doubt,** always use a
dictionary to confirm whether
a word uses *ie* or *ei*.

Single syllable sounds

As mentioned in the rhyme, the sound of the *ie* or *ei* can be used to work out which letter combination is right. There are four main rules to remember if the *ie/ei* is pronounced as one syllable. However, most of the rules have exceptions, which have to be learnt.

Rule 1
If the sound is "ee", the *i* goes before the *e*.

niece, belief, achieve, field

There are numerous exceptions to this rule that have to be learnt.

protein, seize, either, weird, caffeine

Rule 2
If the "ee" sound follows the letter *c*, the *e* goes first.

receive, receipt, deceit, ceiling

One exception to this rule is when the *ci* sounds like "sh".

ancient, conscience, species

The rule also doesn't apply to words ending in *y* that have been modified.

fancied, policies, bouncier

Rule 3
The *e* goes before the *i* if the sound is "ay" or "eye".

weight, height, feisty

Sometimes, the "eye" sound can also be heard when the *i* goes before *e*.

die, pie, lie, cried

Rule 4
The *e* goes before the *i* if the sound is "eh", as in *met*.

heifer, leisure

exceptions to this rule

friend, lieutenant

Double syllable sounds

If the *i* and *e* are pronounced as two different sounds, it is easy to work out which letter comes first. If the "i" sound is pronounced first, then the *i* comes first in the spelling, and vice versa.

di-et, a-li-en, sci-ence, so-ci-e-ty

de-i-ty, see-ing, be-ing, re-ig-nite, here-in

Pronounced *i* then *e*
In these words, the *i* syllable is said first, so the *i* comes first in the spelling.

Pronounced *e* then *i*
In these words, the *e* syllable is said first, so the *e* comes first in the spelling.

Capital letters

THE MOST COMMON USE OF A CAPITAL LETTER
IS AT THE BEGINNING OF A SENTENCE.

In addition to starting sentences, capital letters are used
for the names of people and places, and expressions
of time, such as days of the week.

Starting a sentence

The first word of a sentence begins with a capital letter. This draws the reader's attention and emphasises the beginning of the new sentence. A capital letter follows a full stop, an exclamation mark or a question mark at the end of a previous sentence.

On that

The first word in a sentence begins with a capital letter.

Expressions of time

Days of the week, months of the year and national and religious holidays, such as Christmas, are all written with capital letters. However, the names of the seasons, such as winter, are never capitalised. Historical periods and events, such as the Industrial Revolution and the Olympic Games, are always capitalised.

Saturday

The days of the week are always capitalised.

Bronze Age

Both letters are capitalised for this historical period.

Halloween

Celebrations are always capitalised.

On that Saturday afternoon i
Olivia as she hurried to meet he

• Remember to begin every **quotation** with a capital letter.

A, H, I, M, O, T, U, V, W, X and Y are all **symmetrical** capital letters.

Capital letters and titles

The titles of books, plays, songs, newspapers, films and poems need capital letters. Smaller words within a title, such as the articles *a* and *the*, or the prepositions *of* and *in*, are not usually capitalised unless they are at the start of a title. For example, *The New York Times* has a capital *t* for *The* because it is the first word of the newspaper's title.

• Unlike other pronouns, such as *you*, *he*, *she*, *it* and *them*, *I* is **always spelt** with a **capital letter**.

The English alphabet **originally only had capital letters**. Lower-case letters were introduced in the **eighth century CE**.

Identifying when to use capital letters

It is important to use capital letters correctly so it is clear where one sentence ends and another begins. Proper nouns must also be capitalised, so that the names of people or places, or expressions of time, can be easily distinguished from other common things.

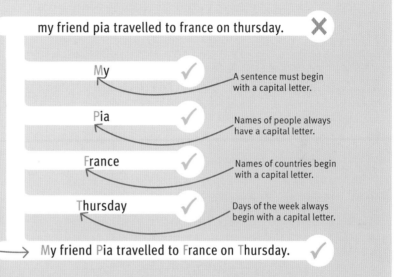

my friend pia travelled to france on thursday. ✗

My ✓ — A sentence must begin with a capital letter.

Pia ✓ — Names of people always have a capital letter.

France ✓ — Names of countries begin with a capital letter.

Thursday ✓ — Days of the week always begin with a capital letter.

All the capital letters are used correctly here.

My friend Pia travelled to France on Thursday. ✓

San Francisco, the rain drenched friends at the Katwalk Café.

People and places

Proper nouns, such as the names of people or places, always begin with a capital letter. A capital letter is also required to describe a specific place, such as "the North", which may refer to the northern region of a country. However, capital letters are not required when indicating a general direction, as in north of the shopping centre.

San Francisco — A city requires a capital letter. For cities with two parts, both words are capitalised.

Olivia — The name of a person must be capitalised.

River Nile — Both parts of this specific river name are capitalised.

Katwalk Café — Both parts are capitalised as they form the name of a place of business.

Disneyland — This theme park is the name of a place, so it is capitalised.

Africa — Names of continents are capitalised.

Silent letters

A SILENT LETTER IS WRITTEN BUT NOT PRONOUNCED.

English includes many words with silent letters. This can sometimes make spelling difficult; however, learning to recognise certain patterns can help with spelling these words.

Silent letters

Letters that do not affect the sound of a word are called silent letters. In many cases, these letters were once clearly heard, but over time the pronunciation of the words has changed, even though the spelling has stayed the same.

condem**n**

If the silent *n* is removed, it does not change the sound of this word – but it would be misspelt.

Letter	When it can be silent	Examples
a	before or after another vowel	**a**isle, coco**a**, he**a**d
b	after *m*	crum**b**, lim**b**, thum**b**
	before *t*	de**b**t, dou**b**t, su**b**tle
c	after *s*	mus**c**le, s**c**ent, s**c**issors
d	before or after *n*	We**d**nesday, han**d**some, lan**d**scape
e	at the end of a word	giraff**e**, humbl**e**, lov**e**
g	before *h*	dau**g**hter, thou**g**h, wei**g**h
	before *n*	campai**g**n, forei**g**n, **g**nome
h	at the beginning of a word	**h**eir, **h**onest, **h**our
	after *ex*	ex**h**austing, ex**h**ibition, ex**h**ilarate
	after *g*	g**h**astly, g**h**ost, g**h**oul
	after *r*	r**h**apsody, r**h**inoceros, r**h**yme
	after *w*	w**h**ale, w**h**eel, w**h**irlpool
k	before *n*	**k**nee, **k**night, **k**now
l	before *d*	cou**l**d, shou**l**d, wou**l**d
	before *f*	beha**l**f, ca**l**f, ha**l**f
	before *m*	a**l**mond, ca**l**m, pa**l**m
n	after *m*	autum**n**, hym**n**, solem**n**
p	before *n*	**p**neumatic, **p**neumonia, **p**neumonic
	before *s*	**p**salm, **p**sychiatry, **p**sychic
	before *t*	**p**teranodon, **p**terodactyl, recei**p**t
t	before *ch*	ca**t**ch, stre**t**ch, wi**t**ch
	after *s*	cas**t**le, Chris**t**mas, lis**t**en
u	with other vowels	b**u**ilding, co**u**rt, g**u**ess
w	before *r*	**w**reck, **w**rite, **w**rong
	with *s* or *t*	ans**w**er, s**w**ord, t**w**o

Auxiliary letters

An auxiliary letter is a type of silent letter that can change the pronunciation of a word. For example, if the letter *a* in *coat* is removed, this would spell another word, *cot*, which sounds different and has a different meaning to *coat*.

Here, the silent *e* is an auxiliary letter because, if it is removed, the sound changes. It would also be confused with the existing word *kit*.

Letter	When it can be silent	Examples
a	after *o*	boat, coat, goat
b	after *m*	climb, comb, tomb
c	before *t*	indict
d	before *g*	badge, dodge, judge
e	at the end of a word	hope, kite, site
g	after *i* and before *n*	benign, design, sign
	after *i* and before *m*	paradigm
h	after *c*	ache
i	only in one word	business
l	before *k*	folk, talk, walk
	before *m*	calm, palm
s	after *i*	aisle, island
w	before *h*	who, whom, whose

Regional variations

One aspect that varies from one accent to the next is the silencing and sounding of particular letters. The English language includes a range of regional accents, each with its own peculiarities. Even so, two people raised in the same region might pronounce the same word differently.

Most speakers don't pronounce the final *r* in this word.

Letter	When it can be either silent or heard	Examples
h	before *e*	herb
	after *w*	which, whip, whisky
r	after a vowel	born, car, star
t	before or after another consonant	often, fasten, tsunami

About **60 per cent** of English words contain a **silent letter**.

• Some words that contain silent letters stem from **other languages**. The words *knife*, *knock* and *know*, which all have a **silent k**, are **Old Norse** words. The words *bright*, *daughter* and *night*, which all contain the **silent gh**, are **Anglo-Saxon** words.

Compound words

A NEW WORD FORMED FROM THE UNION OF
TWO WORDS IS CALLED A COMPOUND WORD.

SEE ALSO

❰ **20–21** Parts of speech
❰ **22–23** Nouns
❰ **38–39** Verbs
❰ **140–141** Roots
Irregular word spellings **164–165** ❱

A compound word is made up of two smaller words that
have been joined together. There are many compound
words in the English language.

Adding detail

Some words are joined to other
words to add detail, making the
resulting compound word more
specific. For example, the word
house can modify the word
boat to create the new compound
word *houseboat*. The word *boat*
can be modified again with other
words, such as *power* and *steam*,
to create new compound words
that describe other types of
boat: for example, *powerboat*
and *steamboat*.

The word *house* modifies the
word *boat* to specify a type
of boat: a *houseboat*.

 house ⟷ boat **houseboat**

The word *cheese* modifies
the word *cake* to specify
a type of cake: *cheesecake*.

 cheese ⟷ cake **cheesecake**

• Most compound words are nouns.
Verbs formed from two words tend
to stay as two words: for example,
the verb *turn around* **can be
distinguished from the compound
word** *turnaround* – a noun that
usually refers to the sudden or
unexpected reversal of something.

GLOSSARY

Noun A part of speech that refers
to a person, place or thing.

Verb A part of speech that describes
an action.

Word 1	Word 2	Compound word
air	craft	aircraft
baby	sitter	babysitter
book	keeper	bookkeeper
card	board	cardboard
dish	washer	dishwasher
fire	place	fireplace
ginger	bread	gingerbread
horse	shoe	horseshoe
key	hole	keyhole
news	paper	newspaper
river	side	riverside
snow	flake	snowflake
sun	rise	sunrise
tax	payer	taxpayer
wall	paper	wallpaper

New meaning

This type of compound word is formed when two smaller words are combined to form a new word that is unrelated to the original words. For example, *hogwash* is made up of two words, *hog* (a type of swine) and *wash* (to cleanse). When combined, these words form the compound word, *hogwash* – a noun that describes something as nonsense.

The word *glove* combines with the word *fox*, resulting in a type of plant: *foxglove*.

The word *tail* combines with the word *pony*, resulting in a type of hairstyle: a *ponytail*.

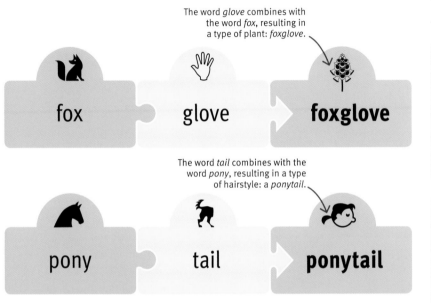

| fox | glove | > | foxglove |
| pony | tail | > | ponytail |

Some languages, such as German and Finnish, **can combine three words**. For example, *Farbfernsehgerät* means **"colour television set"** in German.

• Two words can be joined together to form a compound word if the combination creates **one idea or item**, such as *afterlife* or *backbone*. If two words do not create one idea or item, they should stay separate.

REAL WORLD

Evolving compound words

Some words go together so often that they might at first seem to be compound words, such as *post office*, *half moon* and *ice cream*. Many words begin as two separate words (*wild life*), then become hyphenated (*wild-life*), and then, eventually, become a compound word (*wildlife*).

Word 1	Word 2	Compound word
block	buster	blockbuster
cart	wheel	cartwheel
heart	beat	heartbeat
honey	moon	honeymoon
in	come	income
life	style	lifestyle
lime	light	limelight
master	piece	masterpiece
off	shoot	offshoot
over	come	overcome
scare	crow	scarecrow
show	case	showcase
sleep	walk	sleepwalk
type	writer	typewriter
wind	screen	windscreen

Irregular word spellings

SOME SPELLINGS DON'T FOLLOW ANY RULES.

SEE ALSO

❰ **134–135** Syllables
❰ **138–139** Understanding English irregularities
❰ **156–157** The "*i* before *e* except after *c*" rule

The only way to remember irregular spellings is to learn them. However, there are ways to do this other than just staring at the words.

Weird words

Some words are difficult to spell because they are not spelt like they sound. For example, *said* rhymes with *led* and *fed* but is spelt very differently. Other irregular spellings are tricky because they go against common rules: for example, the word *foreign* does not follow the "*i* before *e* except after *c*" rule.

• One way to learn a spelling is to put up **reminders** everywhere. Write the **troublesome word** in **large letters,** and then put it on the **wall** or anywhere around the house where it will be seen **throughout the day**.

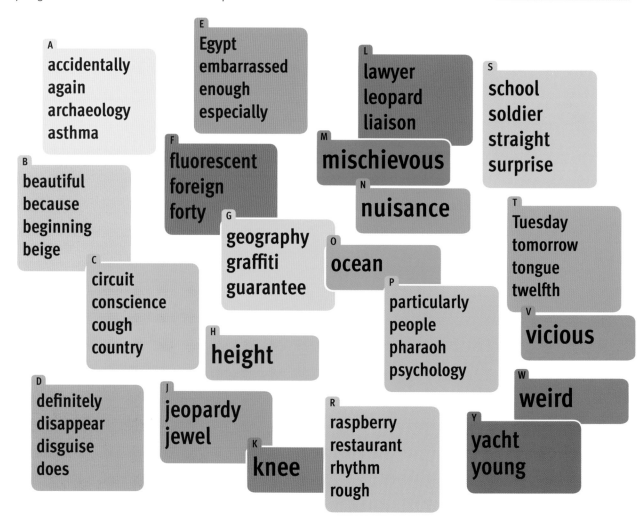

A
accidentally
again
archaeology
asthma

E
Egypt
embarrassed
enough
especially

L
lawyer
leopard
liaison

S
school
soldier
straight
surprise

F
fluorescent
foreign
forty

M
mischievous

B
beautiful
because
beginning
beige

N
nuisance

T
Tuesday
tomorrow
tongue
twelfth

G
geography
graffiti
guarantee

O
ocean

C
circuit
conscience
cough
country

P
particularly
people
pharaoh
psychology

V
vicious

H
height

D
definitely
disappear
disguise
does

J
jeopardy
jewel

R
raspberry
restaurant
rhythm
rough

W
weird

K
knee

Y
yacht
young

Write it out

One technique to learn a spelling is to look at the word, cover it up, write it out from memory, then check it. Do this as many times as necessary.

LOOK

COVER

WRITE

CHECK

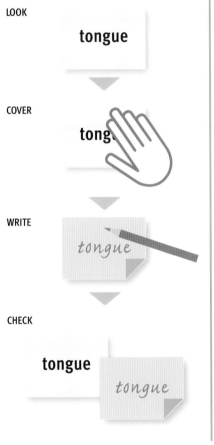

What's the problem?

Another way to learn an irregular spelling is to investigate what makes it so difficult. Look at the word and underline the part that is strange or hard to remember. Highlighting the problem will make it easier to recall.

 le**o**pard

The *o* is silent.

rest**aur**ant

The *aur* sounds like it should be spelt *er*.

It's strange that this word uses an *f* and *th* to make the sound.

 twel**fth**

Speak differently

If a word isn't written how it sounds, say it out loud, pronouncing it so that it does match the spelling.

defin**IT**ely

Stress the *it* to remember that it isn't spelt *at*.

WED NES DAY

Say this word in its separate parts to make it easier to spell.

particul**ARLY**

Start to stress the *arly* to remember that it isn't spelt *erly*.

Words within words

Another trick is to look for smaller words in longer ones. This will associate the longer word with the smaller word. Visualising these small words with pictures will make spelling the longer word much easier.

Draw images like this to visualise the words within words.

 There is a **rat** in sep**arate**

Silly sayings

Making up ridiculous phrases can help people to remember spellings. These are called mnemonic devices. One method is to think of a phrase with a word beginning with each letter in the tricky word. Other sayings can remind people of the number of particular letters in a word.

RHYTHM

Rhythm **H**elps **Y**our **T**wo **H**ips **M**ove

Each word in the saying starts with a letter from the spelling.

BECAUSE

Big **E**lephants **C**an't **A**lways **U**se **S**mall **E**xits

This saying reminds people that the word has one *c* and two *s*'s.

NECESSARY

One **c**offee with two **s**ugars

Homonyms, homophones and homographs

SOME WORDS HAVE THE SAME PRONUNCIATION OR SPELLING BUT MEAN DIFFERENT THINGS.

SEE ALSO

❮ **78–79** Commonly misused words
❮ **140–141** Roots
❮ **142–143** Prefixes and suffixes
❮ **160–161** Silent letters
❮ **164–165** Irregular word spellings
Writing to describe ❯ **208–209**

Variations in pronunciation or spelling are what distinguish homonyms, homophones and homographs. Using the correct word is important for both spoken and written English.

Homonyms

Words with the same spelling and pronunciation, but different meanings, are called homonyms. For example, the word *fair* can refer to an event with games and rides or to the idea of treating somebody in a reasonable way.

The word **homonym** come from the Greek **homos**, which means **"same"**, and **onyma**, which means **"name"**.

Crossword puzzles

Crossword puzzles can be difficult without a good understanding of homonyms, homophones and homographs. The clues in cryptic crosswords take advantage of the confusion caused by these words in order to mislead the reader.

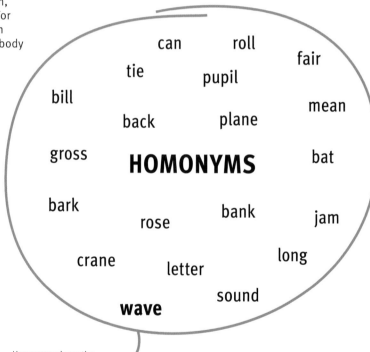

can   roll   fair
tie   pupil
bill
back   plane   mean
gross   **HOMONYMS**   bat
bark
rose   bank   jam
crane   long
letter
sound
wave

Homonyms have the same pronunciation and spelling.

▷ **Wave**
The homonym *wave* has several meanings. These include the kind of wave caused by ocean currents, as well as the movement of a hand as a greeting gesture or signal.

Homophones

Words with identical pronunciation but different spellings and meanings are called homophones, which means "same sound" in Greek. Most homophones come in pairs, such as *reed* and *read*; however, there are also some groups of three words, as in *to*, *too* and *two*.

Homophones have the same pronunciation but different spellings.

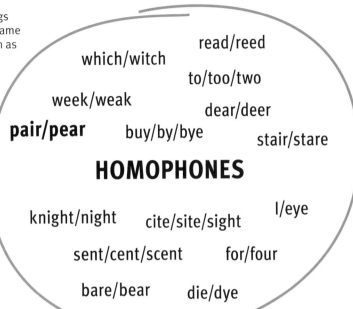

which/witch
read/reed
to/too/two
week/weak
dear/deer
pair/pear
buy/by/bye
stair/stare

HOMOPHONES

knight/night
cite/site/sight
I/eye
sent/cent/scent
for/four
bare/bear
die/dye

△ **Pear and pair**
The words *pear* and *pair* are homophones. The first word refers to an edible fruit, and the second word means two of something.

Homographs

Words that are spelt the same but pronounced differently, with different meanings, are called homographs, which means "same writing" in Greek. For example, the word *tear* can refer to a watery discharge from the eye or a rip in something.

Homographs have different pronunciations but the same spelling.

reject
putting
minute
bow
tear
content
live
lead
object
wind
bass

HOMOGRAPHS

contract
refuse
produce
wound
row
project
close
sow
does

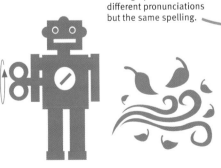

△ **Wind**
The homograph *wind* has two meanings. One relates to a turning or twisting action, and the other refers to a strong breeze.

Confusing words

SIMILAR-SOUNDING WORDS CAN BE DIFFICULT TO SPELL.

English includes many words that look and sound the same, or nearly the same. Recognising small differences in pronunciation can help with spelling.

SEE ALSO	
❮ **136–137** Morphemes	
❮ **142–143** Prefixes and suffixes	
❮ **162–163** Compound words	
❮ **166–167** Homonyms, homophones and homographs	
Other confusing words	**170–171** ❯

Noun and verb confusion

Some nouns and verbs are often confused because of their similar or identical pronunciation. In some cases, a small change in the sound of a word can indicate a different part of speech, as in the noun *advice* and verb *advise*. More often, however, words have the same pronunciation but a different spelling and meaning, as in *drawer* and *draw*.

advice
This noun refers to guidance.

 or

advise
This verb means to offer suggestions.

Their **advice** was helpful.

I asked her to **advise** me.

breath
This noun refers to air taken in or out of the lungs.

 or

breathe
This verb means to take air in and out of the lungs.

She took a deep **breath**.

He had to **breathe** hard while jogging.

ceiling
This noun refers to the upper surface of a room.

 or

sealing
This verb means to close securely.

The new light hung from the **ceiling**.

The plumber is **sealing** the gap.

device
This noun refers to a piece of equipment.

or

devise
This verb means to plan or invent.

I bought a new phone **device**.

The team will **devise** a website.

drawer
This noun refers to a storage compartment.

 or

draw
This verb means to illustrate something.

She put her pen in the **drawer**.

He liked to **draw** buildings.

effect
This noun refers to the result of an action.

 or

affect
This verb means to have an impact on.

The protest had a positive **effect**.

The fight **affect**ed him badly.

lesson This noun refers to a period of teaching.	**or**	**lessen** This verb means to reduce.	

weight This noun refers to mass contained by an object.	**or**	**wait** This verb means to stay or delay an action.	

She enjoyed her piano **lesson**.

I must **lessen** my grip on the rope.

The bag's **weight** is immense.

I must **wait** for my brother.

Commonly misspelt words

There are many other words that sound the same or similar to each other, but have different spellings and meanings. In all cases, it is important to use the correct word in order to be understood, particularly in written form. If uncertain which is the correct word to use, check a dictionary.

Word	Example sentence
are	Those boys **are** always getting into trouble.
hear	I could **hear** the plane flying overhead.
know	The taxi driver did not **know** the way to my house.
lose	There was no way she could **lose** in the finals.
passed	He **passed** the present to his friend.
weather	The **weather** report predicted snowfall.

Word	Example sentence
our	**Our** team was invited to the national championships.
here	**Here** is the latest photo of my family.
now	There is **now** a café where my house used to be.
loose	My friend's **loose** change fell out of his pocket.
past	She drove **past** the park on the way home.
whether	I am not sure **whether** to wear my coat today or not.

One or two words?

Some phrases have different meanings according to whether they are spelt as one word or two. For example, the single word *everyday* means routine or commonplace, whereas *every day* means each day.

Word	Example sentence
anyone	**Anyone** caught smoking will be punished.
already	Our passports have **already** been inspected.
altogether	The song was **altogether** inappropriate.
everyday	I was wearing **everyday** clothes around the house.
maybe	**Maybe** one day they will uncover the truth.

Phrase	Example sentence
any one	**Any one** of those people could be to blame.
all ready	We are **all ready** to board the plane.
all together	The paintings were exhibited **all together** for the first time.
every day	I need to use a hairdryer **every day** after my shower.
may be	There **may be** more than one culprit.

• Learning the meanings of commonly used **roots, prefixes** and **suffixes** can help with confusing words.

Other confusing words

MISSPELT WORDS OFTEN ARISE FROM CONFUSED MEANINGS.

SEE ALSO
❬ **104–105** Apostrophes
❬ **166–167** Homonyms, homophones and homographs
❬ **168–169** Confusing words

Some words are misunderstood and, therefore, spelt incorrectly. Choosing the wrong word can alter the meaning of a sentence, which may confuse the reader.

Confused meanings

Some words are incorrectly spelt because their meanings are not properly understood. In some cases, two words may sound similar, which only adds to the confusion.

With such words, the difference in meaning and spelling has to be learnt; there is no trick or rule to remember. Consult a dictionary if in doubt about which word to use.

adapt **adopt**
This refers to making something suitable. This can mean to follow an idea or method.

A fish can **adapt** to a new habitat.

They will **adopt** the new policy.

conscience **conscious**
This refers to a sense of right or wrong. This means to be aware or awake.

Her **conscience** told her to confess.

He was **conscious** of his faults.

disinterested **uninterested**
This refers to an impartial person. This means having no interest.

The **disinterested** reporter is talking.

He is **uninterested** in the show.

distinct **distinctive**
This refers to something that is different. This means a feature of a person or thing.

There are two **distinct** cell types.

She had a **distinctive** voice.

historic **historical**
This refers to something famous in history. This means something linked to the past.

D-Day is an **historic** event.

The museum held **historical** relics.

regretful **regrettable**
This refers to the feeling of regret. This means to give rise to regret.

She was **regretful** for her actions.

The loss of jobs was **regrettable**.

Triple trouble

Sometimes, three words sound very similar but mean different things. In such cases, be extra careful to understand the differences between the three words and learn the spellings.

though
This means the same as the word *however*.

 or

through
This means into one end and out of the other.

 or

thorough
This refers to something that is well done or complete.

He still wanted to go shopping, **though**.

He walked **through** the crowd.

He conducted a **thorough** investigation.

quit
This means to leave, usually permanently.

 or

quiet
This refers to making little or no noise.

 or

quite
This usually refers to the greatest extent or degree.

The journalist **quit** her job at the newspaper.

It seemed eerily **quiet** along the street.

The story made **quite** an impression on her.

More confused meanings

There are many examples of words that are widely and repeatedly misspelt because their meanings are not clearly understood. Always re-read the sentence to make sure the correct word is used.

Word	Example
accident	The bicycle **accident** left her with a large bruise.
angel	The religious text mentioned an **angel**.
desert	It was very hot in the middle of the **desert**.
elicit	The father tried to **elicit** a response from his son.
envelop	The fog was about to **envelop** the town.
lightening	The hairdresser was **lightening** my hair.
rational	There was no **rational** reason for her behaviour.

Word	Example
incident	There was an **incident** of bullying on the team.
angle	Every **angle** in a square is the same size.
dessert	My favourite **dessert** is key lime pie.
illicit	The airport confiscated **illicit** food from the man.
envelope	He put the letter in an **envelope**.
lightning	The **lightning** storm caused havoc.
rationale	She explained the **rationale** for her decision.

Funny puns

Tabloid newspapers are renowned for their use of puns in headlines. Puns take advantage of the potential confusion between words that sound the same to create jokes or wry commentary.

Abbreviations

A WORD OR PHRASE THAT IS WRITTEN IN A
SHORTENED FORM IS CALLED AN ABBREVIATION.

SEE ALSO

❰ 94–95 Full stops and ellipses
❰ 158–159 Capital letters
❰ 164–165 Irregular word spellings
Picking the right words 182–183 ❱

The English language contains many abbreviations,
which are used to represent longer words or phrases
in speech, or where space is limited. In some cases,
the abbreviation is better known than the full name.

The symbol @ is an abbreviation for
"at" and is used in **e-mail addresses**
and **text messsages**.

Common abbreviations

The way an abbreviation is written
usually depends on the category
to which it belongs. Often, a full
stop is used to represent missing
text. For abbreviated Latin phrases,
full stops are used after each letter.
Abbreviations that are formed from
the initial letters of a group of words
usually don't use full stops.

REAL WORLD

NASA

One of the world's most recognised abbreviations is
the name of the American government agency NASA,
which stands for the National Aeronautics and Space
Administration. The first letter from each word forms
this acronym – an abbreviation that is pronounced as
a word, not as separate letters. The NASA logo shown
here is on the side of a space shuttle.

Abbreviation	Words in full
3-D	three-dimensional
a.m.	*ante meridiem* (Latin); before noon (English)
b.	born (indicating birth date)
BCE	before the Common Era
Brit	British
C	Centigrade or Celsius
CE	Common Era
dept.	department
DIY	do-it-yourself
ed.	edition or editor
e.g.	*exempli gratia* (Latin); for example (English)
est.	established or estimated
EST	Eastern Standard Time
etc.	*et cetera* (Latin); and the rest (English)
EU	European Union
F	Fahrenheit
FAQ	frequently asked questions
GMT	Greenwich Mean Time
HTML	HyperText Markup Language

Abbreviation	Words in full
i.e.	*id est* (Latin); that is (English)
IOU	I owe you
LED	light-emitting diode
long.	longitude
MD	medical doctor
Mr.	Mister
Mrs.	Mistress (referring to wife)
PDF	Portable Document Format
per cent	*per centum* (Latin); in each hundred (English)
p.m.	*post meridiem* (Latin); after noon (English)
PM	Prime Minister
Pres.	President
P.S.	*post scriptum* (Latin); written after (English)
PTO	please turn over
SMS	Short Message Service
UK	United Kingdom
US	United States
USB	Universal Serial Bus
www	World Wide Web

Shortenings

A shortening is a representation of a single word, typically in lower-case letters. Usually, the beginning or the end of a word is dropped; in rare cases, both the beginning and end of a word are omitted. The use of a full stop depends on whether the abbreviation is formal or informal. Occasionally, shortening results in spelling changes, as when *bicycle* is changed to *bike*.

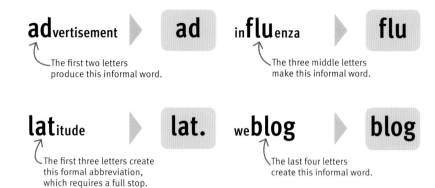

advertisement ▶ **ad**

The first two letters produce this informal word.

in**flu**enza ▶ **flu**

The three middle letters make this informal word.

latitude ▶ **lat.**

The first three letters create this formal abbreviation, which requires a full stop.

we**blog** ▶ **blog**

The last four letters create this informal word.

Contracted abbreviations

A contracted abbreviation occurs when letters from the middle of a word are removed. These words are usually related to a position or qualification. This type of abbreviation usually begins with a capital letter. A full stop is normally used at the end of a contracted abbreviation.

Docto**r** ▶ **Dr.**

Take out the middle four letters to get this abbreviation.

Junio**r** ▶ **Jr.**

Remove the middle four letters to form this abbreviation.

Limit**ed** ▶ **Ltd.**

Remove the letters *imi* and *e* to make this abbreviation.

Ser**g**ean**t** ▶ **Sgt.**

Remove the letters *er* and *ean* to create this abbreviation.

Initialisms

An initialism is created from the first letter of each word. Each letter is pronounced separately and written in capital letters. Initialisms generally don't require full stop between the letters.

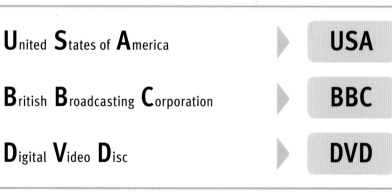

United **S**tates of **A**merica ▶ **USA**

British **B**roadcasting **C**orporation ▶ **BBC**

Digital **V**ideo **D**isc ▶ **DVD**

Acronyms

An acronym is a word formed from the initial letters of a group of words. It is different from an initialism because it's pronounced as it is spelt, not as separate letters. Acronyms are written in capital letters and without full stops.

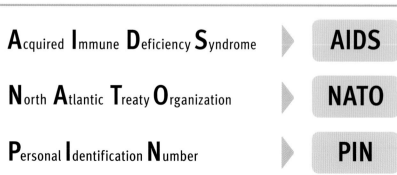

Acquired **I**mmune **D**eficiency **S**yndrome ▶ **AIDS**

North **A**tlantic **T**reaty **O**rganization ▶ **NATO**

Personal **I**dentification **N**umber ▶ **PIN**

British and American spellings

BRITISH AND AMERICAN WORDS ARE OFTEN SPELT
USING DIFFERENT ENDINGS.

In British English, the *l* is often doubled before a suffix, but not in
American English. Words that end in -ise, -yse, -ce, -re and -our
in British English may also be spelt differently in American English.

SEE ALSO

❮ **142–143** Prefixes and suffixes

❮ **154–155** Single and double consonant words

English-language
spelling was first
standardised by the
English writer **Samuel
Johnson** in 1755.

Doubling the letter *l*

Words that are written with a double *l*
in British English are often written
with only a single *l* in American English.
This usually occurs when a suffix,
such as -or, -ed, -er or -ing, is added
to a word ending in a single *l*.

British English	American English
cancelled	canceled
counsellor	counselor
fuelled	fueled
jeweller	jeweler
marvelled	marveled
modelling	modeling
quarrelled	quarreled
traveller	traveler

Words ending in -ise or -ize and -yse or -yze

Most words that end with -ise or -yse in British
English end with -ize or -yze in American
English. However, the -ize and -yze spellings
are also widely used in Britain.

British English	American English
analyse	analyze
criticise	criticize
hypnotise	hypnotize
mobilise	mobilize
modernise	modernize
organise	organize
recognise	recognize
visualise	visualize

Words ending in -ce or -se

Certain words that end with -ce in British
English end with -se in American English.
Depending on the part of speech, some words,
such as *practice* and *licence*, are spelt in two
different ways in British English, whereas
this distinction is ignored in American English.

British English	American English
defence	defense
licence (noun); license (verb)	license (noun and verb)
offence	offense
pretence	pretense
practice (noun); practise (verb)	practice (noun and verb)

Words ending in -re or -er

Many British words that end with -re are spelt with -er in American English. This difference is commonly seen in the spelling of metric measurements, such as *metre* and *litre* in British English, compared with *meter* and *liter* in American English.

British English	American English
calibre	caliber
centre	center
fibre	fiber
lustre	luster
meagre	meager
sombre	somber
spectre	specter
theatre	theater

Words ending in -our or -or

Words that end with -our in British English often end with -or in American English. However, in British English, when one of the endings -ous, -ious, -ary, -ation, -ific, -ize or -ise is added to a noun that ends in -our, the -our is usually changed to -or. For example, *humour* becomes *humorous*, and *glamour* becomes *glamorise*.

British English	American English
behaviour	behavior
colour	color
flavour	flavor
humour	humor
labour	labor
neighbour	neighbor
rumour	rumor
vigour	vigor

Same spelling

Many British and American words are also spelt the same, regardless of the rules. In most cases, there is no reason for this and the words just have to be learnt. If uncertain, check how words are spelt in a dictionary.

rebelled   **endurance**   **feather**

mediocre

advertise   **exercise**

fooling   **actor**

Webster's Dictionary

Noah Webster (1758–1843) is frequently credited with introducing American spelling. Webster wanted to emphasise a unique American cultural identity by showing that Americans spoke a different language from the British. He also advocated spelling words phonetically. In 1828, he published *An American Dictionary of the English Language*, which forms the basis of American spelling to this day.

- American and British spellings are both **correct**, as long as one or the other is used **consistently**.

- Occasionally, American English uses the British spelling for **names**, as in the case of the space shuttle *Endeavour* or **Ford's Theatre** in Washington, D.C.

More British and American spellings

SPELLING DIFFERENCES BETWEEN BRITISH AND AMERICAN
ENGLISH CAN SOMETIMES AFFECT A WORD'S PRONUNCIATION.

SEE ALSO

❬ **142–143** Prefixes and suffixes
❬ **146–147** Words ending in -e or -y
❬ **154–155** Single and double consonant words
❬ **160–161** Silent letters
❬ **162–163** Compound words

Small differences between British and American spellings do not
usually change the meaning of a word. However, British English
may use two words to indicate two meanings, whereas American
English uses the same word for both meanings.

Different sounds or words

A minor change in the spelling of a word
can affect its sound, even if the meaning
is the same. Occasionally, British and
American English use different words
to mean the same thing.

British English	American English
aeroplane	airplane
aluminium	aluminum
disorientated	disoriented
pavement	sidewalk
sledge	sleigh or sled

Different meanings

Sometimes, British English uses two
words that sound the same but with
different spellings to indicate different
meanings. American English uses the
same word for both meanings.

The *Oxford English Dictionary* is widely thought
to be the **authority** on the English language and
includes both **British** and **American** spellings.

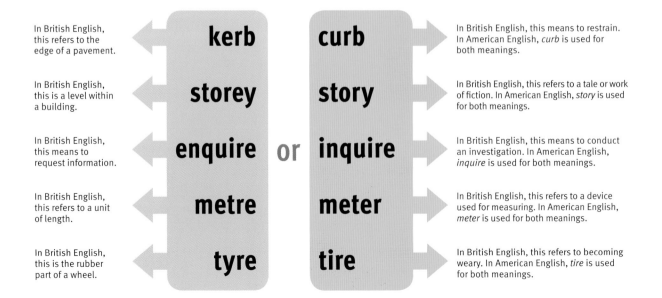

In British English, this refers to the edge of a pavement.

kerb or **curb**

In British English, this means to restrain. In American English, *curb* is used for both meanings.

In British English, this is a level within a building.

storey or **story**

In British English, this refers to a tale or work of fiction. In American English, *story* is used for both meanings.

In British English, this means to request information.

enquire or **inquire**

In British English, this means to conduct an investigation. In American English, *inquire* is used for both meanings.

In British English, this refers to a unit of length.

metre or **meter**

In British English, this refers to a device used for measuring. In American English, *meter* is used for both meanings.

In British English, this is the rubber part of a wheel.

tyre or **tire**

In British English, this refers to becoming weary. In American English, *tire* is used for both meanings.

Silent vowels

In British English, some words have two vowels in a row, one of which is silent. In American English, this silent vowel is usually dropped.

British English	American English
anaemia	anemia
foetus	fetus
manoeuvre	maneuver
paediatric	pediatric
palaeontology	paleontology

Past tenses ending in -ed or -t

When verbs are written in the past tense, their spellings can differ between British and American English. This is mainly the case with verbs in which the last letter is *l*, *m* or *n*. American English uses the regular ending -ed, whereas British English often uses the irregular ending -t.

British English	American English
burnt or burned	burned
dreamt or dreamed	dreamed
learnt or learned	learned
smelt or smelled	smelled
spelt or spelled	spelled

Retaining or dropping the silent -e

Certain words in American English do not have a silent -e ending, while British spelling usually retains the silent -e. This pattern occurs most commonly when a suffix, such as -ment, has been added to a word that ends in a silent -e.

British English	American English
acknowledgement	acknowledgment
ageing or aging	aging
axe	ax
judgement	judgment
useable or usable	usable

• Some words that are **hyphenated** in British English are **compound words** in American English. For example, British English uses *ear-splitting* and *kind-hearted*, while American English uses *earsplitting* and *kindhearted*.

REAL WORLD
Mid-Atlantic English

In the early part of the twentieth century, many American actors, such as Katharine Hepburn, tried to cultivate an accent that was neither obviously American nor British. This was sometimes called "mid-Atlantic English". The fashion for this accent has disappeared, and today the term is used to refer to written English that avoids obvious "Britishisms" or "Americanisms".

Communication skills

Effective communication

GOOD COMMUNICATION SENDS THE RIGHT MESSAGE.

To communicate means to exchange ideas and information with others. Communicating effectively means exchanging ideas and information with others in such a way that they understand precisely what is meant.

Everyday communication

Communicating effectively isn't just about writing an A-grade essay. People need to pass on information in many different scenarios every day. Most communication has a desired effect: for example, to give the recipient information or to persuade them to do something.

> **Sending an invitation**
> Giving a friend advice
> **Making a complaint**
> Giving travel directions
> **Selling an item on the Internet**
> Auditioning for a play

Good communication skills can help in many different situations.

Getting the message

Bad communication will not have the desired effect. For example, an unclear recipe will produce an inedible cake, a lacklustre political speech will lose votes and an incomplete party invitation will confuse the intended guests, who may fail to turn up.

This invitation does not specify what time or where the party is taking place.

I'm having a party next Saturday. It would be great to see you there. Remember to dress up.

The term *dress up* is vague and could even mean fancy dress.

This version gives precise details about the time and location.

Please join me to celebrate my birthday on

Saturday 14 July at 7 p.m.

My address is
13 York Rd, Thornbridge, TH12 2HE.

The dress code is formal.

The exact dress code is specified.

Sending the right message

In order to send clear and effective messages, it's important to consider various factors.

LET'S PARTY!

Don't miss the
celebration of the year on

Saturday 14 July at 7 p.m.

There will be **food,
dancing, fireworks, magic**
and **much, much more.**

My address is
13 York Rd, Thornbridge, TH12 2HE.

HOW TO GET HERE

Tone

Tone refers to the mood or feeling of a piece of writing. The tone should be selected according to the purpose of the text. For example, a party invitation should be enthusiastic, an advice column should be sympathetic and a business letter should be formal and serious.

Language

Effective communication should be written using appropriate language. The choice of vocabulary and sentence structures will help to communicate the right message.

Layout

The font size and colour, the arrangement of text on the page and the use of images can simplify a message or draw attention to pieces of information. The layout of some forms of communication, such as newspaper articles and letters, follows specific conventions.

Method

It's important to pick the right method of communication, such as an e-mail, newspaper article or leaflet. People also communicate verbally in a debate or by giving a speech. Non-verbal methods of communication, such as body language and eye contact, should also be considered.

This sounds fun...

Audience

A message needs to be tailored to its audience. For example, a piece of writing for young children may use simple and fun language, whereas an adult audience will understand more complicated vocabulary.

Purpose

All communication has a purpose. This is the effect that the message should have on the audience. For example, it may be to encourage them to go to a party, to give them advice or to pass on news.

Picking the right words

EFFECTIVE COMMUNICATION USES VARIED AND APPROPRIATE VOCABULARY.

It's important to pick words that are clear and suit the purpose and audience of the text. Using the same words all the time can be boring, so try to use a varied range of vocabulary.

Avoid overused words

Using a wide range of vocabulary makes a piece of writing more entertaining and original. Here are some overused words to avoid, such as *got* and *great*, and some alternatives, known as synonyms.

very

pleasant
charming   agreeable

incredibly   truly
unusually
extremely   delightful

countless
numerous
many
myriad

acquired
obtained
received

nice

thrilling
entertaining
amusing
enjoyable

lots of

wonderful
fabulous   incredible
fantastic

got

great

finally
later   next
then

fun

- **Look up** any **new** words and find out what they mean. Then, write them down and try to use them in the **future**.

Less is more

It's important not to use several words when one will do. Overly long phrases might seem impressive, but they are often unclear. Most long phrases can be replaced with shorter versions.

Military jargon

Members of the armed forces use jargon to communicate with one another for speed and secrecy. Many of these terms are abbreviations of longer phrases. For example, *DPV* is the abbreviation for "Desert Patrol Vehicle".

Unclear version	Concise version
she is of the opinion that	she thinks that
concerning the matter of	about
in the event that	if
regardless of the fact that	although
due to the fact that	because
in all cases	always
he is a man who	he
a small number of	a few

How formal

The words people use depend on the situation they're in and the person they're talking to. In informal situations, people tend to use colloquial words, but when writing to someone they don't know, or someone in authority, they use formal vocabulary.

> Hey, man. This homework sucks. I just don't get it.

A text message to a friend can include slang, such as "Hey, man" and "sucks".

> Dear Mrs. Jones,
>
> Jake experienced some difficulties in completing last night's homework. Although he tried very hard, he could not understand the exercise. He may need some extra help so that he can finish the work.
>
> Yours sincerely,
> Sheila Jessop

A letter to a teacher should be written in formal language.

Word play

Writers also choose words to entertain readers. By using particular combinations of words, they can create humour and sound patterns. There are three main types of word play: puns, alliteration and assonance.

Puns

A pun is a play on words. It exploits the multiple meanings of a word, or similar sounding words, to create humour.

Once **a pun** a time...

Alliteration

Alliteration is the effect created when words next to or close to each other begin with the same letter or sound. It is often used in newspaper headlines.

Thomas Turner tripped over the **table**.

Assonance

Assonance is the effect created by the repetition of vowel sounds. It is often used in poetry.

Is it **true you** like **blue**?

Getting technical

Jargon is the term for words or phrases that are only used and understood by members of a particular group or profession. For example, doctors, lawyers and sports professionals use certain terms to communicate quickly and effectively. However, it's best to avoid using jargon outside of these circles, because it can be meaningless to other people.

Get me his **vitals**.

Doctors use this term to refer to patients' vital statistics, such as their pulse, body temperature and breathing rate.

Making sentences interesting

THE BEST PIECES OF WRITING USE SENTENCES THAT ARE CLEAR BUT ALSO INTERESTING TO READ.

A text containing very similar sentences will be boring to read. Using a variety of sentence types with plenty of detail will make a piece of writing more engaging.

Pick and mix

Good writers vary the types of sentences that they use in their work. Lots of short sentences can make a piece of writing monotonous and disjointed. Using some longer sentences instead helps the writing flow and links ideas together. There are three main types of sentences to choose from.

This compound sentence has two main clauses linked by the conjunction *and*.

This simple sentence contains the subject *monster* and the main verb *was*.

A monster was on the loose. It came out at night and its howls filled the air. People said that the monster had green fur and red eyes, although no one had ever seen it.

This complex sentence contains a main clause and a subordinate clause.

Change of pace

Rather than using a random mixture of sentences, it's possible to select a particular type of sentence for effect – for example, to change the pace or add tension or excitement.

A long sentence in a speech can reinforce the seriousness of a problem.

She began to run. The monster followed. Her heart was racing. The monster wasn't far behind. She had to make a decision. She jumped into the lake.

Pulling herself out of the water, she could see light from the cottage in the distance. She scrambled up the riverbank, and ran through the mud, under the oak trees, around the bend in the road and up the path. She was home.

"If we don't all gather together and track down the bloodthirsty monster, our children will not be safe on the streets and we will not be able to sleep sound in our beds. We need to act now."

A string of short sentences in a story can create excitement.

Using a short sentence after a very long one can relieve tension.

Following the long sentence with a short sentence can make a powerful final point.

A fresh start

Good writers avoid starting all the sentences in a paragraph in the same way because it sounds monotonous. Sentences can easily be rewritten to stop this from happening.

All these sentences start with the same word, *there*.

There was a chill in the air as Jessica walked through the woods. There was nobody around. There was a sudden growl in the distance.

This passage gives exactly the same information, but in a more interesting way.

There was a chill in the air as Jessica walked through the woods. Nobody was around. Suddenly, she heard a growl in the distance.

Add detail

Adding extra detail using adjectives and adverbs will make a sentence more informative and interesting. The position of an adverb can also be changed to vary the sentence structure.

This sentence isn't very interesting.

Jessica backed away from the monster.

Adding an adverb tells the reader about the way the girl is moving. The adjective describes the mood of the monster.

*Jessica **nervously** backed away from the **angry** monster.*

Moving the adverb changes the structure of the sentence.

***Nervously**, Jessica backed away from the **angry** monster.*

GLOSSARY

Main clause A group of words that contains a subject and a verb and makes complete sense on its own.

Subordinate clause A group of words that contains a subject and a verb but depends on a main clause for its meaning.

• Add more detail to a sentence by using **prepositions**, which tell the reader **where** something is or **when** something is happening. Prepositions include *about*, *across*, *after*, *at* and *under*.

• Use a variety of **conjunctions** to link clauses and make sentences **flow** from one to another. These are **connecting words**, such as *so*, *because*, *until*, *whereas* and *but*.

REAL WORLD

Exciting commentary

Sports commentators often describe the events of a game or race with very short sentences. This makes the commentary as fast-paced and exciting as the event itself. It's particularly effective for radio commentaries when listeners can't see the action, but are relying on the commentary to create the mood.

Planning and research

IT'S ESSENTIAL TO PLAN A PIECE OF WRITING.

Good writers always plan their work – on paper rather than in their heads. Planning helps a writer generate ideas, organise them into a clear structure and avoid leaving anything out.

First scribbles

The best way to start planning a project is to jot down any relevant ideas, words and phrases. One method is to use a mind map. At this stage in the planning process, it's useful to think of as many relevant ideas as possible – they can be cut down later.

▷ **Map out ideas**
A mind map is a visual method of writing down notes. The free structure of a mind map can make it a very effective way to generate ideas. However, a simple list is also fine.

Rising obesity levels

Quote from athlete

Make new friends

Why young people need to do more exercise

Improve fitness

Prevent disease

Develop a talent

The idea for the piece of writing goes in the middle.

Ideas are written around the edge.

• Use **official** or well-known publications or websites for research to ensure that the information is **accurate**.

• Try to **cross-reference** any facts or statistics with another source for accuracy.

• Keep a file called "Bibliography" open whenever working on a project and **regularly update** it.

Research

It's important to research a piece of writing in order to gain a good overall understanding of a topic, and to gather specific examples, quotations or statistics. Sources for research include books, websites and newspapers. To avoid plagiarism (copying someone else's work), always rephrase the sentences.

▷ **Neat notes**
Notes should be neat, tidy and as detailed as possible. Untidy or incomplete notes will hinder the writing process, and the information may have to be found again.

Write down the source for each statistic, quotation and fact.

At a later stage, colour code each note to show which paragraph it will be used in.

Put inverted commas around quotations now to avoid plagiarism later.

Worldwide obesity has more than doubled since 1980. (World Health Organization Report, 2012)

"Physical inactivity is an independent risk factor for coronary heart disease – in other words, if you don't exercise, you dramatically increase your risk of dying from a heart attack when you're older."
Dr. John Hobbs

Bibliography

When doing research, it's essential to keep a running list of sources by creating a document called a bibliography. This should include all books, magazines, websites and television programmes used for the project. Each source should go on a single line, with a comma between each detail and a full stop at the end.

Put the author's last name first.

The book title should be in italics or underlined.

Find the publisher and the publication date on one of the first few pages of the book.

Roberts, Alice, _The Complete Human Body Book_, London: Dorling Kindersley, 2010.

John Hobbs, Doctor, interviewed on 3/3/2013.

http://www.who.int/dietphysicalactivity/childhood/en/

Include the full addresses of any websites.

Include the details of any people who were interviewed.

The plan

The next stage is to organise the ideas and research into a clear structure using paragraphs. A piece of writing needs to start with an introduction that states what the work is about. Each new idea forms a new paragraph. Finally, a conclusion sums everything up. Paragraphs need to follow a clear progression: for example, in order of importance or chronology (date order).

A plan should include the main points that will be made in each paragraph.

It isn't necessary to use full sentences in a plan, but always use complete sentences when writing the final piece.

It's useful to give each paragraph a colour and go back to the notes and colour each note according to which paragraph it relates to. This will make it easier to find the right notes during writing.

Introduction
Background information. How young people today do less exercise than ever. This is linked to bad health and delinquency. Include shocking statistics.

1. It's easy to change
Exercise like running, starting a football team and walking is cheap and doesn't need equipment. It doesn't take up much time – give figures.

2. Health benefits
Exercise makes you happier, helps you lose weight, improves fitness levels. Include some statistics.

3. Social benefits
Team sports are sociable – young people will mix with others and make more friends. Keeps young people out of trouble. Encourages healthy competitive and team spirit.

4. Long-term benefits
A generation with fewer health problems. More success in professional sports.

Conclusion
How the worrying situation discussed in the introduction could change. Vision for the future. Quote from Olympic champion.

▷ **Going according to plan**
Using a plan will keep a piece of writing focused. However, it is common to add, take out or move ideas around during writing.

Paragraphing

PARAGRAPHS ARE USED TO ORGANISE A PIECE OF WRITING.

It's important to structure a long piece of writing, such as an essay, article or letter, into paragraphs. This will break up the text into separate points, which will make it easier to read.

SEE ALSO

‹ **58–59** Conjunctions

‹ **184–185** Making sentences interesting

‹ **186–187** Planning and research

Reading and commenting on texts **192–193** ›

> Starting an introduction with a question will catch the reader's attention.

> One way of starting a new paragraph is to indent the first line.

> This paragraph is about the health benefits of exercise.

What's your excuse? Perhaps you don't like getting sweaty, you have no time or you're just plain lazy. Whatever the reason, you're not alone; fewer and fewer young people are doing enough exercise. However, sport offers numerous health and social benefits, so it's time to stop complaining and get moving.

...Thus, regular exercise can not only improve your long-term health, but can also make you feel happier and less stressed out.

In addition to the health benefits, doing sport can improve your social life. It is an opportunity to see your friends on a regular basis and to meet new people by joining a team.

> The next sentence are about social benefits, so they start in a new paragraph.

A good start

The opening paragraph should state what a piece of writing is about. It also needs to grab the reader's attention so that he or she wants to read on. The first line should be something strong and original, such as a quotation, a rhetorical question or a statistic.

The great American basketball player Michael Jordan once said, "I can accept failure, but I can't accept not trying."

> Start an introduction with a famous or memorable quotation.

Are you putting yourself at risk? People who don't do enough exercise dramatically increase their risk of developing heart disease.

> Use a shocking fact to make an impact.

New idea, new paragraph

All the sentences in a paragraph should be related to one another. A new point of discussion requires a new paragraph. Start the new paragraph by indenting the first few words of the text or by leaving a line.

> Another way to start a new paragraph is to leave a line.

...Thus, regular exercise can not only improve your long-term health, but can also make you feel happier and less stressed out.

In addition to the health benefits, doing sport can improve your social life. It is an opportunity to see your friends on a regular basis and to meet new people by joining a team.

Once upon a time...

Fiction writers need to write good opening lines to draw readers into the story. For example, the author J.K. Rowling starts the first chapter of *Harry Potter and the Deathly Hallows* with the lines: "The two men appeared out of nowhere, a few yards apart in the narrow, moonlit lane."

— CHAPTER ONE —

The Dark Lord Ascending

Topic sentences

It can be effective to start a paragraph with a topic sentence. This is a statement that introduces the main idea in the paragraph. The rest of the paragraph needs to expand or give evidence to back up the topic sentence. This method can help to keep a piece of writing focused.

The health benefits of regular exercise cannot be ignored.

This bold statement is a topic sentence. The rest of the paragraph will discuss the health benefits that it refers to.

Overall, there is no excuse. Doing regular exercise will reduce your chances of developing heart disease and other serious illnesses. In the short term, it will make you fitter, happier and more energetic. Finally, it is an excellent way to meet new people, have fun and perhaps discover a new talent.

A conclusion should make a decisive final statement.

Link a conclusion back to points in the introduction to give the piece cohesion.

• Referring **back** to points made in previous paragraphs makes a piece of writing more **connected** because it shows that the piece has been considered as a whole.

• Do not make **completely new** points in a conclusion.

Seamless links

A good piece of writing should be cohesive. This means that the sentences, paragraphs and ideas are all linked together in a flowing way. Sentences and paragraphs can be connected using linking words or phrases. However, use these sparingly.

A lasting impression

A conclusion should summarise the main points made in a piece of writing and make a decisive judgement about the topic. It should refer back to the original question and, ideally, any points made in the introduction. A sophisticated conclusion can end by referring to the wider implications of the question, and leave the reader with something to think about.

A conclusion should repeat the main points.

If you start now, perhaps you could be climbing the Olympic podium one day.

A final, memorable statement in a piece of writing is sometimes called a "clincher".

on the other hand **by contrast** **however** **nevertheless**	**therefore** **thus** **as a result of** **accordingly**
to contrast one idea with another	to give logical reasons
first **next** **first of all** **finally**	**also** **moreover** **furthermore** **in addition**
to order ideas in a sequence	to develop an idea

Genre, purpose and audience

ALL NON-FICTION TEXTS HAVE A CLEAR GENRE, PURPOSE AND AUDIENCE.

SEE ALSO

❮ **86–87** Colloquialisms and slang
❮ **180–181** Effective communication
❮ **182–183** Picking the right words
❮ **186–187** Planning and research
Reading and commenting on texts   **192–193** ❯

Writers need to consider what type of text they are writing, as well as for whom they are writing and why. These factors influence the presentation style and language used.

Genre

A non-fiction text is one based on facts, rather than a story. The different types, or genres, of non-fiction text all have their own features and conventions. For example, a newspaper or magazine article will have a headline at the top and text written in columns, whereas a letter includes the sender's address at the top.

Newspaper stories are written in columns with a headline at the top.

Leaflets are sheets of paper folded into three, with information on each segment.

Letters can be formal or informal, but both types are laid out with the sender's address at the top.

Advertisement

Website

Newspaper article

Blog

Leaflet

GENRE

Script

Speech

Letter

The genre, purpose and audience of a text need to be considered together. All three factors influence the features of a piece of writing.

Purpose

The purpose of a text is the reason that it was written. For example, an encyclopedia entry about Paris is supposed to inform the reader, whereas an advertisement for a holiday in Paris is intended to persuade the reader to visit. Even though they are about the same subject, these two texts would have very different features.

Texts written to inform contain lots of facts and need to be very clear.

Pieces of advice will have a sympathetic tone.

Persuasive texts contain opinions.

• Sometimes a text can be written for **more than one purpose**. An advertisement for spot cream might give customers **advice** about their skin, but will also try to **persuade** them to buy the product.

To inform

To advise

PURPOSE

To influence

To analyse

To describe

GLOSSARY

Adjective A describing word that tells the reader more about a noun.

Colloquialism A word or phrase used in informal speech.

Fact A statement that can be proved.

Jargon Specialist terms that are understood and used by a select, often professional, group of people.

Slang Words and phrases that are used in informal speech and often only understood by a select group of people.

REAL WORLD
Television audiences

Television advertising executives design advertisements to appeal to their target audience. For example, they might use actors who remind viewers of themselves. They will also aim to show the advertisements during television programmes that are related to their product. So, advertisements for new food products might be shown during the break in a cookery show because people who watch cookery shows are more likely to buy food products.

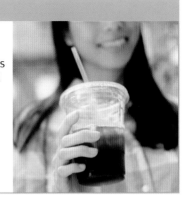

Teachers

Adults

A text written for a particular group of professionals can use terms that only they will understand.

Environmentalists

A piece written for a group of people who believe in something strongly can reinforce and flatter their opinions.

AUDIENCE

General public

Something written for a general audience should be simple enough to be understood by everyone. However, it should not be patronising, because it needs to appeal to adults as well as children.

Teenagers

Young children

In some languages, such as French, speakers use **different words** depending on **who** they are talking to. For example, the French word for "you" is *tu* in an **informal** situation, but it is *vous* in a **formal** situation.

Audience

A non-fiction text always has a target audience. For example, it might be for adults, teenagers or children. It could be for people with a particular interest or specialist knowledge, or it may be designed to appeal to a general audience. The key aspects of the text need to be tailored to attract this target audience.

Audience	Some common features
Adults	Sophisticated vocabulary, longer sentences, detailed subject matter, smaller font size, longer pieces of writing, formal tone and language
Young children	Simple vocabulary, short sentences, larger font size, simple subject matter, pictures and colour to keep them interested
Teenagers	Slang, colloquial language, informal tone, humour, subject matter that seems relevant to them
Professionals	Jargon or specialist terms that are understood by them

Reading and commenting on texts

IT'S USEFUL TO BE ABLE TO INTERPRET AND WRITE ABOUT
DIFFERENT PIECES OF WRITING.

SEE ALSO

❮ **88–89** Direct and indirect speech

❮ **102–103** Colons

❮ **108–109** Inverted commas

❮ **190–191** Genre, purpose and audience

Layout and presentational features **194–195** ❯

Writing to influence **202–203** ❯

When answering a question about a text, a writer needs to understand
the question, find the right information in the text and use it to write
a focused answer.

Understand the question

The first step is to read the question
and understand what it is asking.
Even a well-crafted answer will get
no marks if it does not answer the
question. Underlining the key words
in the question will make it easier
to focus on what is being asked.

This question only asks about
the opening paragraph, so don't make
comments about the rest of the text.

What do you learn from the opening paragraph about...

What are the four main reasons that the writer gives...

How does the writer use language to persuade the reader that...

This question is asking specifically
about language, so there is no need
to write about presentation.

The right information

The next stage is to read the text and
look for the relevant information or
features. It is useful to underline
the words, sentences or passages
that will help answer the question.
Sometimes a question will refer to
two texts.

TEXT 1

Are your parents always nagging you to eat breakfast?
Well, this time they're right. In the morning, your body
needs fuel, just like a car. Once you've filled up, you'll
be ready to hit the road.

compares the body to a car

Underline sections
that will be useful
when writing
an answer.

Write observations
and notes around
the text.

This extract has the same subject
matter as Text 1, but is written in
complex, scientific language.

• **Read** the whole text first. It
is important to get an **overall idea**
of what the text is about before
analysing the details.

• Refer to the text frequently, but be
selective – don't copy out whole
chunks of text.

• Become more **familiar** with
different types of texts and the
techniques they use by **reading**
texts from **everyday life**, such as
newspapers and even junk mail.

TEXT 2

Recent studies outline the many health benefits of eating a
nutritious breakfast. In the morning, the body's glycogen
stores start to deplete. Without breakfast, a person soon
begins to feel fatigued.

Provide evidence

When writing about a text, every point made must be backed up with evidence. This can be made up of a quotation (the exact words from the text), or a reference (a description of the pictures, structure or layout). A quotation must be surrounded by inverted commas to separate it from the answer.

The first extract was written to persuade young children to eat a healthy breakfast. It starts by asking the reader a question: "Are your parents always nagging you to eat breakfast?" The writer has also used phrases such as "fuel", "filled up" and "hit the road", to compare the process of eating breakfast to the process of filling a car up with fuel.

Long quotations need to be preceded by a colon. If it is longer than four lines, leave a line before the quotation.

Short quotations can be embedded in the text.

Explain why

After giving an example, it is essential to explain what it shows about the text. This will make the point clear.

This answer gives an example.

The writer has used words such as "fuel", "filled up" and "hit the road" to compare eating breakfast to filling a car up with fuel. This simple comparison makes the process easier for young children to understand. It also makes the text more fun, so it will hold a young audience's attention.

It then explains why this feature of the text is effective.

Fact or opinion?

Facts are pieces of information that can be proved. Opinions are what people believe or think. It is important to see the difference between fact and opinion when figuring out the purpose of a text. In general, informative texts use facts, whereas persuasive texts use personal opinions. Sometimes a text will use both.

This statement is presented as a fact, but it is actually an opinion because not everyone would agree with it.

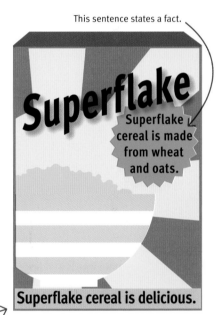

This sentence states a fact.

Superflake

Superflake cereal is made from wheat and oats.

Superflake cereal is delicious.

Comparing texts

When comparing two texts, do not write about one text and then the other. Comparisons must be drawn between the two, which means picking out the similarities and differences. Some useful terms for making comparisons include *both texts*, *similarly*, *by contrast*, *on the other hand*, *whereas* and *in comparison*.

These words help to compare and contrast the two texts.

***Both** texts are about the importance of a nutritious breakfast and both try to persuade the reader to eat more healthily. However, they use very **different** language techniques. **Whereas** the first text, for young children, uses simple language and basic explanations, the second text, for adults, goes into much **more** detail and uses scientific terms such as "glycogen stores"...*

Layout and presentational features

THE WAY THAT A TEXT IS PRESENTED ADDS TO ITS OVERALL IMPACT.

Layout refers to the way that a text is organised on a page. Presentational features are the individual elements, such as pictures, headlines, fonts and colour.

Headline
Headlines sit at the top of newspaper and magazine articles, leaflets and sometimes advertisements. Headlines are usually in bold text and capital letters so that they stand out and attract the reader's attention.

Font
The font refers to the size, shape and colour of the text. Large fonts are often used for children because they are easier to read. Coloured text and fun shapes are also used for a young audience, whereas serious pieces of writing are printed in a small standard font. Bold and italic fonts are used to draw attention to headings or certain words and phrases.

MYSTERIOUS INTRUDERS

This subheading could be printed in a fun font if the article were for children.

Bullet points
Bullet points are used to break up a dense block of text into a clear list of individual points. This makes the information easier to read and absorb.

SUPERNATURA

Recently revealed statistics show a record number of supernatural sightings in the local area. The police have recorded 31 ghost sightings in the past five years, along with 25 reports of UFOs, 15 zombies, 10 vampires and eight witches.

MYSTERIOUS INTRUDERS

Often the calls appear to be serious incidents, such as intruders at a property, but then turn out to be something more mysterious. The police claim that the time spent answering the calls costs the force thousands of pounds every year.

More strange sights
• There have been 14 sightings of big cats in the past five years, as well as eight reported injuries blamed on big cats.

• Six people have claimed that they have seen a sea monster. Apparently, it resembles a huge alligator with purple scales.

• A ghost ship has been seen on four occasions on the harbour rocks. In 1876, a ship was wrecked on this exact spot.

Effective images

Charity advertisements often show images of the people or animals that they want to help. These are effective because they make the issue more real for the audience, and let them imagine the positive effect that their money would have for the cause.

We promise we'll never put down a healthy dog.

Please promise to help us with a gift in your Will.

Every year, Dogs Trust cares for around 16,000 dogs in our 18 rehoming centres across the UK. We never put down a healthy dog. By leaving a gift in your Will, your love of dogs can live on and help us make the world a better place for them.

IGHTINGS SURGE

| Ghosts | UFOs | Zombies | Vampires | Witches |

The most common supernatural sightings are of ghosts.

ZOMBIE WAS FILM EXTRA

Most of the sightings are easily and quickly explained. In 2011, a reported zombie sighting turned out to be a film extra taking his lunch break. Another caller raised the alarm after seeing something suspicious floating in the air on a Saturday night: "I saw a big, orange, glowing sphere rising from the ground." The sighting turned out to be a Chinese lantern.

"I saw a big, orange, glowing sphere rising from the ground."

• When analysing the layout of a piece, **don't just identify** the features – **explain why** they are **effective**.

Photographs and graphics

Images can be used for effect or to give more information. For example, an advertisement for a hair product might show a picture of a model with extremely glossy hair to persuade the audience to buy a new shampoo. A newspaper report about a terrible flood might show a photograph of the affected area to demonstrate exactly what has happened. Graphs and diagrams are used to make complicated topics or statistics clear.

Caption

Photographs and diagrams are usually accompanied by a short sentence that explains what the image is about. This is called a caption.

Subheading

Subheadings are used to break up a long text into shorter chunks, so that it's easier to read. They also summarise the content of the next paragraph, which helps the reader to find the section they're interested in reading.

Pull quote

Newspaper and magazine articles often include quotes from eyewitnesses or experts. To draw attention to particularly interesting quotes, the words can be lifted out from the article and repeated elsewhere on the page, usually in bolder or larger type.

Writing to inform

THE MAIN PURPOSE OF SOME PIECES OF WRITING IS TO GIVE THE READER INFORMATION.

Informative texts, such as leaflets, encyclopedias, newspaper reports and letters, give the reader information about a topic. Some texts also tell the reader how to do something, by giving instructions.

SEE ALSO

❮ **54–55** Voices and moods
❮ **116–117** Bullet points
❮ **194–195** Layout and presentational features
Newspaper articles   **198–199** ❯
Letters and e-mails   **200–201** ❯

Simple but detailed

Informative writing needs to give readers the details they need to know, and do so clearly. It should include lots of facts, presented in short paragraphs and using simple vocabulary.

Sierra Nevada of California

3.7 million visitors

A headline at the top of a leaflet tells the reader what it is about.

YOSEMITE
NATIONAL PARK

Yosemite National Park covers nearly 761,268 acres (3,081 sq km) of mountainous terrain in the Sierra Nevada of California. The park attracts more than 3.7 million visitors each year.

There are countles[s] ways to explore an[d] have fun in Yosem[ite] National Park.

Pictures of the place show the reader what it looks like and make the leaflet look attractive.

REAL WORLD

DIY dilemma

Sometimes people buy furniture in separate parts to be put together at home. The buyer needs to follow a set of instructions in order to assemble the item. Often, the instructions are not very clear, which can lead to a great deal of frustration.

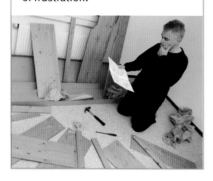

Bite-sized chunks

It's effective to break down detailed text into short sections, so that the information is easy to find and absorb. Subheadings are useful for guiding readers through the text and leading them to important details. Bullet points divide up the information even further.

Please remember:
- Stay on the trails.
- Drink plenty of water.
- Do not litter.

Bullet points divide up the information.

- Avoid using unnecessarily **complicated** language that may **obscure** the information.

- Use **adverbs**, such as *carefully* or *quickly*, in **instructions** to give the reader more information on **how** to do something.

Here are some of the activities we have to offer:

Biking
More than 19 km (12 miles) of paved cycle paths are available in the park.

Birdwatching
Try to spot some of the 262 species of birds recorded in Yosemite.

Hiking
Get your hiking boots on and explore the park by foot.

Fishing
Following the regulations, see what you can catch in the lakes and rivers.

Horse riding
Saddle up and enjoy the park's majestic views on horseback.

Please remember:
- # Stay on the trails.
- # Drink plenty of water.
- # Do not litter.

HOW TO GET HERE

Driving instructions
From San Francisco

1. Take the Bay Bridge (Interstate 80) east.
2. Take Interstate 580 east, following signs for Tracy/Stockton to Interstate 205.
3. Follow Interstate 205 to Highway 120.
4. Take Highway 120 into Yosemite National Park.

Numbered steps create an easy-to-follow sequence.

Not just a pretty picture

Adding images and colour makes an informative text look more fun, but can also make the details clearer. Diagrams and maps show the reader something, rather than just telling them.

Easy instructions

Instructions are a type of informative text. They include travel directions, recipes and product manuals. They are usually written in a numbered, step-by-step format. Commands are also used to give firm and clear instructions.

Commands tell the reader what to do.

Take Highway 120 into Yosemite National Park.

Newspaper articles

NEWSPAPERS INFORM AND ENTERTAIN THE READER.

Journalists use certain techniques to inform and engage their readers. The specific content and language used in an article depend on the type of publication and the intended audience.

Which paper?

Some newspapers focus on serious, in-depth articles, while other papers run more sensational stories, such as political scandals or celebrity gossip. The scope of a paper also affects its content. National newspapers report on national or global events, but regional newspapers focus on local community finances, politics and events, which are more relevant to local people.

MARKETS FALL AS ECONOMIC CRISIS CONTINUES

↖ Some newspapers choose to run serious stories.

HOLLYWOOD COUPLE SPLITS

↖ Other newspapers focus on celebrity stories.

SCHOOL TO CLOSE

↖ Local newspapers report local news.

A local grandmother was rescued from h[er] burning home on Saturday by her pet do[g]. Shirley Williams, 65, was in bed with the f[lu] when the blaze broke out at approximate[ly] 2 p.m., following an electrical fault.

Her golden retriever, Star, was in t[he] garden, but risked his life by boundi[ng]

Details, details, details

News articles need to explain what happened, where, why and who was involved. All good journalists include as many details as possible in their stories, such as names, ages and times.

Shirley Williams, 65, was in bed with the flu when the blaze broke out at approximately 2 p.m., following an electrical fault.

Drama

Newspapers often use exaggerated or dramatic language to catch the reader's attention and make an article more exciting to read.

blaze ↖ The word *blaze* sounds more dramatic than *fire*.

GLOSSARY

Alliteration The repetition of certain letters or sounds for effect.

Headline The statement at the top of an article that tells the reader what it is about.

Pun The use of a word or phrase that has two meanings for comic effect.

Quote To repeat the words of a person. Quotations need to be surrounded by inverted commas.

Sales of **printed newspapers** have **declined** in recent years because many people read the news **online.**

ERALD VH

RDOG

AVES SICK

GRANNY

the fire. He led her to safety through smoke and flames. Local firefighter Joe who later arrived at the scene, said, would have got there too late. That saved her life."

Shirley is recovering in hospital. The or has commended Star for his bravery.

Headlines

Headlines tell the reader what a story is about. They are short and dramatic and often use techniques such as alliteration or puns to grab attention and sell copies.

SUPERDOG SAVES SICK GRANNY

Using three words in a row beginning with the letter *s* creates a snappy headline.

Stay active

The news is usually written in the active rather than the passive voice. This is because sentences in the active voice are shorter, easier to read and convey a sense of immediacy, which makes the news sound more exciting.

he led her

The active voice makes the story sound immediate.

she was led

The passive voice would make the story less engaging.

In their words

Journalists quote experts to give a news story authority. They also interview and quote the people who were involved. This makes the story seem more real for the reader.

"That dog saved her life."

Short and snappy

People often read newspapers in a rush, so journalists need to get the information across quickly and simply. Sentences and paragraphs should be short and clear.

Shirley is recovering in hospital.

Letters and e-mails

LETTERS AND E-MAILS ARE FORMS OF CORRESPONDENCE
ADDRESSED TO A SPECIFIC PERSON OR GROUP.

Different types of correspondence are used in certain
situations, for different purposes. It is important to set
out each type correctly.

SEE ALSO

❮ **118–119** Numbers, dates and time
❮ **188–189** Paragraphing
❮ **196–197** Writing to inform
Writing to influence   **202–203** ❯
Writing to explain or advise   **204–205** ❯
Writing from personal experience   **210–211** ❯

Formal letters

Formal letters are written to someone the writer doesn't
know, or to someone in authority, such as a teacher or a
politician. Examples of formal letters include job application
letters and complaint letters. People send complaint letters
about faulty products or bad service in a hotel or restaurant.

The **first e-mail** was sent
in **1971**. Today, more
than **294 billion** e-mails
are sent every day.

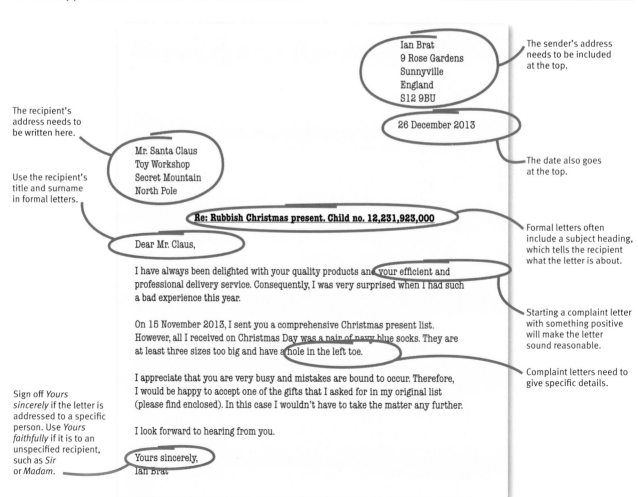

The sender's address
needs to be included
at the top.

Ian Brat
9 Rose Gardens
Sunnyville
England
S12 9BU

26 December 2013

The recipient's
address needs to
be written here.

The date also goes
at the top.

Mr. Santa Claus
Toy Workshop
Secret Mountain
North Pole

Use the recipient's
title and surname
in formal letters.

Re: Rubbish Christmas present. Child no. 12,231,923,000

Dear Mr. Claus,

Formal letters often
include a subject heading,
which tells the recipient
what the letter is about.

I have always been delighted with your quality products and your efficient and
professional delivery service. Consequently, I was very surprised when I had such
a bad experience this year.

Starting a complaint letter
with something positive
will make the letter
sound reasonable.

On 15 November 2013, I sent you a comprehensive Christmas present list.
However, all I received on Christmas Day was a pair of navy blue socks. They are
at least three sizes too big and have a hole in the left toe.

Complaint letters need to
give specific details.

I appreciate that you are very busy and mistakes are bound to occur. Therefore,
I would be happy to accept one of the gifts that I asked for in my original list
(please find enclosed). In this case I wouldn't have to take the matter any further.

I look forward to hearing from you.

Sign off *Yours
sincerely* if the letter is
addressed to a specific
person. Use *Yours
faithfully* if it is to an
unspecified recipient,
such as *Sir*
or *Madam*.

Yours sincerely,
Ian Brat

Informal letters

Informal letters are used for someone the sender knows, such as a friend, a family member or a person of the same age or younger. They might describe a place or experience, pass on news or thank the recipient for something. Informal letters have a chattier tone, but still follow a set layout.

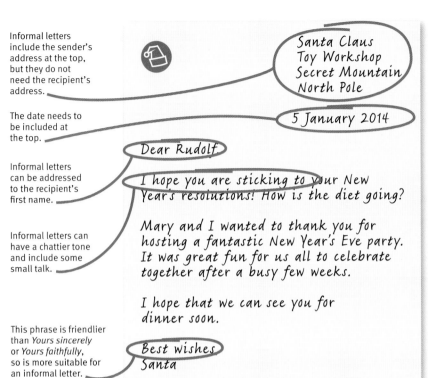

Informal letters include the sender's address at the top, but they do not need the recipient's address.

The date needs to be included at the top.

Informal letters can be addressed to the recipient's first name.

Informal letters can have a chattier tone and include some small talk.

This phrase is friendlier than *Yours sincerely* or *Yours faithfully*, so is more suitable for an informal letter.

> Santa Claus
> Toy Workshop
> Secret Mountain
> North Pole
>
> 5 January 2014
>
> Dear Rudolf
>
> I hope you are sticking to your New Year's resolutions! How is the diet going?
>
> Mary and I wanted to thank you for hosting a fantastic New Year's Eve party. It was great fun for us all to celebrate together after a busy few weeks.
>
> I hope that we can see you for dinner soon.
>
> Best wishes
> Santa

- A **job application** letter gives an employer the **first impression** of a candidate, so it needs to be perfect.
- A complaint letter should be **firm but polite**. A **rude** letter will only **annoy** the recipient and reduce the chance of an apology or compensation.

E-mails

E-mails to friends or family don't have to follow any particular rules. However, e-mails to people whom the sender doesn't know should use appropriate language and have a clear structure. More and more correspondence is now sent via e-mail, so writing an e-mail isn't an excuse to be sloppy.

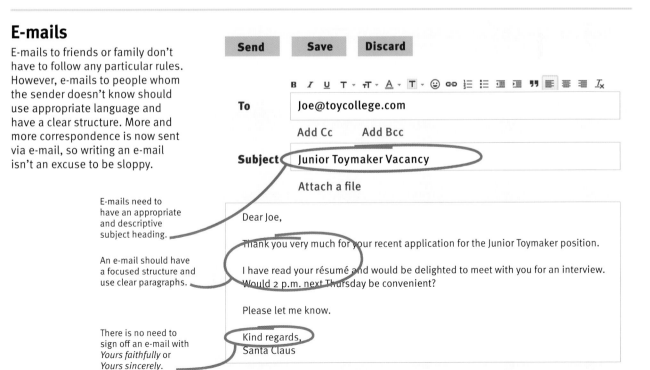

E-mails need to have an appropriate and descriptive subject heading.

An e-mail should have a focused structure and use clear paragraphs.

There is no need to sign off an e-mail with *Yours faithfully* or *Yours sincerely*.

Send **Save** **Discard**

To Joe@toycollege.com

Add Cc   Add Bcc

Subject Junior Toymaker Vacancy

Attach a file

Dear Joe,

Thank you very much for your recent application for the Junior Toymaker position.

I have read your résumé and would be delighted to meet with you for an interview. Would 2 p.m. next Thursday be convenient?

Please let me know.

Kind regards,
Santa Claus

Writing to influence

SOME TEXTS SEEK TO CHANGE AN AUDIENCE'S VIEWS
OR BEHAVIOUR.

Pieces of writing that argue or persuade seek to influence
the audience. However, there are subtle differences between
arguing and persuading.

SEE ALSO	
❰ **186–187** Planning and research	
❰ **188–189** Paragraphing	
❰ **190–191** Genre, purpose and audience	
Writing to describe	**208–209** ❱
Writing a speech	**226–227** ❱

A strong argument

An argument tends to acknowledge
the opposite opinion while providing
well-reasoned arguments against it.
For example, if someone were to
argue that cats were better than
dogs, that person would not simply
list all the good things about cats.
He or she would acknowledge why
some people prefer dogs, then
argue against those points.

Reasons why people prefer dogs to cats
- *Dogs are more intelligent than cats.* Cats are smart enough to hunt, wash and fend for themselves.
- *Cats are unkind because they bring dead mice into the house.* This is their way of showing affection.
- *Cats are unsociable.* They are friendly but don't demand constant attention – an annoying characteristic of dogs.

To plan an argument, list the reasons why
people take the opposite point of view.

Try to disprove each point
with a counter-argument.

Powers of persuasion

A persuasive piece is more one-sided and emotional than an
argument. It often coaxes the audience to act: for example, to buy
a product, join an organisation or donate money to charity.

Persuasive writing
does not accept
the opposite
opinion.

This type of writing
coaxes the reader
to act now.

- Persuasive writing should be firm but **not aggressive**.
- **Real-life stories** add emotion to a piece of writing.
- Use **confident language**, such as *you will* and *definitely*, rather than *you might* and *possibly*.

GLOSSARY

Exaggeration Representing something
as larger or better than it actually is.

Hyperbole An extreme form of
exaggeration that is not necessarily
taken seriously, but grabs the
reader's attention.

Rhetorical question A question that
does not need an answer but is used
for effect.

Superlative The form of an adjective
or adverb that suggests the greatest or
least of something.

Get your own way

Writers use particular methods to influence their audiences' opinions. These are called rhetorical devices. Writing that persuades uses more of these techniques than writing that argues.

Repetition rules

Sometimes a word, phrase or structure is repeated to make an idea stick in the audience's mind, and convince them that it's true. Lists of three are a particularly common technique.

Dogs are loyal. Dogs are friendly. Dogs are the best!

Ask the experts

Writers use facts, statistics and quotations from reliable and authoritative sources to back up their points and make them sound more convincing.

According to one recent study at Queen's University, Belfast, dog owners suffer from fewer medical problems than cat owners.

The **Ancient Greeks** called the art of using language to persuade **"the art of rhetoric"**.

Tearjerkers

Some words and phrases make the reader feel an emotion, such as pain, sadness, guilt or anger. Once the reader is feeling this way, they are often more susceptible to persuasion.

Cats bring comfort and friendship to the old, frail and lonely.

Rhetorical questions

A rhetorical question is a question that does not require or expect an answer. However, it makes the reader reflect on points that he or she may not have considered.

Is a cat fun? Can you play fetch with a cat?

Getting personal

Addressing the audience directly with *you* will make them feel more involved. Using *we* can form a relationship between the writer and audience, and encourage the audience to trust and believe the writer.

We all know that you don't have to take cats for constant walks.

Simply the best

Exaggeration is used to emphasise a point and to grab an audience's attention. Exaggeration often includes superlatives, such as *the best*, *the worst* and *the cheapest*. Extreme exaggeration is called hyperbole.

I couldn't live without my cat. My cat is my whole world.

REAL WORLD

I'm talking to you

This poster from 1914 was used to persuade men to join the British army in World War I. It shows Lord Kitchener, the then British Secretary of State for War, telling the audience that their country needs them. By looking directly at the audience and addressing them with the word *YOU*, Lord Kitchener made a very effective appeal.

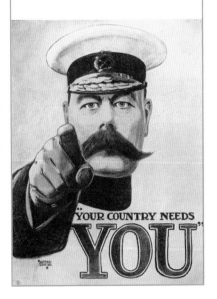

YOUR COUNTRY NEEDS "YOU"

Writing to explain or advise

EXPLANATIONS AND PIECES OF ADVICE GIVE THE READER MORE THAN THE BASIC FACTS.

SEE ALSO

❰ **186–187** Planning and research
❰ **188–189** Paragraphing
❰ **190–191** Genre, purpose and audience
❰ **192–193** Reading and commenting on texts
❰ **196–197** Writing to inform
❰ **202–203** Writing to influence

Writing to explain and writing to advise can be confused with writing to inform. However, explanations and pieces of advice include reasons, feelings and suggestions, as well as information.

Extra explanation

An explanation gives reasons. For example, it can explain why or how an event has happened, or why someone feels a certain way.

Explaining experiences

People are sometimes asked to explain their views on a topic, or the reason an experience was important or difficult. These types of explanations should not only describe the topic or event, but also the feelings involved.

I've lost all my confidence

How and why

Explanations tell the reader how or why something happened, not just what happened. They use linking words and phrases to show cause and effect.

this is because
as a result of this
therefore

STOP THE STENCH!

Dear Annie,

I have a serious problem with smelly feet. It sounds silly, but it has an impact on my entire life. Not only does the smell irritate me, but other people have started to notice and make jokes. I've lost all my confidence and I can't even go to my friends' houses anymore because I'm too frightened to take off my shoes. What can I do?

Anonymous, 14

Dear Anonymous,

Don't worry – you're not alone! Stinky feet are a common problem. This is because there are more sweat glands in the feet than anywhere else in the body. When your feet release sweat, bacteria on the skin break it down. This process releases that cheesy smell.

Good advice

A piece of advice tells someone the best, easiest or quickest way to do something, or suggests how to solve a problem.

• A good explanation must be **well structured** in order to deliver the information in a **clear** and **logical** way.

Sympathy

Advice needs to be authoritative but friendly. Using a sympathetic and positive tone will encourage the reader.

the good news is   don't worry

The good news is that there are lots of simple ways to stop the stench. First of all, you should wash your feet and change your socks every day. You could also try special foot deodorants, but I find spraying normal deodorant on your feet works just as well. A guaranteed way to get rid of the smell is to wash your feet with an antibacterial soap. If you do this twice a day, you should banish smelly feet within a week.

Here are some other useful tips:

- Wear socks and shoes made from natural fibres because they let your feet breathe, unlike synthetic materials.
- Wear open-toed sandals in the summer and go barefoot at home in the evenings.
- See a doctor if these simple measures don't help.

Good luck.

Best,

Annie

Personal pronouns

A writer can address the reader directly by using *you*, or refer to his or her personal opinion with *I*. This helps to build a relationship with the reader, who should then be more receptive to the advice.

you could   I find

Suggestions

Strong suggestions such as *you should* are effective because they encourage the reader to act. However, it's best to include a few gentler suggestions, such as *you could* or *you might*, to maintain a friendly tone.

you should wash your feet

Strong suggestions tell the reader what to do.

Guaranteed results

The text needs to show how the advice will help. It should emphasise what will happen if the advice is or is not followed.

If you do this twice a day, you should banish smelly feet within a week.

Bullet points

Advice leaflets or columns often break down the information into bullet points, so that the reader can read and follow the pieces of advice easily.

Writing to analyse or review

THESE TWO TYPES OF WRITING BREAK DOWN A TOPIC AND DISCUSS ITS KEY PARTS.

Both an analysis and a review discuss a subject in depth. However, whereas an analysis gives a balanced judgement, a review is usually opinionated and personal.

SEE ALSO

❬ **42–43** Simple tenses
❬ **186–187** Planning and research
❬ **188–189** Paragraphing
❬ **190–191** Genre, purpose and audience

GLOSSARY

First person narrative When an author writes a piece from his or her point of view, using *I* and *my*.

Objective When a piece of writing is not influenced by personal opinions.

Subjective When a piece of writing is influenced by personal opinions.

Third person narrative When an author writes from a detached or outside point of view.

Balanced judgement

An analysis is an investigation of a topic. Unlike a persuasive piece of writing or a review, an analysis remains objective, which means that it is not influenced by personal feelings. It will look at the good and bad points of a subject, and come to a fair conclusion. A useful way to plan a balanced analysis is to use a table, listing arguments for and against.

Against reality television	For reality televison
Television producers make shows vulgar and offensive in order to boost ratings.	Reality television is popular and producers should give viewers what they want.
It encourages people to pursue celebrity status, rather than success through education and hard work.	If someone doesn't want to watch a show, they can change the channel or turn off the television.
The contestants are humiliated and treated poorly, which sets a bad example for viewers.	Some shows tackle important problems in society, such as unhealthy eating.
All the shows follow the same formula, and no creativity is involved in the making of a programme.	Reality television tells us more about human nature, and how people behave in certain situations.

Distant and detached

To maintain the objectivity of an analysis, it's best to write in the third person and with an impersonal tone. For example, starting a sentence with the words *It is often argued* does not reveal the writer's personal opinion.

It is often argued...

It seems likely...

There is evidence to suggest...

Many people believe...

It is sometimes stated...

Rave reviews

A review is a piece of writing that provides a focused description and evaluation of an event or a publication, such as a book or a film. It is much more subjective than an analysis, and is therefore written in the first person, with many personal opinions.

The travel website **TripAdvisor** contains more than **75 million** consumer **reviews** and opinions.

Sneak preview

The first part of a review should give a short summary of the film, book, show or other event without giving everything away. It should give the reader a general idea of what it is about.

Film preview

TAKE
TO THE FLOOR 2

The rooftop tango scene is stunning and very moving.

Take to the Floor 2 is the latest in a series of teen dance dramas to spin into cinemas. As usual, the story focuses on two young dancers from the opposite sides of town. When street kid Chad wins a scholarship to a prestigious dance school, he finds it hard to fit in. Then, one day, he catches the eye of ballet dancer Ellie, who is wowed by his moves.

Many of the dance scenes are spectacular, from a rooftop tango in the pouring rain to a shopping mall salsa extravaganza. The cast members are all highly trained movers; however, their acting skills were left at the stage door. Ellie and Chad fail to bring their sizzling dance-floor chemistry into the dialogue, which is disappointing.

Take to the Floor 2 is nothing new; the plot certainly doesn't offer any surprises. However, the film is saved by its show-stopping dance scenes and pumping soundtrack. Overall, it's incredibly fun to watch, even if you end up feeling like you've seen it all before.

The good and the bad

The middle part of a review should go into more detail about the strengths and weaknesses of the subject. It might discuss the acting in a play, the quality of writing in a book or the use of special effects in a film. It's important to back up any comments with examples.

The verdict

The final paragraph in a review should be a summative statement about the subject, and an overall recommendation – a final judgement on whether the subject is worth watching, seeing or reading.

• An analysis should be **structured** clearly, using **paragraphs**. Discuss one point of view first, followed by the other. Finally, come to a **balanced conclusion**.

• When writing a review, think about the **audience** and what they will **want to know** about the subject being reviewed.

Writing to describe

DESCRIPTIVE WRITING TELLS THE READER WHAT SOMETHING
OR SOMEONE IS LIKE.

Many types of writing use description, from stories to advertisements.
Descriptive writing uses particular words to paint a vivid image of
something in the reader's head.

SEE ALSO

❮ **26–27** Adjectives

❮ **40–41** Adverbs

❮ **84–85** Idioms, analogies and figures
of speech

❮ **182–183** Picking the right words

❮ **184–185** Making sentences interesting

Writing a narrative　　　　**212–213** ❯

The senses

When writing to describe, it's important to appeal to the reader's senses.
By describing what something looks, sounds and feels like, a writer can
allow the reader to imagine something in detail. Not all of the senses
may be relevant, but try to think about as many as possible.

• One way to structure a description
is to describe it **location by
location**, as if moving around
a scene with a video camera.

Barbara walked into the kitchen and was confronted by a **rush of
warm air** and the **smell of something sweet**. On the counter was
a **triple-layer chocolate cake** with **fudge icing oozing** down the
sides. She **eagerly cut** a slice and **stuffed** it into her mouth. The
chocolate sponge was **rich** and **bitter** with a slight **nutty** flavour.
The **sugar sprinkles crackled** in her mouth and got **stuck in her
teeth**. Suddenly, the **doorbell buzzed**. Barbara jumped, and her
cake splattered across the floor.

Describe what something
looks, feels, smells,
tastes and sounds like.

REAL WORLD

Too good to miss

Advertising executives use description to
create tempting pictures in an audience's
mind to persuade them to buy something.
For example, they might describe hair as
smooth, *glossy* and *rich* to sell a new
shampoo or hair dye. Alternatively,
an advertisement for a beach resort could
include descriptions such as *azure blue*,
gently lapping waves and *golden sands*.

Descriptive details

Readers won't be able to imagine something unless they are given details. By selecting particular words, writers can add extra information and make a sentence more descriptive.

She reached for a slice of cake and put it in her mouth.

△ **Lacking detail**
This sentence doesn't tell the reader very much about the scene.

adverb   adjective

*She reached **quickly** for a **big** slice of **sticky, delicious** cake and **eagerly** put it in her mouth.*

△ **Adjectives and adverbs**
The addition of adjectives and adverbs instantly makes the sentence more evocative.

Using this word is a more precise way to decribe the big slice.

*She **grabbed** a **wedge** of **sticky, delicious chocolate** cake and **stuffed** it in her mouth.*

△ **Precise vocabulary**
Sometimes it's better to use precise vocabulary that includes description within the words themselves.

*She **tentatively** reached for a **sliver** of **fattening** cake and **sneakily popped** it in her mouth.*

△ **Different choices**
By using different descriptive words, a writer can give a sentence a totally different feel.

Figurative language

Figurative language is an exaggerated style of writing that draws comparisons between things to create a more vivid description.

Simile
A simile compares one thing to another by using the words *as* or *like*.

Her cheeks were pink **like** strawberries.

Metaphor
A metaphor is a word or phrase that describes something as if it were something else.

A **wave** of terror washed over him.

Personification
Personification is when human actions or feelings are given to objects or ideas.

The wind **screamed** and **howled**.

Onomatopoeia
Onomatopoeia is when a writer uses words that mimic the sound they stand for.

The leaves **crunched** underfoot.

Writing from personal experience

WHEN SOMEONE WRITES ABOUT THEIR LIFE OR PERSONAL EXPERIENCES, IT'S CALLED AUTOBIOGRAPHICAL WRITING.

Autobiography is a genre in itself, but it can also be used in other types of writing, such as a speech or an advice leaflet, to give a more personal touch.

A life less ordinary

Everyday life may not seem very interesting, but readers find other people's lives fascinating. Earliest memories, embarrassing incidents, or particularly happy, sad, scary or proud moments all make good topics. Readers also enjoy finding out about experiences that are very different from their own, such as celebrating certain festivals or living in different places.

This is my life

When writing a complete autobiography (from birth to the present day), it's important to work out the right order of events. One way to do this is to create a life map. This is a visual way of plotting events, and can be accompanied by pictures to suggest memories. Rather than listing every single memory, writers often give an autobiography a theme. For example, it might focus on a struggle from rags to riches or a love of sport.

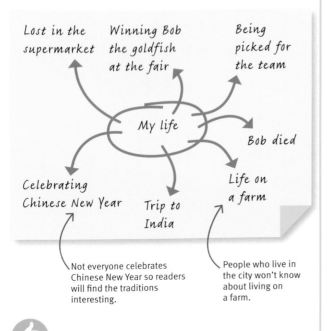

Not everyone celebrates Chinese New Year so readers will find the traditions interesting.

People who live in the city won't know about living on a farm.

Life map

I began to support the local team.

I started to play with a ball in the yard.

I got my first real ball.

My team lost in the final.

• Don't make up a whole experience, but it is acceptable to **embellish** a story slightly if it is going to make the story more **dramatic** or **entertaining**.

Travel writing

Travel writing is very different from the text found in travel guide books, which usually lists information. Pieces of travel writing recount the author's own travel experiences, including his or her feelings, opinions and amusing anecdotes.

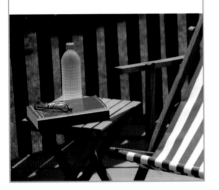

Edited highlights

Autobiographical writing is informative but also needs to be entertaining, so it shouldn't list boring details. For example, there's no need to give a minute-by-minute account of a game. It's much more interesting to tell the reader about feelings and reactions, such as fear, pride or disappointment.

> *I felt sick and panicky all morning before the big game. We needed to win and I'd finally made the team. I had everything to prove.*

Make it real

An autobiography tells stories, and the best stories include plenty of description. Describing sights, sounds, emotions and tastes will allow the reader to picture the experience as vividly as the writer can remember it.

> *It was a hot night in the stadium. The noise of the supporters was deafening, and their chants boomed across the field like a roll of thunder in a storm.*

Add character

Autobiographical writing needs to showcase the writer's unique personality. Therefore, it often includes his or her personal opinions, likes and dislikes, strange habits and favourite vocabulary. Funny details add humour and give the piece character.

> *I was wearing my lucky socks. I had eaten my usual peanut butter sandwich and stroked the cat three times. I was ready to play the game of my life!*

You and me

An autobiography will naturally include the words *I* and *my*, but it can also be effective to address the reader using *you*. This is called direct address and helps to create a relationship with readers, making them feel more involved in the story.

> *I'm sure you've been on the losing side before, or watched your team miss that crucial shot. So you know what it feels like to be emotionally crushed by a loss.*

I was picked for the class team.

Age 12

10 **Age 11**

I met my team's famous captain.

I played for the school.

Age 13

I broke my leg in a game.

Writing a narrative

A NARRATIVE IS A PIECE OF WRITING THAT TELLS A STORY.

A story is an account of events linked by cause and effect. All stories need a narrator, a plot, characters and a setting. Some stories also include dialogue to show conversations between characters.

SEE ALSO

❮ **34–35** Pronouns
❮ **108–109** Inverted commas
❮ **182–183** Picking the right words
❮ **184–185** Making sentences interesting
❮ **208–209** Writing to describe

Whose view?

The narrator is the person telling the story. If the narrator is a character in the story recounting the events from his or her point of view, the narrative is in the first person. If the narrator is uninvolved in the story and always refers to characters as *he*, *she* or *they*, then the story is written in the third person.

The word *my* shows that this story is in the first person.

My master is the most fearsome pirate sailing the seven seas.

First person (main character)
Stories in the first person are often narrated by the main character, or protagonist, of the story.

First person (minor character)
Not all stories in the first person are told by the main character. Using a minor character as a narrator gives a different angle.

The scoundrels had deceived **me**, so **I** made them walk the plank!

Third person
A narrative written in the third person tells the story from the author's or an outsider's point of view.

The word *his* shows that this story is in the third person.

The ruthless captain made **his** crew walk the plank.

Don't lose the plot

The plot is what turns a list of events into a story. All the events happen for a reason and are caused by the actions and decisions of the characters. A good plot needs to have a clear beginning, middle (usually the main part of the action) and end.

△ **Beginning**
The beginning introduces the main characters and the situation that they are in. One classic plot line starts with the main character facing a problem.

△ **Middle**
The middle of the plot often shows the character trying to overcome the problem. The main event or turning point in the plot usually happens in the middle of the story.

△ **End**
The end brings the story to a resolution. The main character may have solved his or her problem. Alternatively, a plot "twist" may introduce an unexpected ending.

Heroes and villains

A good story needs to have interesting characters that the reader cares about. Usually, there is a main character, or hero. There are also villains, who stop the hero from reaching his or her goals, and allies, who help the hero. Each character should be distinctive, with unique physical or personality traits.

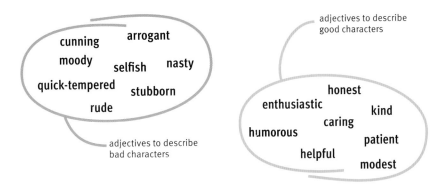

cunning
arrogant
moody
selfish
nasty
quick-tempered
stubborn
rude

adjectives to describe bad characters

adjectives to describe good characters

honest
enthusiastic
kind
caring
humorous
patient
helpful
modest

The perfect setting

The setting is the time, place and situation where the action happens. The right setting will give the story mood and atmosphere. For example, a pirate story could be set on a deserted tropical island in the seventeenth century. Describing a setting in detail will enable the reader to imagine what it is like.

The island was **deserted,** except for the **multicoloured** birds **circling** overhead. The **golden** sandy beach was **fringed** with **coconut** trees and **tropical** plants. A **ghostly** shipwreck in the distance was being **pounded** against the **craggy** rocks by **crashing** waves.

Words that contain description, such as sounds, paint a vivid picture of the scene.

Dramatic dialogue

Using dialogue in a story can reveal more about the characters and advance the plot. It should be concise and dramatic – overly long or pointless pieces of dialogue should be avoided. Choosing phrases such as *he grumbled*, *he screamed* or *he gasped* instead of *he said* also adds more drama.

Pieces of dialogue need to go in inverted commas.

"Is that you, Captain?" shouted the first mate.
"Of course it is. Now, hurry up and lower a boat to fetch me," bellowed the captain.

A new speaker's dialogue needs to go on a new line.

Use more interesting words as an alternative to *said*.

- Use a mixture of **long** and **short** sentences to build up **tension** and **suspense**.
- **Figurative language** such as the simile *as fast as a cheetah* can enrich the description in a narrative. However, use it **sparingly** – too much description can **distract** the reader from the action.

Writing for the Web

WRITING FOR THE WEB IS VERY DIFFERENT FROM WRITING FOR PRINT.

Online readers are usually trying to find specific information and will move on if the website isn't clear or doesn't tell them what they need to know. Web writers use specific techniques to keep readers interested.

Business websites sometimes include company logos.

Easy on the eye

Reading words on a screen is harder than reading them on a printed page, so if online readers find something too difficult to read, they will click away. Therefore, online text should always be written in short and clear sentences and paragraphs.

Key words

The Web is huge and full of websites on the same topics. Web writers have to make their content easy to find by including the "key words" that users search for on search engines. This is called Search Engine Optimization (SEO). It means that headlines and subheadings should be obvious rather than obscure.

Go to kangaroo country

This title is fun but would not always be found in searches for "Australia".

Go to Australia

The word *Australia* will be picked up by search engines.

Attractive images make the website and the places look appealing.

Go Travel

FLIGHTS | HOTELS | TOURS | INSURANCE | AROUND THE WORLD | BUS/TRAIN

Australasia travel guides

If you really want to get away from it all, you can't get much further away than Australasia. Ride the waves on Australia's Gold Coast, hike through the mountains in New Zealand or just relax on the beach in Fiji. Start planning your trip of a lifetime here.

Go to Australia

Australia has it all, from hip cities to idyllic islands to the remote outback. Scuba dive at the Great Barrier Reef, party in Sydney or check out some fascinating wildlife.
Find out more...

Go to New Zealand

New Zealand is a thrill-seeker's paradise. Get your adrenaline rush from skydiving, white-water rafting or bungee jumping. Or just take in the beautiful scenery.
Find out more...

Go to Fiji

If you want to relax on a stunning beach, Fiji won't disappoint. It has more than three hundred islands with crystal clear waters and beautiful coral reefs.
Find out more...

Blogs

Blogs are a type of online journal written for an audience. They are usually written in an informal and personal style and should be entertaining to read. Bloggers often write in the style of casual speech (although blogs should still be grammatically correct), so it's helpful to read a blog out loud to make sure that it has the right tone.

Tabs along the top of the page take the user to different sections of the site.

People read **online text** about **25 per cent slower** than they can read printed material.

GLOSSARY

Blog An online journal containing the author's comments and reflections. It is updated regularly.

Hyperlink A word, phrase or icon on the World Wide Web, which, if clicked, takes the user to a new document or website.

SEO Standing for "Search Engine Optimization", this is the process that increases the online visibility of a website so more Web users will visit it.

ESSENTIALS | PLANNING | DESTINATIONS | VOLUNTEER | WORK

The Go Travel blog

Surfing at Bondi

I've finally made it Down Under!

It's early in the morning here, but I'm not on Aussie time yet so I thought I would update you all on my trip. Yesterday, I decided to cure my jet lag by throwing myself into the pounding surf at Bondi Beach!

Read more....

Blogs can include some slang. This is short for "Australian".

Give it some space

A clear layout also makes online text easier to read. It is often broken up into small paragraphs and bullet points and surrounded by plenty of white space. People often scan read when they are reading online, so clear and descriptive subheadings can help them to find the information that they need.

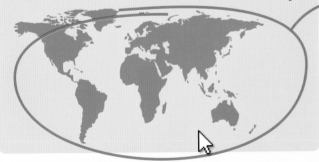

Click on our interactive destination map

Interactive graphics present information in a more entertaining way and keep readers interested.

Act now

All writing has a purpose, whether to give readers information, or to make them buy something. The Web, more than any other medium, can allow readers to act on what they have read straight away. It is therefore important to include active hyperlinks that take readers to extra information or to the checkout page.

Get a quote by e-mail
Ask one of our team

Add to basket

Ask one of our team

Websites use links like this to encourage users to buy something.

Writing a script

VOICE-OVERS AND DRAMATIC SCRIPTS HAVE TO BE EFFECTIVE
WHEN READ ALOUD.

The words in a script are spoken to an audience, so they have to
be easy to understand. Scripts also need to be laid out in specific
ways, and include instructions for the people involved.

Voice-overs

A voice-over is the audio commentary
that accompanies a short video, such as a
documentary, an advertisement or a charity
campaign film. A useful way to lay out a voice-over
script is to use a table with columns.

Easy listening

A voice-over needs to be written in simple language so
that listeners will understand what is said immediately.
They can't go back and read sections again. Using simple
sentences and words will also make a script easy for
narrators to read, so they won't stumble over their words.

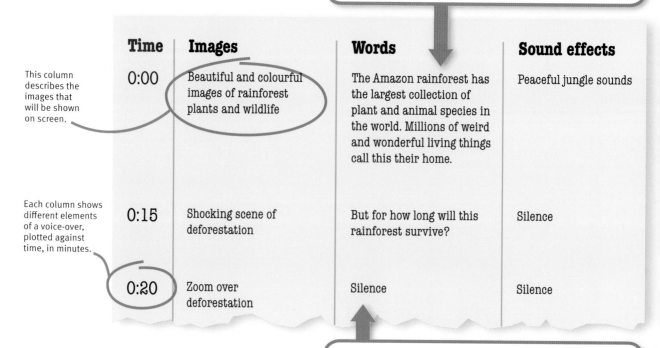

This column
describes the
images that
will be shown
on screen.

Each column shows
different elements
of a voice-over,
plotted against
time, in minutes.

Time	Images	Words	Sound effects
0:00	Beautiful and colourful images of rainforest plants and wildlife	The Amazon rainforest has the largest collection of plant and animal species in the world. Millions of weird and wonderful living things call this their home.	Peaceful jungle sounds
0:15	Shocking scene of deforestation	But for how long will this rainforest survive?	Silence
0:20	Zoom over deforestation	Silence	Silence

Words and pictures

In a voice-over script, the words need to relate
to the images on screen, giving extra information about
them. However, it is often effective to include occasional
silences, so the audience can focus on and absorb what
they can see.

• The best way to test a voice-over is to read it **out loud**. If the narrator **runs out of breath**, or gets **confused**, the script needs to be **rewritten**.

On average, a narrator can read **180 words** out loud **per minute**.

Dramatic scripts

A dramatic script tells a story. However, unlike a written narrative, a script will be performed. Dramatic scripts can be for the theatre, television, radio or film. Each type has slightly different conventions, but they have some common features.

Directions

A script should include directions that tell everyone involved what to do. Directions indicate when actors should enter and exit, and in what tone they should perform a line. Other directions relate to lighting, sound effects or camera shots, such as close-ups.

The title of the piece goes at the top.

PROTEST

Scene A park that is going to be demolished to make way for a shopping centre. There are protest chants.

The setting and the characters involved in the scene are listed at the top.

Characters

MEADOW An environmental activist
DETECTIVE STUBBS A police officer

Directions show when characters enter and exit the scene. They should be in brackets.

(MEADOW starts to climb a tree.)
(Enter DETECTIVE STUBBS)

Directions also include adverbs that tell actors how to perform their lines.

DETECTIVE STUBBS: What do you think you're doing?
MEADOW: (angrily) Saving our trees!
DETECTIVE STUBBS: Get down immediately!

(MEADOW laughs and scrambles to the top of the tree.)

DETECTIVE STUBBS: Hey you, come back!

Dialogue

The dialogue refers to the conversation between characters. In a play, the plot is controlled by the dialogue and action, so the words need to tell the audience what is happening. The speech also needs to be convincing, so it should reflect the age, nationality, personality and mood of each character.

Re-creations

THE REWRITING OF A TEXT IN A DIFFERENT FORM IS CALLED
A RE-CREATION.

A piece of writing can be restyled in a variety of ways. For instance,
a text such as a story could be rewritten as an autobiography or
a newspaper article.

SEE ALSO

❮ 42–43 Simple tenses

❮ 190–191 Genre, purpose and audience

❮ 194–195 Layout and
presentational features

❮ 198–199 Newspaper articles

❮ 212–213 Writing a narrative

Transforming texts

A re-creation is turning one type of text
into another. This can be done by simply
changing the narrative viewpoint. For
example, a third-person narrative could be
turned into a first-person narrative. Similarly,
a story could be retold in a different tense.
A piece of writing can also be rewritten in
a completely different form – a poem could
inspire a story, or a play could become
a newspaper article.

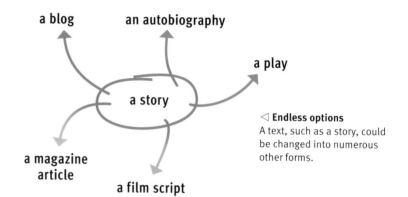

a blog

an autobiography

a play

a story

a magazine article

a film script

◁ **Endless options**
A text, such as a story, could
be changed into numerous
other forms.

REAL WORLD

Revised and updated

Sometimes writers rework classic
stories to appeal to modern
audiences. The action and
characters are often moved into
a modern setting. For example, the
musical *West Side Story* is loosely
based on William Shakespeare's
Romeo and Juliet, but it is set in
1950s New York City.

The original

The best way to start a re-creation is to read and understand
the original text. The rewritten form must include key details
from the original version, such as events in the plot and the
main characters. However, also think about minor details,
such as the mood and atmosphere of the piece.

Highlight the important plot
details in the original text.

extract from
Cinderella

The king's son, who was told that a great princess,
whom nobody knew, had arrived, ran out to receive her. He
gave her his hand as she alighted from the coach, and led her
into the hall, among all the company. There was immediately
a profound silence. Everyone stopped dancing, and the violins
ceased to play, so entranced was everyone with the
singular beauties of the unknown newcomer.

Also look out for
smaller details.

The makeover

The next stage is to think of an original way to transform the text into something else. It is best to choose a form that will suit the main events and characters in the original text. The revised version should use the correct features and layout for the new form.

• Be **creative** but stick to the important details. The new version should show an **understanding of the original text**.

Adding extra descriptive detail shows creativity.

Include details from the original text.

That night changed my life forever. I felt dizzy with excitement as I entered the ballroom. Women in multicoloured dresses sashayed across the floor under sparkling chandeliers. The room was filled with the sound of guests chattering and violins playing. Then everything went silent. Everyone was looking at me.

◁ **Cinderella's story**
The story *Cinderella* could be rewritten as her autobiography. In this case, it should be narrated in the first person and include her thoughts and feelings.

▷ **Royal scoop**
Cinderella could also inspire a scandalous newspaper article. In this case, the new text should be laid out with a headline and in columns, and the language should be short and snappy.

THE CASTLE

Front-page stories usually have an eye-catching headline.

WHO IS SHE?

The secret stunner left the ball in a hurry just before midnight.

PARTY PRINCE SPOTTED WITH MYSTERY WOMAN

Newspaper articles often include alliteration (the use of words beginning with the same letter or sound).

It was a sight that broke hundreds of hearts. Prince Charming, 24, was seen dancing the night away with a new woman on Saturday evening.

The prince, who has publicly announced his intention to wed this year, was apparently bewitched by the beautiful blonde. Dressed in a floor-length metallic gown and glitzy glass slippers, she was the centre of attention at the prince's annual ball.

One attendee said, "Everyone went silent when she entered the room. We were all entranced by her beauty."

These details come from the original text.

There have been more than **400** feature-length film and television **adaptations** of **William Shakespeare's** plays.

Checking and editing

CHECKING AND EDITING WILL IMPROVE A PIECE OF WRITING.

All writers make mistakes or have better ideas. It's important to leave enough time after finishing a piece of work to check for errors and improve the quality of the writing.

The right answer

Even a perfect piece of writing will be poorly received if it answers the wrong question. When reviewing a piece of work, look at the question again, and make sure that the answer fulfils the brief.

The answer should discuss language and presentational features.

Discuss how the website uses language and presentational features to persuade readers to visit the theme park.

The answer should focus on how these features persuade the reader.

Discuss how the website uses language and presentational features to persuade readers to visit the theme park.

This website is designed to lure people to the Wild Waves Water Park. It is particulery aimed at young people who are on school holidays. The range of images are persuasive. The selection shows groups of people who are obviously

Tricky words

One of the most important things to do is to check for spelling mistakes. To correct a spelling in handwritten work, put the mistake in brackets, draw a line through it and write the correct version above. Do not rely on spellcheckers – it's better to identify mistakes and learn the correct versions.

particularly
It is (particulery) aimed

Good grammar

Some grammatical mistakes to look out for include incomplete sentences, incorrect word order and errors of verb agreement.

is
The range of images (are) persuasive.

The subject *range* is singular, so the verb needs to be singular too.

Strict structure

Structuring a piece of text using paragraphs is very important. A new point of discussion requires a new paragraph. If a paragraph break is missing in a piece of handwritten work, mark it in with two diagonal slashes.

reader's attention. // The language used

Use this symbol to show that there should be a new paragraph.

Perfect punctuation

Punctuation marks may look small, but they need to be used correctly. It's easy to make mistakes when writing quickly, so look out for errors such as misused commas and apostrophes.

The coloured text is really eye-catching, and it immediately grabs the reader's attention.

The two clauses need to be joined with a conjunction or a semi-colon, not just a comma.

enjoying themselves and the reader will want to join the fun. The coloured text is really eye-catching, it immediately grabs the reader's attention. The language used on the website is really persuasive. For example, the text is full of verbs suggest movement. The writer has used rhetorical questions to challenge the reader, such as "Do you dare to ride the rapids?"

Varied vocabulary

A polished piece of writing should contain a good range of vocabulary. Repeatedly used words should be replaced with synonyms or similar appropriate words to add variety. Adverbs, such as *very* and *really*, should not be overused.

The language used on the website is convincing.

The word *persuasive* can be replaced with a synonym. The adverb *really* can be cut out.

Something missing?

If a word has been left out in handwritten work, insert a caret symbol (∧) where the words should go and write them neatly above. To insert a longer passage, put an asterisk (*) where the new text should start, put another asterisk at the bottom or side of the work and write the extra text next to it.

that
The text is full of verbs ∧ suggest movement*.

Use the asterisk for longer passages.   Use this mark to add in single words.

*, such as "splash", "zoom", "race" and "spin".

REAL WORLD

George W. Bush

The former US president George W. Bush didn't always check his work. He is famous for making grammatical errors, such as "Rarely is the question asked: is our children learning?" He also once said, "The goals of this country is to enhance prosperity and peace."

The spoken word

THE SPOKEN WORD IS DIFFERENT FROM WRITTEN LANGUAGE
IN MANY KEY RESPECTS.

A person's speech is influenced by various factors, such as where
he or she is from and to whom he or she is talking. It's important
to consider these factors when writing or analysing spoken language.

Standard English

Standard English is often considered the "correct"
form of English, because it is grammatically correct and
does not use any slang. It is usually spoken in a neutral
accent without any regional pronunciation; this is called
Received Pronunciation in the UK, General American in
North America and General Australian in Australia.
Standard English is used in formal situations, by public
officials, and traditionally by the media.

Good evening. Welcome to the nine o'clock news.

Standard English uses formal,
unabbreviated vocabulary
and correct grammar.

Dialect and accent

Varieties of spoken English have developed in different
English-speaking countries across the world, and in the regions
and communities within them. Each variety has its own colloquial
vocabulary and grammatical constructions. These varieties are known
as dialects. An accent is the way in which language is pronounced.
People use dialectal words and constructions in informal situations.

Hello, my friend. How are you?

This person is talking
in Standard English,
but it sounds odd in
an informal situation.

G'day, mate. How ya goin'?

This is Australian slang
for *hello*. It is a
contraction of the
greeting *good day*.

This is slang for *friend*.

The words *you* and
going are spelt like
this to show how they are
pronounced in Australia.

Hey, dude. What's up?

This is another slang
word for *friend*, more
commonly used in
North America.

REAL WORLD

Soap operas

The actors in television soap
operas set in a particular location
will use the accents from that
place. For example, the actors
in the show *Dallas* have Texas
accents. This makes the dialogue
seem more authentic. If the actors
don't speak like this themselves,
they have to learn the accent.

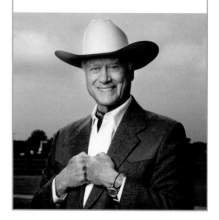

Tone and pitch

Speakers adjust the tone and pitch of their voice according to what they are saying. For example, someone might sound sad and low-pitched if delivering bad news, but delighted and high-pitched if discussing good news.

Bao Bao, the world's oldest panda, has died at the age of 34.

In other news, the weather is going to be fantastic this weekend.

This sentence would probably be delivered in an upbeat tone.

Pauses and fillers

When people are thinking about what to say next, or lose their train of thought, they pause. Sometimes people fill the silence with a hesitation device, such as *er* or *huh*, or with a sigh.

Structure

People often leave out words and use incomplete sentences when they are having spoken conversations. Contractions such as *haven't* and *couldn't* are used more frequently in speech than in written text, because the words are easier to say and help make a conversation flow.

So...why did your team play so badly tonight?

Did you see the game last night?

An ellipsis stands for a pause when spoken language is written down.

Er...we...have no excuse.

Awesome, wasn't it?

Yeah.

This isn't a full sentence. The speaker is relying on what was said before for his or her words to make sense.

GLOSSARY

Accent The way in which a language is pronounced.

Colloquial A word used to describe the language that is used in informal, everyday speech.

Contraction A word that has been shortened by removing letters.

Dialect The informal vocabulary and grammar used by a particular social or geographical group of people.

Pitch The height of a sound.

Tone The feeling or mood projected by a voice, for example, happy, sad, angry or excited.

Reckon we're going to win the league now.

The word *I* has been left out, and *we're* has been used instead of *we are*. The informal verb *reckon* is often used in colloquial speech.

Debates and role plays

DEBATES AND ROLE PLAYS ARE TYPES OF CONVERSATIONS
THAT ARE PREPARED FOR IN ADVANCE.

SEE ALSO
❮ **202–203** Writing to influence
❮ **206–297** Writing to analyse or review
❮ **216–217** Writing a script
❮ **222–223** The spoken word
Presentation skills   **228–229** ❯

A prepared conversation is very different from an informal chat with
friends. Participants need to think about what they are going to
say in advance, and consider how they should react to others.

• A **formal discussion** requires
formal language so try to use
Standard English.

The big debate

A debate is a formal discussion or argument about a topic.
Participants need to express their own opinions confidently,
and listen and respond to others.

I think Powerman is the best
superhero because he has
the most superhuman
powers. He is **incredibly
strong** and can **fly at
supersonic speeds**.

Always back up an
opinion with evidence.

Acknowledge the
opposite point
of view before
disagreeing with it.

**I understand your point.
However,** I think Birdman's
lack of superpowers makes
him more inspirational,
because he has had to
overcome challenges and
learn his skills.

▷ **Prepare**
Participants need to convey their
ideas and opinions. The best way to
do this is to research the topic in
detail, and consider the different
points of view related to it. The most
effective discussions will cover as
many viewpoints as possible.

◁ **Listen and respond**
Listening is just as important as
talking. Participants should show
that they are listening to others by
responding appropriately and asking
relevant questions. They should either
agree with someone and add to
the point, or disagree and say why.

So, Melvin, **what do you
think?** Maybe you prefer
someone else, such
as Tigerwoman?

Coax other
participants to
join in by asking
questions.

Avoid hostile
body language.

▷ **Involve others**
It's important to involve all the
participants in a discussion and to
act as a group. Everyone should be
allowed to speak, without someone
else talking over them. Quieter
members of the group may need
encouragement to join in.

◁ **Body language**
Body language helps participants to
interact with one another. Nodding
in agreement is a simple way to do
this. Making eye contact with
everyone in the group, especially
the speaker, is also effective. If
someone folds their arms, it looks
as if they don't want to be there.

Role plays

A role play is a made-up scenario in which participants each play a character. There isn't a script, so everyone needs to act spontaneously. The best way to prepare is to think about the character's personality, and how they would behave in the specific situation.

The first **American presidential debate** was between the candidates **John F. Kennedy** and **Richard Nixon** in 1960. It was one of the **most-watched** broadcasts in US television history.

Get inside their head

A good way to start is to imagine what the character would be thinking. Reflect on the person's story so far, and what they would think about the current situation. Consider their relationships with the other characters, and how they will behave around them.

Talk the talk

To make characters convincing, it's important to talk like them. An angry person might shout, a shy character might mutter his or her words, and an excited person might talk quickly. Use an appropriate accent if the person is from a particular country or region, and use the right vocabulary for the character's age group.

Walk the walk

The character's personality or mood should be reflected with appropriate body language. For example, a confident character would hold her head up high and her shoulders back and might walk with a swagger. A timid or uncomfortable character would look down at the ground, shuffle, slouch and avoid eye contact.

Not you again!

In court

A criminal trial is a type of debate because the barristers argue about whether a defendant is guilty or not guilty. The prosecution and defence barristers take turns making their points and giving evidence. A judge, and sometimes a jury, will then give a verdict. A barrister's ability to persuade can make all the difference in a trial's outcome.

• Introduce some **controversial points of view** in a discussion. Even if no one agrees with them, unusual ideas can get a debate going.

• Do not **shout**. Even if there is a disagreement, it's important to remain **polite**.

Writing a speech

A SPEECH IS A TALK ON A PARTICULAR SUBJECT TO AN AUDIENCE.

People make speeches for many different reasons, but they are often for work or social occasions. The techniques used for writing a speech are similar to those used in written work, but a speech must be effective when read aloud.

SEE ALSO

❮ **34–35** Pronouns
❮ **182–183** Picking the right words
❮ **188–189** Paragraphing
❮ **202–203** Writing to influence
❮ **222–223** The spoken word
Presentation skills **228–229** ❯

Talking point

Every speech needs to have a clear and passionate message for its audience. For example, a politician makes speeches to persuade people to vote for him or her, or to support his or her policies. Activists speak to raise awareness about an issue, such as animal rights.

• Informal speeches can include some **slang**, but it's best to use **Standard English** so that the audience will **understand** what is **being said**.

GLOSSARY

Alliteration The repetition of certain letters or sounds for effect.

Pronoun A word that takes the place of a noun, such as *I*, *me* or *she*.

Rhetorical question A question that does not require an answer but is used for effect.

Slogan A short but memorable statement that sums up a message.

Standard English The form of English that uses formal vocabulary and grammar.

Ideas for my speech:

- *Save the Brussels sprout!*
- *When I met my favourite sports star.*
- *Mullet hairstyles are a fashion disaster.*
- *Why I should be the next James Bond.*
- *Mobile phones should not be banned in school.*

Structure

Like any piece of writing, a speech needs to have a focused structure, with a clear beginning, middle and end.

I have a shocking secret. I like Brussels sprouts!

Brussels sprouts are incredibly good for you. There is more vitamin C in a sprout than an orange.

So, next time you tuck into dinner, give the little green things a chance.

△ **Beginning**
The opening lines should capture the audience's attention, with a joke, a surprising statistic or an inspirational quote.

△ **Middle**
The middle part of the speech should deliver the main points, one by one. Each point should be backed up with evidence.

△ **End**
The last section needs to sum up the message of the speech and ideally end with something memorable.

Smooth talker

Speech-writers use particular techniques to create interesting speeches that will engage an audience. Most importantly, they consider what the words will sound like when they are spoken out loud.

Rhetorical questions

Sometimes, a speaker will ask the audience a question, often without expecting an answer. Posing questions makes listeners feel involved and encourages them to think about something in depth.

You say that you hate Brussels sprouts, but have you ever given them a chance?

Repetition and lists

Repeating words and phrases gives a speech a good rhythm and emphasises important words and ideas. Patterns of three are particularly common in speech writing. Listing subjects, places or names can reinforce how many there are of something.

Sprouts are bursting with goodness. They are packed with **vitamin C, vitamin A, potassium, calcium, iron and protein.**

Emotive and sensational language

A speech isn't just a list of events or a logical argument. It needs to appeal to the audience. Speech-writers use emotive language to evoke a response in the audience, such as sympathy, guilt or excitement.

Every year, thousands and thousands of untouched Brussels sprouts are **thoughtlessly dumped** in the rubbish bin.

Pronouns

Using the pronouns *I*, *you* or *we* in a speech can make it more personal. Speakers also use friendly terms of address, such as *friends* or *comrades*, to relate to the audience.

I changed my mind about Brussels sprouts. **You** can, too. **Together we** can make this vegetable popular again.

Slogans

Speeches often contain memorable statements called slogans, which sum up an argument. They are usually short and powerful, and sound good when spoken out loud, often because they use alliteration.

Bring **b**ack the **B**russels!

The best speeches are often **short**. **Abraham Lincoln's Gettysburg Address**, one of the most famous speeches in history, lasted for less than **three minutes**.

REAL WORLD

I would also like to thank...

Actors often give speeches when they win prizes at awards ceremonies. The Academy Awards have become famous for having overly long and emotional speeches. The record for the longest speech is still held by Greer Garson, who rambled on for seven minutes in 1942. Since then, ceremony organisers have imposed a 45-second rule, so speeches longer than 45 seconds are cut off by the orchestra.

Presentation skills

THE BEST PUBLIC SPEAKERS ARE CLEAR AND ENGAGING.

Even a well-written speech will be dull if it is badly presented. It's important to speak clearly and to engage an audience with the right tone of voice, body language and even props.

SEE ALSO

❰ 116–117 Bullet points
❰ 202–203 Writing to influence
❰ 222–223 The spoken word
❰ 224–225 Debates and role plays
❰ 226–227 Writing a speech

Flash cards

It's tempting to read out a speech word by word, but a spontaneous delivery is more entertaining for an audience. It's best to learn as much of a speech as possible, and prepare small cards with the important points, quotations and statistics to use as prompts.

Write the important points on a flash card. These can be written in note form.

Include statistics because they are easy to forget.

Why I love Brussels sprouts
- I have a secret. I love Brussels sprouts!
- The day I changed my mind
- They have a bad reputation but don't deserve it
- Largest producer is the Netherlands, with 82,000 tons a year

Speak up

A speaker should never shout, but should project his or her voice so that it can be heard around the room. It's also important not to speak too quickly, as the audience may find it difficult to keep up. In fact, pausing occasionally can be very effective because it gives an audience time to think about what is being said. Finally, there is no need to hide an accent, but the pronunciation should be clear.

Some nutritional facts about Brussels sprouts
- Brussels sprouts contain more vitamin C than oranges. (pause)
- There is almost no fat in Brussels sprouts. (pause)
- Unlike most vegetables, Brussels sprouts are high in protein. (pause)

Include pauses on a flash card to show when to break for a few seconds.

Intonation

When people talk, their voices go up and down and get louder and quieter. This natural variation is called intonation. If a person's voice stays the same, it will sound robotic and send the audience to sleep. Stressing important words or phrases helps to create a good rhythm, and will emphasise those points.

Underline or highlight important words or phrases that need to be stressed.

History of Brussels sprouts
- Forerunners to the Brussels sprout were cultivated in Ancient Rome.
- American Founding Father Thomas Jefferson grew Brussels sprouts.
- Today, production is huge. Approximately 32,000 tons are produced in the United States every year.

Gestures and movement

Gestures can make a presenter seem more enthusiastic and engaging. Speakers often wave their hands around to emphasise certain points and catch an audience's attention. Walking around a room makes a delivery more personal because the speaker moves closer to certain individuals. Making eye contact with individuals in an audience is also important.

- A speaker must sound **enthusiastic**. If he or she sounds bored, the audience will be, too.
- It can be useful to **practise** a speech in front of a **mirror**.

Maintain eye contact to engage the audience.

△ **Enthusiasm**
Enthusiastic gestures, such as punching the air or waving, can make a speaker seem more passionate.

△ **Big ideas**
Some actions – for example, spreading out the arms – can emphasise the size of an issue.

△ **Distraction**
It's important not to move around too much. Awkward movements can distract an audience from what the speaker is saying.

Visual aids

Sometimes speakers use visual aids to engage their audiences. These include images, graphs and diagrams that explain complicated information or make it more interesting. Summarising key points on a projector slide or handout will also emphasise the most important details, and help the audience to remember them.

Vitamin C: 85 mg

Carbohydrates: 8.95 g

Fibre: 3.8 g

Protein: 3.38 g

Sugars: 2.2 g

Fat: 0.3 g

Energy: 179 kJ (43 kcal)

Nutritional value per 100 g (3.5 oz)

REAL WORLD

Dressing down

Public speakers even think about the way they dress when speaking to an audience. Some politicians or business professionals decide not to wear a suit and tie when making a speech to the public. By wearing more casual clothes, they hope that they will look more relaxed and approachable, so the audience will relate to them.

Reference

Grammar reference

Parts of speech

The different types of words that make up sentences are called parts of speech. Only nouns and verbs are essential elements of a sentence, but other parts of speech – such as adjectives and adverbs – can make a sentence more descriptive.

Part of speech	Meaning	Examples
noun	A name	cat, Evie, girl, house, water
adjective	Describes a noun or pronoun	big, funny, light, red, young
verb	Shows action or a state of being	be, go, read, speak, swim, walk
adverb	Describes verbs, adjectives and other adverbs, giving information on where, when and how much	briskly, easily, happily, here, loudly, quite, rather, soon, together, very
pronoun	Takes the place of a noun	he, she, you, we, them, it
preposition	Relates a noun or pronoun to another word in the sentence	about, above, from, in
conjunction	A joining word, used to link words and phrases	and, because, but, while, yet
interjection	An exclamation or remark	ah, hey, hi, hmm, wow, yes
article	Used with a noun to specify whether the noun is a particular person or thing, or something general	a, an, the
determiner	Precedes a noun and puts the noun in context	all, her, my, their, your

Negative and positive words and phrases

Some words have negative meanings – for example, *no*, *none*, *not*, *insult* and *deny*. Other words can be made negative by adding a negative prefix, such as anti-, dis- or un-, or suffix, such as -less. These words can then be used to make a sentence structure positive, which helps to simplify the sentence and make it easier to understand.

Negative structure	Positive structure
was not typical	was atypical
is not social	is antisocial
have no defences	is defenceless
was not hydrated	was dehydrated
does not approve	disapproves
was not legal	was illegal
is not balanced	is imbalanced
was not direct	was indirect
was not spelt correctly	was misspelt
does not exist	is non-existent
was not happy	was unhappy

Irregular verbs

Not all verbs follow the rules: regular verbs follow a specific spelling pattern when they are converted into the past tense, but irregular verbs do not. Here are some of the irregular verbs and their past-tense and past-participle spellings.

Infinitive form	Simple past tense	Past participle
awake	awoke	awoken
bear	bore	borne
beat	beat	beaten
bend	bent	bent
bind	bound	bound
bite	bit	bitten
burn	burned/burnt	burned/burnt
deal	dealt	dealt
dig	dug	dug
dream	dreamed/dreamt	dreamed/dreamt
feed	fed	fed
fight	fought	fought
forbid	forbade	forbidden
forget	forgot	forgotten
forgive	forgave	forgiven
forsake	forsook	forsaken
grind	ground	ground
hide	hid	hidden
hit	hit	hit
hurt	hurt	hurt
kneel	knelt	knelt
leap	leaped/leapt	leaped/leapt
light	lit	lit
overdo	overdid	overdone
prove	proved	proved/proven
read	read	read
ring	rang	rung
seek	sought	sought
shine	shone	shone
slay	slew	slain
stink	stank	stunk
tread	trod	trodden
wake	woke	woken
weave	wove	woven

Pronouns

Pronouns are used to represent nouns, so that sentences do not become repetitive. Singular nouns should be replaced by singular pronouns, and plural nouns should be replaced by plural pronouns. Some pronouns can be singular or plural.

Type	Singular	Plural
personal pronouns	I you he she it me him her	we you they us them
possessive pronouns	mine yours his hers its	ours yours theirs
relative pronouns	that what which who whom whose	that what which whose
reflexive pronouns	myself yourself himself herself	ourselves themselves
demonstrative pronouns	this that	these those
interrogative pronouns	who whom what which whose	what which
indefinite pronouns	all another any anyone anything each more most neither nobody none no one nothing other some somebody	all any both few many most none others several some

Common grammatical errors

Dangling participles

The introductory phrases in the first two sentences below set the sentence up for a noun that doesn't follow. This is called a "dangling participle" because the first part of the sentence is left dangling, with nothing to support or explain it. The noun that starts the second part of the sentence must be the noun that relates to the first part.

✗ **Smiling** from ear to ear, **the school** confirmed Jo's position on the debate team.

✗ **Smiling** from ear to ear, **Jo's position** on the school debate team was confirmed.

✓ **Smiling** from ear to ear, **Jo** heard that her position on the school debate team was confirmed.

Double negatives

Two negatives make a positive in maths, and the same is true in language – two negative words in a sentence cancel each other out to upset the intended meaning.

✗ Charlie **couldn't** have **none** of the sweets.

✓ Charlie **could** have **none** of the sweets.

✓ Charlie **couldn't** have **any** of the sweets.

Incomplete sentences

A complete sentence must make sense, and to do this it must contain a subject and a verb. Even though the second sentence below is made up of only two words, it is complete because it has a subject and a verb. The first sentence is incomplete because it doesn't have a subject.

✗ Where is.

✓ I slept.

Misuse of *me*, *myself* and *I*

If the following sentence is split into smaller parts, the sentence "Me travelled by train" is wrong.

✗ Luke and **me** travelled by train.

✓ Luke and **I** travelled by train.

Likewise, if this sentence is split into smaller parts, the sentence "It was a long journey for I" is wrong.

✗ It was a long journey for Luke and **I**.

✓ It was a long journey for Luke and **me**.

Myself always needs to have a subject to refer back to. There is no *I* or *me* in the first of the following sentences, so the use of *myself* in this instance is wrong.

✗ Luke wondered about **myself** in the same situation.

✓ I wondered about **myself** in the same situation.

Misplaced modifiers

A modifier needs to be close to the word that it is modifying; otherwise, confusion can occur. In the following sentence, the modifier *hot* should refer to the warmth of the porridge that Becky eats every morning, and not the heat of the bowl.

✗ Becky ate a **hot** bowl of porridge every morning.

✓ Becky ate a bowl of **hot** porridge every morning.

Misusing gender-neutral pronouns

Some pronouns, such as *they*, don't specify a gender. *They* is a plural pronoun and is sometimes misused in sentences where a singular pronoun is needed. In the following sentence, *they* is wrong because it is plural while the subject *someone* is singular. *They* should be replaced with *he or she,* or the sentence should be rewritten.

✗ If **someone** did that, then **they were** wrong.

✓ If **someone** did that, then **he or she was** wrong.

Split infinitives

An infinitive is the simplest form of a verb, such as *to run* or *to have*. It is preferable to keep the word *to* with the infinitive verb in a sentence. In the first sentence below, the adverb *secretly* has separated *to* from the verb *like*. This is a split infinitive and should be avoided.

✗ She used **to** secretly **like** football.

✓ She secretly used **to like** football.

Subject-verb disagreement

In the example below, the subject has been misidentified as *presents* – a plural noun – so the plural form of the verb (*were*) has been used. The subject of the sentence is actually the singular noun *sack*, so the singular form of the verb (*was*) should be used instead.

✗ The **sack** of presents **were** delivered late.

✓ The **sack** of presents **was** delivered late.

Non sequiturs

Literally translated, *non sequitur* means "it does not follow" and is an instance where one statement or conclusion doesn't logically follow what was previously said or argued. Here are some examples:

You have a big nose. Therefore, your face looks young.

I will win the game. I have a hat.

Commonly misused words and expressions

Using *bored of* instead of *bored by* or *bored with*

✗ She was bored **of** studying.

✗ He was bored **of** the classes.

✓ She was bored **with** studying.

✓ He was bored **by** the classes.

Confusing *compared to* and *compared with*

Compared to should be used when asserting that two things are alike. In this sentence, Jess was like the best in the class.

✓ The teacher compared Jess **to** the best in the class.

Compared with should be used when comparing the similarities and differences between two things. In the sentence below, the teacher was considering how similar Jess was to the best in the class.

✓ The teacher compared Jess **with** the best in the class.

Using *different to* instead of *different from*

✗ The left side is different **to** the right side.

✓ The left side is different **from** the right side.

Using *like* as a conjunction instead of *as if* or *as though*

Like is correctly used as a preposition in the final example sentence; it should not be used as a conjunction.

✗ He acted **like** he didn't care.

✓ He acted **as though** he didn't care.

✓ It looks **like** a turtle.

Using *or* with *neither*

Either and *or* go together, and *neither* and *nor* go together.

✗ Use **neither** the left one **or** the right one.

✓ Use **either** the left one **or** the right one.

✓ Use **neither** the left one **nor** the right one.

Using *should of*, *would of* and *could of* instead of *should have*, *would have* and *should have*

Of is often wrongly used to mean *have* in spoken English.

✗ Steve **should of** stood up for himself.

✓ Steve **should have** stood up for himself.

✓ Steve **should've** stood up for himself.

Using *try and* and *go and* instead of *try to* and *go to*

The conjunction *and* is often wrongly used instead of the preposition *to* with the verbs *try* and *go*.

✗ We should **try and** change our flights.

✓ We should **try to** change our flights.

✗ I'll **go and** see the show.

✓ I'll **go to** see the show.

Using nouns as verbs

In spoken English, especially jargon, it is common for nouns to be used as verbs. This practice is best avoided.

✗ The fire will **impact** on the environment.

✓ The fire will have **an impact** on the environment.

Rules for forming sentences

• A sentence must always contain a subject and a verb, start with a capital letter and end with a full stop, question mark or exclamation mark. A sentence may also contain an object.

• The basic structure for a sentence to follow is subject–verb–object.

• Never join two main clauses using only a comma. Either separate the clauses into two separate sentences by using a full stop or a semi-colon, or add a joining word such as *and* or *but* after the comma.

• Ensure that a sentence makes sense. If it doesn't make sense, one of the essential ingredients is probably missing, so the sentence is incomplete. For example, a subordinate clause does not make a complete sentence on its own; the main clause is also needed.

• Make sure that the subject and verb match. If the subject is singular, then the verb should be singular; if the subject is plural, then the verb should be plural.

• Use the active voice instead of the passive voice. The active voice is simpler, so the meaning is conveyed more clearly.

• Use positive sentence structure instead of negative sentence structure whenever possible in order to simplify sentences and make them easier to understand.

• Sentences should have a parallel structure. This means that the same patterns of words should be used to show that different parts of the sentence have equal importance.

✗ Darcy likes swimming, running and to ride her bike.

✓ Darcy likes to swim, run and ride her bike.

Punctuation reference

Punctuation mark	Name	How to use
.	full stop	• marks the end of a complete statement • marks the end of an abbreviated word
...	ellipsis	• marks where text has been omitted or an unfinished sentence
,	comma	• follows an introductory word, phrase or clause • can be used as brackets, to separate a non-essential part of a sentence • can be used with a conjunction to join two main clauses • separates words or phrases in a list • represents omitted words to avoid repetition in a sentence • can be used between an introduction to speech and the direct speech
;	semi-colon	• separates two main clauses that are closely related • precedes adverbs such as *however*, *therefore*, *consequently* and *nevertheless* to connect clauses • separates items in a complex list
:	colon	• connects a main clause to a clause, phrase or word that is an explanation of the main clause or that emphasises a point in the main clause • introduces a list after a complete statement • introduces quoted text
,	apostrophe	• marks a missing letter • indicates possession • creates plural forms if just adding an *s* is confusing
-	hyphen	• links two words in compound modifiers • can be used in fractions and in numbers from twenty-one to ninety-nine • joins certain prefixes to other words
" "	inverted commas	• can be used before and after direct speech and quoted text • separates a word or phrase in a sentence • can be used around titles of short works
?	question mark	• marks the end of a sentence that is a question
!	exclamation mark	• marks the end of a sentence that expresses strong emotions • can be used at the end of an interruption to add emphasis
( )	brackets	• can be used around non-essential information in a sentence • can be used around information that provides clarification
—	dash	• can be used in pairs around interruptions • marks a range of numbers (5–6 hours) • indicates direction of travel (Trys–Qysto route)
•	bullet point	• indicates a key point in a list
/	slash	• can be used to show an alternative instead of using the word *and* or *or*

Contractions

	be	will	would	have	had
I	I am I'm	I will I'll	I would I'd	I have I've	I had I'd
you	you are you're	you will you'll	you would you'd	you have you've	you had you'd
he	he is he's	he will he'll	he would he'd	he has he's	he had he'd
she	she is she's	she will she'll	she would she'd	she has she's	she had she'd
it	it is it's	it will it'll	it would it'd	it has it's	it had it'd
we	we are we're	we will we'll	we would we'd	we have we've	we had we'd
they	they are they're	they will they'll	they would they'd	they have they've	they had they'd
that	that is that's	that will that'll	that would that'd	that has that's	that had that'd
who	who is who's	who will who'll	who would who'd	who has who's	who had who'd

Verbs and *not*	Contraction
is not	isn't
are not	aren't
was not	wasn't
were not	weren't
have not	haven't
has not	hasn't
had not	hadn't
will not	won't
would not	wouldn't
do not	don't
does not	doesn't
did not	didn't
cannot	can't
could not	couldn't
should not	shouldn't
might not	mightn't
must not	mustn't

Auxiliary verbs and *have*	would have	should have	could have	might have	must have
Contraction	would've	should've	could've	might've	must've

Common punctuation errors

Comma splice

A comma between two clauses creates a "comma splice" if it is used without a conjunction. The comma needs to be replaced with either a semi-colon or a full stop, or the text can be rewritten to use a comma and a conjunction.

✗ You cook**,** I'll do the dishes.

✓ You cook**, and** I'll do the dishes.

Greengrocer's apostrophe

An unnecessary apostrophe incorrectly placed before the plural *s* is called a "greengrocer's apostrophe".

✗ carrot**'**s ✗ apple**'**s

✓ carrots ✓ apples

Hyphen in a compound modifier

Using a hyphen in a compound modifier that includes an adverb ending in -ly is incorrect. These compound modifiers are never hyphenated.

✗ cleverly-planned meeting

✓ cleverly planned meeting

Misuse of *your* and *you're*

Confusion between *your* and *you're* can be avoided by remembering that "you're" is a contraction made up of two separate words: *you* and *are*.

✗ It's in **you're** bag. ✗ **Your** mistaken.

✓ It's in **your** bag. ✓ **You're** mistaken.

Spelling reference

Commonly misspelt words

There are many difficult words in the English language that people struggle to spell correctly. Here are some of the most commonly misspelt words, with handy tips on how to spell them correctly.

Correct spelling	Spelling tips	Common misspelling
accommodation	there are two *c*'s and two *m*'s	accomodation
apparently	*ent* in the middle, not *ant*	apparantly
appearance	ends -**ance**, not -**ence**	appearence
basically	ends -**cally**, not -**cly**	basicly
beginning	double *n* in the middle	begining
believe	remember the "*i* before *e* except after *c*" rule	beleive or belive
business	starts with **busi-**	buisness
calendar	ends with -**ar**, not -**er**	calender
cemetery	ends with -**ery**, not -**ary**	cemetary
coming	there is only one *m*	comming
committee	double *m*, double *t* and double *e*	commitee
completely	remember the last *e*; ends -**tely**, not -**tly**	completly
conscious	remember the *s* before the *c* in the middle	concious
definitely	*ite* in the middle, not *ate*	definately
disappoint	there is one *s* and two *p*'s	dissapoint
embarrass	there are two *r*'s and two *s*'s	embarass
environment	remember the *n* before the *m*	enviroment
existence	ends with -**ence**, not -**ance**	existance
familiar	ends with -**iar**	familar
finally	there are two *l*'s	finaly
friend	remember the "*i* before *e* except after *c*" rule	freind
government	remember the *n* before the *m*	goverment
interrupt	there are two *r*'s in the middle	interupt
knowledge	remember the *d* before the *g*	knowlege
necessary	one *c* and two *s*'s	neccessary
separate	*par* in the middle, not *per*	seperate
successful	two *c*'s and two *s*'s	succesful
truly	there is no *e*	truely
unfortunately	ends with -**tely**, not -**tly**	unfortunatly
which	begins with **wh**	wich

Two words or one?

Some words in the English language are often used together, so it's easy to mistake them for a single word. Here are some phrases that many people fall into the trap of writing as one word instead of two.

a lot	full time	home page	real time
bath time	half moon	ice cream	seat belt
blood sugar	hard copy	life cycle	side effect
cash flow	high chair	never mind	time frame
first aid	hip bone	post office	time sheet

Commonly confused words

The English language is full of similar-sounding words that have different meanings. It is essential, therefore, to spell the words correctly to achieve the correct meaning in a sentence. Here are some of the most commonly confused words that sound alike, with examples of their correct usage.

accept and **except**
I **accept** your apology.
Everyone was on the list **except** for me.

adverse and **averse**
She was feeling unwell due to the **adverse** effects of her medication.
He was lazy and **averse** to playing sport.

aisle and **isle**
The bride walked down the **aisle**.
They visited an **isle** near the coast of Scotland.

aloud and **allowed**
She read the book **aloud**.
He was **allowed** to choose which book to read.

amoral and **immoral**
Her **amoral** attitude meant that she didn't care if her actions were wrong.
He was fired from the firm for **immoral** conduct.

appraise and **apprise**
The manager needed to **appraise** the employee's skills.
The lawyer arrived to **apprise** the defendant of his rights.

assent and **ascent**
He nodded his **assent**.
They watched the **ascent** of the balloon.

aural and **oral**
The **aural** test required her to listen.
The dentist performed an **oral** examination.

bare and **bear**
The baby had a **bare** bottom.
The large **bear** roamed the woods.

break and **brake**
The chocolate was easy to **break** apart.
The car didn't **brake** fast enough.

broach and **brooch**
He decided to **broach** the subject for discussion.
She wore a pretty **brooch**.

cereal and **serial**
He ate a bowl of **cereal** for breakfast.
She found the **serial** number on her computer.

complement and **compliment**
The colours **complement** each other well.
He paid her a **compliment** by telling her she was pretty.

cue and **queue**
The actor waited for his **cue** before walking on stage.
The checkout **queue** was very long.

desert and **dessert**
The **desert** is extremely hot and dry.
She decided to have cake for **dessert**.

draught and **draft**
There was a **draught** coming from under the door.
He had written a **draft** of the letter.

pore and **pour**
He had a blocked **pore** on his nose.
She helped **pour** the drinks at the party.

principle and **principal**
The man believed in strong **principles**.
He was given the role of the **principal** character.

stationary and **stationery**
The aircraft landed and remained **stationary**.
She looked in the **stationery** cupboard for a pen.

Tricky capitalised words

Certain words sometimes begin with a capital letter and at other times they don't. It's important to know when to use a capital letter, so that written sentences make sense.

In some cases, capital letters are the only distinguishing factor between two words that are spelt in the same way, but mean very different things.

Confused words	Lower-case meaning	Capitalised meaning
alpine and **Alpine**	relating to mountainous areas	relating to the Alps
august and **August**	majestic	the eighth month of the year
cancer and **Cancer**	a disease	a constellation and astrological sign
china and **China**	porcelain	a country in eastern Asia
earth and **Earth**	soil, dry land	the planet we live on
jack and **Jack**	a device for lifting heavy items	a male name
italic and **Italic**	a sloping typeface	relating to Italy
lent and **Lent**	the past tense of the verb *lend*	in Christianity, the period preceding Easter
march and **March**	to walk briskly and rhythmically	the third month of the year
marine and **Marine**	relating to the ocean	a member of the Marine Corps
mercury and **Mercury**	a chemical element	the closest planet to the Sun
nice and **Nice**	pleasant	a city in the south of France
pole and **Pole**	a long cylindrical object	a person from Poland
swede and **Swede**	a vegetable	a person from Sweden

Common Latin and Greek roots

Latin root	Meaning	Examples
act	do	**act**ion, en**act**
ang	bend	an**g**le, trian**g**le
cap	head	**cap**ital, de**cap**itate
dic	speak	**dic**tate, pre**dict**
imag	likeness	**imag**e, **imag**ination
just	law	**just**ice, **just**ify
ques	ask, seek	**ques**tion, re**ques**t
sci	know	con**sci**ence, **sci**ence

Greek root	Meaning	Examples
arch	chief	**arch**bishop, mon**arch**
auto	self	**auto**biography, **auto**matic
cosm	universe	**cosm**opolitan, **cosm**os
gen	birth, race	**gen**eration, **gen**ocide
log	word	apo**log**y, dia**log**ue
lys	break down	ana**lys**is, cata**lys**t
morph	shape	meta**morph**osis, **morph**ology
phon	sound	sym**phon**y, tele**phon**e

Prefixes and suffixes

Prefixes	Meanings	Examples
aero-	air	**aero**plane, **aero**sol
agri-	of earth	**agri**business, **agri**culturalist
ambi-	both	**ambi**guous, **ambi**valent
astro-	star	**astro**logy, **astro**naut
bio-	life, living things	**bio**diversity, **bio**fuel
contra-	against, opposite	**contra**band, **contra**dict
deca-	ten	**deca**de, **deca**hedron
di-, du-, duo-	two	**di**oxide, **du**et, **duo**tone
electro-	relating to electricity	**electro**lysis, **electro**magnet
geo-	relating to Earth	**geo**graphy, **geo**logy
hydro-	relating to water	**hydro**electricity, **hydro**power
infra-	below, beneath	**infra**red, **infra**stucture
kilo-	one thousand	**kilo**gram, **kilo**metre
mal-	bad	**mal**aise, **mal**nourished
maxi-	large	**maxi**mise, **maxi**mum
multi-	many	**multi**cultural, **multi**ply
nano-	one-billionth, extremely small	**nano**second, **nano**technology
ped-	foot	**ped**estrian, **ped**ometer
proto-	first	**proto**col, **proto**type
sy-, syl-, sym-, syn-	together, with	**sy**stem, **syl**lable, **sym**bol, **syn**thesis
tele-	distant	**tele**phone, **tele**scope

Suffixes	Meaning	Examples
-ade	action	block**ade**, masquer**ade**
-an	person, belonging to	guardi**an**, histori**an**
-ancy, -ency	state	vac**ancy**, ag**ency**
-ar, -ary	resembling	line**ar**, exempl**ary**
-ard, -art	characterise	wiz**ard**, bragg**art**
-ence, -ency	state	depend**ence**, emerg**ency**
-ess	female	lion**ess**, waitr**ess**
-fy	to make into	beauti**fy**, simpli**fy**
-iatry	healing, medical care	pod**iatry**, psych**iatry**
-ile	having the qualities of	project**ile**, sen**ile**
-our	condition	hum**our**, glam**our**
-ory	having the function of	compuls**ory**, contribut**ory**
-phobia	fear of	agora**phobia**, arachno**phobia**
-ure	action	expos**ure**, meas**ure**
-wise	in the manner of	clock**wise**, like**wise**

Homonyms

Homonyms are words that have the same spelling
and pronunciation, but different meanings.

Homonym	Meaning 1	Meaning 2	Meaning 3	Meaning 4
back	a person's back, from shoulders to hips	the back part of an object, opposite to the front	to go backwards	in return
board	a thin, flat piece of wood	a decision-making body	regular meals	to get on to a ship or train
bore	to make a hole	a hollow part of a tube	a dull person or activity	to make someone weary
cast	to throw forcefully in a specific direction	to cause light or shadow to appear on a surface	to register a vote	actors in a drama
clear	easy to interpret or understand	having or feeling no doubt or confusion	transparent	free of obstacles
course	a route or direction	a dish forming one of the parts of a meal	the way in which something develops	a series of lessons on a particular subject
dock	an enclosed area of water in a port	the place in a court where defendants stand	to deduct, usually money	to cut short, for example, an animal's tail
fair	treating people equally or appropriately	light hair colour or complexion	fine and dry weather	stalls and amusements for public entertainment
tie	fabric worn around neck	to fasten with string or cord	the same score in a game	a bond that unites people

Homophones

Homophones are words with identical pronunciations,
but different spellings and meanings.

Spelling 1	Meaning 1	Spelling 2	Meaning 2	Spelling 3	Meaning 3
aisle	a passage	isle	a small island	I'll	Contracted form of *I will*
buy	to purchase	by	means of achieving	bye	short for *goodbye*
cent	a monetary unit	scent	an odour	sent	past tense of the verb *send*
cite	to mention	sight	vision	site	a place
for	in support of	fore	situated in front	four	the number (4)
meat	animal flesh as food	meet	to get together	mete	to dispense a punishment
rain	precipitation from the sky	rein	a strip attached to a horse for guidance	reign	the period of rule by a monarch
raise	to lift something	rays	beams of light	raze	to completely destroy or demolish
vain	conceited	vane	a device for showing wind direction	vein	a blood vessel

Useful spelling rules

• The "**ee**" sound at the end of a word is almost always spelt with a **y**, as in *emergency* and *dependency*. There are exceptions to this rule, such as *fee* and *coffee*.

• When *all* and *well* are followed by another syllable, they only have one *l*, as in *already* and *welcome*.

• When *full* and *till* are joined to a root syllable, the final *l* should be dropped, as in *useful* and *until*.

• When **two vowels** go walking, **the first one** does the talking. This means that when there are two vowels next to each other in a word, the first one represents the sound made when spoken, while the second vowel is silent, as in *approach* and *leather*. There are some exceptions to this rule, including *poem* and *build*.

• When words end in a **silent -e**, drop the **silent -e** when adding endings that begin with a vowel: for example, when adding **-ing** to *give* to form *giving*. Keep the **silent -e** when adding endings that begin with a consonant: for example, when adding **-s** to *give* to form *gives*.

• If a word ends with an "**ick**" sound, spell it using *ick* if it has one syllable, as in *click* and *brick*. If the word has two or more syllables, spell it using *ic*, as in *electronic* and *catastrophic*. Some exceptions to this rule include *homesick* and *limerick*.

• The letter *q* is usually followed by a *u*, as in *quiet* and *sequence*.

Mnemonics and fun spelling tips

ocean
Only **c**ats' **e**yes **a**re **n**arrow.

affect and effect
Affect is the **a**ction; **e**ffect is the **re**sult.

dilemma
Emma faced a dil**emma**.

soldier
Sol**die**rs sometimes **die** in battle.

misspells
Miss Pells never misspells.

desert and dessert
What's the difference between deserts and desserts? Desserts are sweeter with **two s's** for sugars.

island
An island **is land** that is surrounded by water.

difficulty
Mrs. **D**, Mrs. **I**, Mrs. **FFI**, Mrs. **C**, Mrs. **U**, Mrs. **LTY**.

height and weight
There is an **eight** in h**eight** and w**eight**.

secretary
A **secret**ary must keep a **secret**.

measurement
You should be **sure** of your mea**sure**ments before you start work.

piece
You have to have a **pie** before you can have a **pie**ce.

hear
H**ear** with your **ear**.

Communication skills reference

Synonyms

Good writers use a wide range of vocabulary. Rather than using the same word repeatedly, try to use different words that mean the same thing. These are known as synonyms. Some alternatives may give more information than the original choice: for example, *she whispered* tells the reader much more than *she said*.

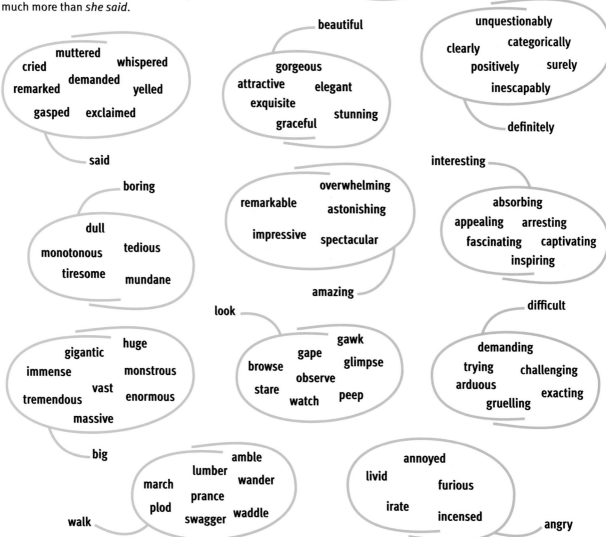

exciting

dramatic   thrilling

sensational

beautiful

unquestionably

clearly   categorically

positively   surely

inescapably

definitely

muttered
cried   whispered
demanded
remarked   yelled
gasped   exclaimed

said

gorgeous
attractive   elegant
exquisite
graceful   stunning

boring

dull
monotonous   tedious
tiresome   mundane

overwhelming
remarkable   astonishing
impressive   spectacular

amazing

interesting

absorbing
appealing   arresting
fascinating   captivating
inspiring

difficult

huge
gigantic
immense   monstrous
vast
tremendous   enormous
massive

big

look

gawk
gape
browse   glimpse
observe
stare   peep
watch

demanding
trying   challenging
arduous
gruelling   exacting

amble
lumber
march   wander
prance
plod   waddle
swagger

walk

annoyed
livid
furious
irate
incensed

angry

Adjectives to describe characters

The best stories include unique characters. Use unusual adjectives to describe a character's mood and personality.

absent-minded	flamboyant	materialistic
argumentative	generous	morose
bossy	glamorous	optimistic
charismatic	gregarious	responsible
considerate	intelligent	ruthless
eccentric	intuitive	witty

Tautologies

Some phrases say the same thing twice. These are called tautologies and should be avoided because they are unnecessary.

Tautology	Reason
tiny little baby	*tiny* and *little* mean the same thing
a round circle	circles are always round
an old antique	an antique has to be old
an unexpected surprise	all surprises are unexpected
yellow in colour	something can't be yellow in anything other than colour
month of May	May is always a month
new innovation	an innovation has to be new

Clichés

A cliché is a colloquial expression that has been overused. Clichés should be avoided because they make a piece of writing unoriginal, and because they are informal and often ambiguous.

face the music

as light as a feather

up in the air

at the end of the day   at all costs

in a nutshell

on a roll   cost an arm and a leg

Emotive language

Writers use emotive language to have a greater emotional impact on their audience. This technique is useful when trying to persuade or entertain an audience. It's important to be aware of the effect this language can have in order to analyse and write emotive texts.

Normal version	Dramatic version
she cried	she wailed
a good result	a staggering result
disturbance in town centre	riot in town centre
school fire	school blaze
brave person	heroic citizen
unhappy workers	furious workers
animals killed	animals slaughtered
house prices fall	house prices plummet
problems in schools	chaos in schools

Less wordy

Using more words than necessary can obscure the meaning of a phrase. Concise writing is both clearer and more stylish.

Wordy version	Concise version
a considerable number of	many
are of the same opinion	agree
as a means of	to
at the present time	currently, now, today
at this point in time	now
give an indication of	show
has a requirement for	requires, needs
has the ability to	can
in close proximity to	near
in the absence of	without
in the course of	during
in the majority of instances	usually
in the very near future	soon
is aware of the fact	knows

Cover letters

A cover letter is a formal letter written to accompany a résumé for a job application. It should be laid out like any formal letter, and include certain details that will promote the application. A good cover letter should be concise and no more than one page long.

The applicant's details go at the top right.

Joe Elf
Hollow Tree
Snowy Forest
Lapland

The date needs to be included under the applicant's address.

15 September 2013

The employer's details go at the top left.

Mr. Santa Claus
Toy Workshop
Secret Mountain
North Pole

The first paragraph should state which role the applicant is applying for, and where he or she saw the vacancy.

<u>Junior Toymaker Vacancy</u>

The vacancy details go in the subject line.

Dear Mr. Claus,

I would like to apply for the position of Junior Toymaker advertised in the *Lapland Chronicle*. As requested, I have enclosed my résumé and two references.

The role would be an excellent opportunity for me to start my career in toy manufacturing. I believe that my impressive education and examination results from the Toy College would make me an asset to the company.

The middle of the letter needs to explain why the applicant wants the job, and what skills and experience he or she has.

I can be contacted at the address and phone number on my résumé. I am available for interview next week.

Ending with a positive phrase will show enthusiasm.

I look forward to discussing this role with you soon.

Yours sincerely,

Joe Elf

Joe Elf

Referencing

In academic work, writers have to reference their sources. This is to prove that they have not copied another scholar's writing, taken credit for someone else's ideas or made up information. A reference needs to be added if another writer's direct words have been quoted, or his or her original ideas or findings are described. Statistics also need to be referenced. There are several referencing systems to choose from; however, the same system must be used throughout a piece of writing.

▷ **Numbering system**
In a numbering system, a small number is placed after each fact or quotation that needs to be referenced. This corresponds to a numbered source placed at the bottom of the page, called a footnote. The details are repeated in the bibliography at the end of the work.

Pizza purists argue that pizzas should only be topped with tomatoes, herbs and sometimes mozzarella. According to the Italian food writer, Gennaro Rossi, "There are only two types of pizza – Marinara and Margherita. That is all I serve."[1]

1 Gennaro Rossi, *The Perfect Pizza* (London: Pizza Press, 2010), p.9.

The title of the book is written in italics.

The location and name of the publisher appear in brackets, separated by a colon. A publisher's name is followed by a comma and the publication date.

The specific page reference(s) should also be included. If the reference is to a single page, *p.* should be used. If a reference is made to several pages, *pp.* is used.

▷ **Bracket system**
In a bracket system, the author and date are cited in brackets within the text. This way of referencing is often called the "Harvard system" because it originated at Harvard University.

The full year of the source is included.

The exact page reference is also added.

Pizza purists argue that pizzas should only be topped with tomatoes, herbs and sometimes mozzarella. According to the Italian food writer, Gennaro Rossi (Rossi 2010, p.9), "There are only two types of pizza – Marinara and Margherita. That is all I serve."

Only the surname of the author is included.

There should be no comma between the name of the author and the date, but the date and page reference should be separated by a comma.

▷ **Reference list**
When using the bracket system, the rest of the information about the sources needs to be included in a reference list at the end of the assignment. Unlike a bibliography, a reference list only includes the sources that have been quoted or paraphrased; it does not list books used for background research.

Romano, S. (1982) *The History of Italian Cooking*, Rome: Food Books.
Rossi, G. (2010) *The Perfect Pizza*, London: Pizza Press.
Smith, J. (2006) *My Love of Pizza*, New York: Big Fat Publishing.

The sources should be listed alphabetically by the author's surname.

The date of the work goes after the author's name in brackets.

The title is italicized.

The publisher's details are separated by a colon.

End each entry with a full stop.

Glossary

abbreviation
A shortened form of a word, often with one or more full stops to represent missing letters.

abstract noun
The name given to something that cannot be touched, such as a concept or a sensation.

accent
The way in which a language is pronounced, which varies across geographic areas.

acronym
An abbreviation made up of the initial letters of the main words in a phrase. These letters are pronounced as a word (rather than as separate letters), which represents the meaning of the original phrase.

active voice
When the subject of a sentence is performing the action of the verb, and the object is receiving it.

adjectival phrase
A group of words that describe a noun or pronoun.

adjective
A word that describes a noun.

adjective prepositional phrase
A prepositional phrase that describes a noun.

adverb
A word that modifies the meaning of an adjective, verb or other adverb.

adverb prepositional phrase
A prepositional phrase that describes a verb.

adverbial phrase
A group of words that behave in the same way as an adverb and answer questions such as: How? When? Why? Where? How often?

alliteration
The repetition of certain letters or sounds for effect.

Arabic numerals
Everyday numerals such as 1, 2 and 3.

attributive position
When an adjective is placed directly in front of the noun or pronoun that it is modifying.

auxiliary verb
A "helping" verb such as *be* or *have* that joins the main verb in a sentence to the subject. Auxiliary verbs are also used with other words to form contractions and negative sentences.

bibliography
A list of all the sources used in a piece of academic work.

blog
An online journal that contains the writer's comments and reflections. It is updated regularly.

cardinal number
A counting number such as *one*, *two*, *ten* or *twenty-one*.

clause
A grammatical unit that contains a subject and a verb. Sentences are made up of one or more clauses.

collective noun
The name given to a collection of individuals – people or things.

colloquial language
The language that is used in everyday speech.

colloquialism
A word or phrase used only in informal speech.

command
A sentence that gives an instruction.

common noun
The name given to everyday objects, places, people and ideas.

concrete noun
The name given to an ordinary, physical thing, such as an object or animal.

conjunction
A word or phrase used to connect words, phrases and clauses.

consonant
A letter of the alphabet that is not a vowel.

contraction
A shortened form of a word or words, in which letters are omitted from the middle and replaced with an apostrophe.

co-ordinating conjunction
A word that connects words, phrases and clauses of equal importance.

dangling participle
When a modifying phrase or clause that starts with a participle is put in the wrong place in a sentence, and has no subject to hold on to.

dialect
The informal vocabulary and grammar used by a particular social or geographic group.

direct object
The person or thing directly affected by the action of the verb.

direct speech
Text that represents spoken words and is written in inverted commas.

exaggeration
When something is represented as larger or better than it actually is.

exclamation
A sentence that expresses a strong emotion, such as surprise, or a raised voice, and ends in an exclamation mark.

fact
A statement that can be proved.

first person narrative
When an author writes a piece from his or her point of view, using *I* and *my*.

gerund
The name given to the present participle when it is used as a noun.

headline
The statement at the top of an article that tells the reader what the article is about.

hyperbole
An extreme form of exaggeration that may not be taken seriously, but grabs the reader's attention.

hyperlink
A word, phrase or icon on the World Wide Web, which, if clicked, takes the user to a new document or website.

indefinite pronoun
A pronoun such as *everyone* that refers to nobody or nothing specific.

indirect object
The person or thing indirectly affected by the action of the verb.

indirect question
A sentence that reports a question that has been asked, without expecting an answer, and ends in a full stop.

infinitive
The simplest form of a verb: the form that is used in dictionaries.

interjection
A word or phrase that occurs alone and expresses emotion.

intonation
The variation of pitch and loudness in a person's voice.

intransitive verb
A verb that does not require an object.

italics
A style of type in which the letters are printed at an angle to resemble handwriting.

jargon
A type of slang that includes specialist terms that are used and understood by a select, often professional, group of people.

linking verb
A verb, such as *be*, that joins the subject of a sentence to a word or phrase – often an adjective – that describes the subject.

main clause
A group of words that contains a subject and a verb and makes complete sense on its own.

metaphor
A word or phrase that is used to describe something as if it were something else.

misplaced modifier
A modifier that has been placed so far from the person or thing it is intended to modify that it appears to modify a different person or thing.

modal auxiliary verb
An auxiliary verb such as *could* that is used with an action verb to express a command, an obligation or a possibility.

morpheme
The smallest meaningful part of a word.

noun
A part of speech that refers to a person, place or thing.

noun phrase
Several words that, when grouped together, perform the same function as a noun.

number
The term used to identify a noun or pronoun as singular or plural.

object
The person or thing (a noun or pronoun) that is receiving the action of the verb.

objective
When a piece of writing is not influenced by the writer's personal opinions.

onomatopoeia
The use of words that mimic the sounds they represent.

opinion
A statement based on someone's personal view.

ordinal number
The form of a number that includes *first*, *second*, *tenth* and *twenty-first*.

participle
The form of a verb that ends in -ing (present participle) or -ed or -en (past participle).

passive voice
When the subject in a sentence is receiving the action of the verb, and the object is performing it. It is formed using the auxiliary verb *be* and the past participle.

past participle
The form of a verb that usually ends in -ed or -en. It is used with the auxiliary verbs *have* and *will* to form the perfect tenses, and with the auxiliary verb *be* to form the passive voice.

personal pronoun
A pronoun such as *she* that takes the place of a noun and represents people, places or things.

personification
When human actions or feelings are given to objects or ideas.

pitch
The height of a sound.

plural noun
When more than one person or thing is being described.

possessive determiner
A word that is used before a noun to show ownership.

predicate position
When an adjective follows a linking verb at the end of a sentence.

prefix
A group of letters attached to the start of a word that can change the original word's meaning.

prepositional phrasal verb
A verb followed by a preposition, which together act as a single unit to describe an action.

prepositional phrase
A preposition followed by a noun, pronoun or noun phrase that together act as an adjective (describing a noun) or an adverb (describing a verb) in a sentence.

present participle
The form of a verb that ends in -ing. It is used with the auxiliary verb *be* to form the continuous tenses.

pronoun
A word, such as *I*, *some* or *who* that takes the place of a noun.

proper noun
The name given to a particular person, place or thing, which always starts with a capital letter.

pun

The use of a word or phrase that has two or more meanings for comic effect.

question

A sentence that asks for information.

quotation

Text that reproduces another author's exact words, and is written in inverted commas.

quote

To repeat the words of a person.

relative pronoun

A pronoun such as *which* that links one part of a sentence to another by introducing a relative clause, which describes an earlier noun or pronoun.

rhetorical question

A question that does not require an answer but is used for effect.

Roman numerals

Numbers represented by certain letters of the alphabet, such as *i* (one), *v* (five) and *x* (ten).

root

A whole word or part of a word that can attach to a suffix or prefix.

SEO

Standing for "Search Engine Optimization", this is the process that increases the online visibility of a website, so more Web users will visit it.

simile

A phrase that compares one thing to another using *as* or *like*.

slang

Words and phrases that occur in informal speech and are often only used by a select group of people.

slogan

A short but memorable statement that sums up a message.

Standard English

The form of English that uses formal vocabulary and grammar.

statement

A sentence that conveys a fact or piece of information.

subject

The person or thing that is performing the action of the verb.

subjective

When a piece of text is influenced by the writer's personal opinions.

subordinate clause

A group of words that contains a subject and a verb but depends on a main clause for its meaning.

subordinator

A conjunction used to connect words, phrases and clauses of unequal importance.

suffix

An ending made up of one or more letters that is added to a word to change its form or its meaning.

superlative

The form of an adjective or adverb that suggests the greatest or least of something.

syllable

A unit of pronunciation that has one vowel sound.

synonyms

Words that have the same or similar meanings.

tautology

Saying the same thing more than once using different words.

tense

The form of a verb that indicates the timing of an action.

third person narrative

When an author writes from a detached or outside point of view, using *he/his* or *she/her*.

tone

The feeling or mood projected by a voice: for example, happy, sad, angry or excited.

transitive verb

A verb that must be used with an object.

verb

A part of speech that describes the action of a noun or pronoun, or a state of being.

vowel

One of the five letters *a, e, i, o* or *u*.

Index

Acknowledgements

DORLING KINDERSLEY would like to thank David Ball and Mik Gates for design assistance, Mike Foster and Steve Capsey at Maltings Partnership for the illustrations, Helen Abramson for editorial assistance, Jenny Sich for proofreading, and Carron Brown for the index.

The publisher would like to thank the following for their kind permission to reproduce their photographs:

(Key: a-above; b-below/bottom; c-centre; f-far; l-left; r-right; t-top)

29 Alamy Images: Niday Picture Library. **39** Alamy Images: Moviestore Collection Ltd. **45** Alamy Images: Kumar Sriskandan. Alamy Images: Kumar Sriskandan. **45** Alamy Images: Kumar Sriskandan. Alamy Images: Kumar Sriskandan. **54** Fotolia: (c) Stephen Finn. **63** Corbis: Bettmann. **69** Corbis: Susana Vera / Reuters. **75** Alamy Images: Vicki Beaver. **80** Corbis: Michael Ochs Archives. **84** Alamy Images: Stephen Finn. **86** Alamy Images: Jon Challicom. **98** Alamy Images: Papilio. **101** Corbis: Ken Welsh / * / Design Pics. **104** Alamy Images: Jamie Carstairs. **109** Getty Images: NBC. **111** Alamy Images: Eddie Gerald. **112** Alamy Images: flab. **121** Alamy Images: incamarastock. **134** Alamy Images: Phillip

Augustavo. **138** Corbis: National Archives / Handout / Reuters. **143** Alamy Images: David Page. **156** Corbis: Franck Guiziou / Hemis. **158** Alamy Images: Martin Shields. **163** Dreamstime.com: Urosr. **166** Corbis: Darren Greenwood / Design Pics. **172** Corbis: Richard T Nowitz. **175** Getty Images. **177** Corbis: Bettmann. **182** Alamy Images: Paul David Drabble. **185** Dreamstime.com: Shariffc. **191** Corbis: JGI / Jamie Grill / Blend Images. **195** Used with kind permission of Dogs Trust, the UK's largest dog welfare charity with 18 rehoming centres nationwide and they never put down a healthy dog. **196** Alamy Images: Alistair Scott. **203** Alamy Images: Mary Evans Picture Library. **208** Corbis: Frank Lukasseck. **211** Alamy Images: Nancy G Photography / Nancy Greifenhagen. **214** Getty Images: Darryl Leniuk (b); Nicholas Pitt (t); Jochen Schlenker (c). **218** Corbis: John Springer Collection. **221** Alamy Images: Kristoffer Tripplaar. **222** The Kobal Collection: Warner Horizon TV. **225** Corbis: Heide Benser. **227** Corbis: GARY HERSHORN / X00129 / Reuters. **229** Corbis: Joshua Bickel

All other images © Dorling Kindersley
For further information see: **www.dkimages.com**